THE EDUCATOR:

OR

HOURS WITH MY PUPILS.

BY MRS. LINCOLN PHELPS.

AUTHOR OF "LINCOLN'S BOTANY," AND A SERIES OF WORKS FOR SCHOOLS,
ON BOTANY, NATURAL PHILOSOPHY, CHEMISTRY, ETC.,
"THE FIRESIDE FRIEND," "IDA NORMAN," ETC.

New York:
A. S. BARNES & COMPANY.
1876.

TO

MRS. EMMA WILLARD,

THE GUIDE OF MY EARLY YEARS, MY EDUCATOR, MY AFFECTIONATE FRIEND AND BELOVED SISTER,

This Volume is Dedicated:

LET US ENCOURAGE EACH OTHER IN OUR MUTUAL LABORS,

ADOPTING THE SENTIMENT OF THE POET:

" Fear not to cast
Thy bread upon the waters, sure at last
In joy to find it after many days.
The work be thine, the fruit thy children's part:
Choose to believe, not see ; sight tempts the heart
From sober walking in true Gospel ways." *

ALMIRA LINCOLN PHELPS.

EUTAW PLACE, *Baltimore, Maryland.*
March 28th, 1859.

* Keble's Christian Year.

SYNOPSIS OF CONTENTS.

FIRST SERIES.

CONTENTS.

ADDRESS XIII.

ADDRESS XIV.

ADDRESS XV.

ADDRESS XVI.

ADDRESS XVII.

ADDRESS XVIII.

INTRODUCTION.

"HOURS WITH MY PUPILS!" How do these words, as they touch a spring in memory's casket, people my solitary apartment with living forms! Bright young faces appear before me, a mass of heads with raven locks or flaxen curls, and the bloom of health upon the rounded cheek. Their countenances are turned towards me in the attitude of attention. Such was the scene presented in the weekly assemblages at the Patapsco Institute, where for many years, I labored in my mission of educator. The "Assembly," as those meetings were called, was held in the chapel, and was considered an important occasion by all the inmates of the establishment.

Of this institute, I will say to those of my readers to whom its location and scenery may not have been familiar, that it is situated on an elevated table-land overlooking the Patapsco River. Its massive granite buildings stand alone in solitary grandeur, giving to the indwellers a sense of elevation and upliftedness, which harmonizes with the sublimity of the surrounding scenery. The deep recessed windows in the massive walls with the huge chimneys, combine to give the impression of a Gothic castle of the middle age. Here passed fifteen years of my life, and under my watch and care, grew from small beginnings, a large and flourishing institution, numbering about one hundred and fifty inmates, including besides pupils, various officers of the institution, teachers and servants. One mind directed all, and its labors were crowned with success by Him who ordereth all events.

On the days of "assembly" the inmates of the entire establishment were impressed with a sense that there must be quiet; servants about the premises checked their accustomed mirth, their laughter or singing, and if there chanced to be one forgetful of the occasion, there was ever some mentor at hand to put the finger on the lip and point to the chapel, or to say, "hush, they are in assembly." These quiet *hours with my pupils* stand out in bold relief as one of the distinguishing features of the whole period of my life at Patapsco. As the bell struck on Friday at four o'clock P.M., might have been seen pouring from the various parts of the building its many inmates, who were soon, under the eye of the presiding teacher, seated in their proper places. Even the sable handmaid of the Principal felt that she had an important part to act, inasmuch as she was sure beforehand to remind her mistress that it would soon be four o'clock; and when the clock struck to bring forward from its place the formidable book of Teachers' Reports, which with the written Address she had seen in progress, she would gravely carry to the chapel and place upon the desk, going out with the solemnity of one who has fulfilled a serious duty. The Principal having taken her seat, the Vice-Principal or Presiding Teacher, amidst profound and anxious silence, read the reports of the progress, conduct, etc., of the pupils during the preceding week, after which the Principal read an Address, often interspersed with extempore remarks. This volume will contain the spirit of those addresses. The occasion naturally suggested the subjects discussed. The mother (for the time being) of nearly one hundred young girls, separated from the busy scenes of the world, its follies and temptations, and yet knowing that her daughters must soon become actors in these scenes, could never be at loss what to say. Her own large and varied experience of life, with habits of reflection and observation, should have qualified her to direct them wisely. The characters and conduct of the women who were educated by her must be the test. Yet we would object to those cases being taken as a criterion where the pupil was but a short time under the influence of the system of education pursued at Patapsco, where the previous training had been defective, or where the influences on leaving school were unfavorable. A few years of a different training could not be expected entirely to change early habits of thought, and subsequent worldly temptations. Yet, in my declining years, I may indulge the thought that there are wives and mothers, who, amidst their duties, bless their early friend and preceptress for teaching them how to act their part in life's changing scene, giving them rules and principles to be applied to those various occurrences which could only have been foreseen by Almighty prescience. There are teachers, too, who in their high and responsible duties, may refer to her who, according to her best ability, taught them how to teach, and inspired them with lofty ideas of the mission to which they had devoted themselves. Are there not, too, ladies walking in single blessedness, fancy free, who can refer to impressions derived from my instructions, that there might be a course of life, dignified and useful, above the trivialities of fashion and folly, devoted to the study of the true and beautiful, to the cultivation of the mind and taste, and to the doing good to others, making happy those who come within the charmed circle of their influence? Such were the objects in view in the addresses to my pupils, which will appear in the following pages.

HISTORICAL SKETCH.

The educational labors of the author of this volume commenced at an early age. After the decease of her husband, Simeon Lincoln of Connecticut, she became connected with her sister, Mrs. Emma Willard, in the Troy New York Female Seminary, of which institution Mrs. Phelps was Acting Principal in 1830 and '31, during a visit of her sister to Europe.

On her marriage with the Hon. John Phelps, of Vermont, in 1831, she removed to that State, where, during the seven following years, she prepared for publication her "Female Student; or, Fireside Friend," "Caroline Westerly; or, the Young Traveller," "Geology, Botany, Natural Philosophy, and Chemistry, for Beginners," with "Lectures on Natural Philosophy and Chemistry, and Progressive Education, with a Mother's Journal." Severe mental labor and close application, with consequent sedentary habits, having seriously affected her health, a change of climate and mode of life seemed desirable. About this time, an invitation to Mrs. Phelps to organize and preside over a seminary in West Chester, Pa., was regarded favorably by her husband, as offering a desirable opportunity for the exercise of her educational tastes and experience in a sphere where *doing* would be united with *thinking*, and active duties surrounded by the young, would take the place of solitary study and reflection.

The new seminary was opened in October, 1838, under flattering auspices; but, while the public were looking to its brilliant success, the Principal of the Educational Department (as Mrs. Phelps was called) saw the elements of its dissolution in the hostility of some of the trustees to religious instruction and worship; and finding that no influence of hers—no success, however flattering, could induce a change in their settled determination to counteract, if they did not exclude, religious teaching, she resolved to withdraw from her connection with this institution; though it was not without sorrow of heart that she left the warm-hearted girls who had come together to be under her care, and the intelligent and hospitable social circle of friends which had welcomed her coming among them, and deeply regretted the cause of her departure.

Undertaken with no regard to improvement, but as a grand speculation, the West Chester Seminary contained within its own organization the elements of decay. The Girard College, with its no-religion, had been the great model of some of its founders;—but without the Girard funds to sustain the splendid but hollow fabric, it fell to ruin. When too late, the stockholders and trustees appointed a committee to wait on the late Principal of the Educational Department, and offer to her the uncontrolled direction of the establishment; but she had already made for herself and many attached pupils a pleasant home in Rahway, N. J. Here she proposed to complete the scholastic course of certain normal pupils who had accompanied her from New England, and, after seeing them established in their chosen profession, to return to the home in Bratleborough, Vermont, to which she had ever expected to retire. But the Lord had other designs.

An invitation jointly from the bishop of the diocese of Maryland, and the trustees of the Patapsco Female Institute, in 1841, induced Mr. and Mrs. Phelps to remove from New Jersey to establish in Maryland a school for Christian education. They were accompanied by most of their teachers, with a large number of former pupils from New England, Pennsylvania, and New Jersey.

We have given a brief sketch of the steps which, under the guidance of God's providence, led the author to that beloved spot, where, during her life's meridian, she enjoyed her labors of love in the companionship of the young, the beautiful, and the gifted. If all were not such as we might have wished, there were none who had not some redeeming traits of character. Removed from kindred, and dependent on my care and affection, they were my daughters. Was there not love between us? How often does the beaming forth of some almost forgotten countenance remind me that nothing is lost—that no love which has ever been felt can be blotted out of the heart's memory.

It was here that the spirit of my husband serenely passed away from earth, like the calm sun-set of an October evening, when the hills and forests which skirt the western horizon of Patapsco are tinted with heavenly radiance. And then, after some years had passed, another spirit was called away. She who might well serve for a model of what woman should be—who was admired, loved, and almost revered by those who saw her beautiful life, who heard her sweet music on many instruments, and the touching tones of her voice ; whose life was harmony, uniting learning and accomplishments with piety and all womanly virtues ; she was suddenly called for—and, in a moment, nothing was left but the empty shrine of the departed spirit.

It was not in her home at Patapsco that this change came. It was when travelling* with her invalid mother, watching with anxiety the effect upon her of change of air and scene after a protracted illness—it was then, that God called her to himself, and doubtless with that ready obedience which ever characterized her, her spirit responded, " Lord, here am I."

A few months after this affliction, the Author, yielding to the pressure of sorrow, and the ever-present consciousness of a support taken away, made arrangements for resigning the charge of the Patapsco Institute. Established on the basis of Christian principles, and blessed with Christian worship and ordinances, it had flourished and taken firm root as a standard collegiate institution for the daughters of the South. That this religious culture should be continued by her successor, was the first stipulation made by the Principal, and it is the testimony of her experience, that no system of education not based upon religion can be permanently successful.

* The death of Jane P. Lincoln, the eldest daughter of Mrs. Phelps, occurred by the railroad calamity of August 29, 1855, near Burlington, N. J.

A FAREWELL TO VERMONT.

Land of the *Mountains Green** and rugged soil;—
Of cascades wild, of swiftly gliding streams;—
Of darkly waving pines, and stately firs;—
Of gloomy ravines, and romantic dells;—
Of haunted glens, and sweetly smiling dales!
Land of my beauteous, mountain home, farewell!

Yet still I linger—for, to me, thou art
A land of beauty, picturesque, and rich
In native charms—a land for Poet's dreams,
For patriot's visions, and for angel's thought.
Methinks there's inspiration in the breeze
Reflected from yon mountain's pine-clad side,
Breathing aërial music to my soul—
Then dying 'mid the groves, with cadence sweet.

Yet in these shades, where Poesy might dwell,
And Fiction weave her ever-varying web,
No magic lyre has struck; no fairy bands
Have issued forth to charm the wond'ring world.

* Vermont was originally called by the French Verd Mont, or the Green Mountain State.

Is it that in my soul the chord is broke,
That once could harmonize with nature's charms,
And poesy, with youth, has passed away?
It is not this, methinks, but that fair Truth,
With her pure, steady light, has seemed more bright
Than Fiction's flickering torch, and gilded ray.
To study nature, and God's providence,
As manifest in these material things,
And having learn'd, t' impart to other minds
Knowledge so wond'rous, this, I've better deem'd
Than pencilling fantastic imagery.

There's poetry in science, when it leads
To gaze upon the rainbow's glorious arch,
To follow Echo to her grottos wild,
To trace the circling planets in their course,
And watch the bud first bursting into bloom.
Nature, I owe thee much;—if I have felt
Aught of the firm resolve, or wish sublime,
'Tis that I drank from thee the heavenly draught,
And gave thy moral image to the world.
And, oh ye venerable oaks! whose shade
Embosoms the dear spot I now must leave,
Adieu, ye ancient friends! and may, sometimes,
Thy feather'd songsters thrill in pensive notes
Their sorrow for me, gone! for dear to me
Their matin song and vesper hymn have been.

Sweet home, adieu! flowers that I've loved to tend,
Watching with care maternal for your bloom;
Others may cull your sweets, enjoy your charms,
May twine my woodbine o'er the trellis neat,
May guide the Lonicera's * spiral way,

* Trumpet honeysuckle.

Or train the pensile Lycium's * graceful stalk.
Oh, ye have been my pride, ye twining race,
Who have so beautified and cheer'd my bow'rs
And I have fancied, as I've seen you climb,
'Twas *gratitude* that urged your upward way,
And gave luxuriant blossoms for my care.
E'en on the very verge of winter's frost,
Your bloom still lingers, as if fain ye would
Cheer nature's gloom, and soothe this parting hour.

My grateful flower, methinks I hear thee ask
Why thus I leave thee to a stranger's care;
Perchance, uncared for, trampled under foot
By the rude hind, as valueless and naught.
My honeysuckle sweet, list to my words:
Thou'rt a dear, docile plant, and pleasant 'tis
To train thee in the way that thou should'st go.
But I must tell thee, there are *flowers* on earth
Created for far purer skies than these.
They are allied to thee in outward form,
Being made of earth and beautified by God
With shape and color, lovely to the eye.
But God to these sweet flowers has given
Immortal spirits to survive decay.
In yon fair sylvan† land a garden blooms
Of those immortal plants, and fitting 'tis
That skillful, patient hands should lend their aid
To train them for the ends which God ordains.
As step by step, thy upward way I've train'd,
So must I guide them in their onward course
Up learning's height, and virtue's rugged way.—
Such labor calls me hence, but yet, methinks,

* Tea-vine.

† Penn-sylvania or Penn's sylvan-land.

When frost of time shall settle on my brow,
And age asks respite from the cares of life,
Like Noah's wand'ring dove, my flowers, my birds,
My ancient trees, again I'll come to you.

Here stands *my home*, above the busy town,
Peeping through clustering oaks with col'mns white
And fair proportions. Quick the eye of taste,
Beholding from the bustling street below,
Pauses to mark its beauty, and admire
A scene so fair. Ionian portico, and verdant lawn,
Piazzas, gravel'd walks, and garden fair,
All, all, adieu! I may not linger more
Within these halls, sacred to studious thought,
To social converse, and the heart's repose.

But thou, my native stream!* I turn to thee,
As to an early friend;—what though thy wave
First met my view, where stands the Charter Oak†
(That patriotic tree of olden time),
And where sweet Sigourney now tunes her harp;—
What, though changing time my home has placed
In regions distant from that honored land,
For steady habits erst so much renown'd,
And strait-hair'd Puritans, a goodly race;
Yet *nearer* to *thine own birth-place*,‡ thou'rt still
My native stream; and onward mak'st thy way
Laving the soil, where, in their last repose,

* The Connecticut River.

† The hollow oak in which was concealed the Charter of Connecticut when Sir Edmund Andross, commanded by James II., went to Hartford, Conn., to seize upon that instrument. N.B.—This hollow tree, of 1687, flourished in a green old age, the pride of Connecticut, until 1857, when it was prostrated by a violent wind.

‡ The Connecticut River rises in the north part of Vermont.

My lov'd ones rest, father, and kindred near;
And dearer names, that memory garners up
'Mid her mysterious and spectral throng,
Shadows of youthful hope, and youthful love.
As *theirs*, I would that *my* last rest might be
Beside my native stream.

How oft, at pensive twilight, has my gaze,
Wandering beyond the cheerful village scene,
Sought yonder hill, whose monumental stones,
Their snowy whiteness blending with the skies,
Speak to the heart the vanity of earth.
It is a beauteous spot, fit place for rest,—
And such, methinks, the dreamless, quiet sleep
Which human care or woe shall ne'er disturb.
There, still, perchance, beside my native steam,
Beneath those sacred shades, I may repose.

Fain would I linger to survey the scene,
The lovely, variegated landscape round;*
The verdant hills where echo loves to dwell,
The mountains hoar,† seen in the distance far;
And tributary waters, whose meand'ring course
Is marked by waving lines of silvery tint.
The village spires pointing towards the skies,
Mark where the voice of heavenly wisdom sounds.
Full many a dwelling peers upon my sight,
Where warm hearts cluster and kind thoughts abound,
And where, methinks, when I am far away,
My name will not be strange upon the ear,
Nor utter'd but in friendship's kindest tone.

* The tourist who has visited Brattleborough, Vermont, may have recognised the scenes here described.

† The White Hills of New Hampshire.

Friends! in whose converse I had thought to pass
Life's future days, from you, time's restless wave,
Which late has thrown me midst your pleasant scenes,
Now bears me onward!—
And thus, with me, this world has ever been,
Like rushing river, in its rapid course.
Fain would I, as the calm and placid lake,
Which never leaves its fond encircling shade,
Rest 'mid these cheerful bowers and solemn groves;—
But God directs our pathway, and His will
Should be our guide. Then let me nerve my heart,
And turn me from my dear, my mountain-home.

ADDRESSES.

We commence "HOURS WITH MY PUPILS" with Addresses of the second year at Patapsco, those of the first year having been seldom committed to writing; though the weekly assembly, with its customary exercises, was from the first always held with undeviating regularity. The extempore Addresses, or Talks to the Pupils, were perhaps not less effective than written essays, though, in the latter, it was intended to keep up attention by a colloquial style and familiar manner.

HOURS WITH MY PUPILS.

ADDRESS I.

SKETCH OF PATAPSCO IN THE AUTUMN OF 1841.

Changes—Problem to be wrought out in regard to the Education of Women.

My Dear Pupils :

One year has passed since we commenced our labors in this place, with the view of establishing an Institution for the Christian education of girls, upon an enlarged plan and liberal principles, giving to our sex corresponding advantages with those enjoyed by young men in colleges. And yet we have endeavored to keep in view the great difference in the future destiny of the two sexes, so that we may not disturb the order and harmony of social life, in attempting to turn the future woman from her proper sphere of duty. We would not be instrumental in educating masculine women, but we seek to enlighten, refine and elevate the female mind and character.

You will not, therefore, expect in this place to hear much upon the *rights of woman,* while her *duties* will claim most of our attention; and your course of education will be directed to fit you to become useful rather than brilliant, patient rather than presuming.

One year has passed rapidly away, since most of us came hither as strangers. We have seen great changes in the appearance of our home, both within and abroad; and the wilderness has literally been made to blossom as the rose. Some of you, brought to my care from distant regions, accompanied me hither, other pupils joined us here, and so we began to live together and to make a new home; strangers to each other, with different habits of thinking and acting, with much to learn, and something to forget.

But we will look back through memory's stereoscope to the entrance into this place of those who came from a distant region, to commence anew the work of education. In October of 1841, a weary company of travellers were climbing the steep ascent which leads to our granite edifice, that, like some feudal castle of the Rhine, overlooks the surrounding country. The hectic flush of decay had passed over the landscape, and from the old forest trees upon the hill-side and the mountains, the autumnal blasts were strewing the withered leaves upon the ground, preparatory to their returning again to their native earth. An equinoctial storm which had met the travellers on their journey, still lingered in the horizon, and the dark heavy clouds seemed to weep as if in harmony with the scene. The pathway up the hill was tangled with briars, and rough with broken fragments of rock; and around the mansion were heaps of unremoved stones, which had been left there on the erection of the building. In front of our classic portico, at the base of the massive granite steps, a drove of ill-favored swine were rooting up the ground, their gutteral exclamations little resembling the dulcet notes of the piano or harp, with which our halls now resound. No welcome of friends awaited the travellers as they entered their new home; gloomy and desolate seemed its spacious apartments.

But the sky was once more serene, the beauties of the scenery gradually unfolded themselves, every point of view showed some new object of interest, and the uninterrupted prospect of the heavens, as seen from this great observatory, gave to the mind new elevation and expansion. Nowhere does the Indian-summer appear more delightful than in this picturesque region.

After a few weeks of great labor and effort, the Institute was prepared for the reception of pupils. But often did the unbelieving doubt arise in my mind, will parents come hither with their daughters? I recalled my first impressions of the wildness of the scenery, of the seclusion of the place, and "How hard it was to climb, etc.," But if I had doubts I did not express them, and when any one said to me, "*If* you succeed here," I would reject any *supposition*, and say, "we will succeed."

There was work done by faithful laborers, without on the grounds, and in the interior, to render the abode pleasant and comfortable. Load after load of furniture found its way into the house, which at length began to look like a home. And so I trust those of you who were with us last year have found it, as well as a literary institution where the mind has received its due share of attention.

The new Patapsco Institute opened encouragingly; travelling from afar were seen pupils,—from Canada and the southern States, from the Atlantic and the Mississippi, and even the Cherokee nation; they met here—and here they have lived together as a band of sisters under the care of their common parents. Most of them are now before me, ready to welcome with kind greeting the new sisters who have joined them in this beginning of a new school year.

But unexpected events have prevented the return of some. Among these the first who came hither to welcome the founders of the new Institute was a widowed mother, bringing her two lovely daughters. She was enthusiastic in the cause of the education of woman, and ready to make sacrifices to promote the improvement of her daughters. Her enlightened and judicious opinions, so earnestly expressed, were highly encouraging in respect to the success of the undertaking. Superior to narrow views, and highly appreciating intellectual efforts and zeal in a good cause, Mrs.——'s companionship was of no small value to her, who was deeply sensible of the many obstacles to be overcome in the accomplishment of her objects. She was a woman of feeble frame and delicate heath, the sole parent of a large family, but her comprehensive and far-seeing mind looked beyond present scenes, and she perseveringly followed out for herself that course which her judgment had decided on. With no pretensions to being a literary woman, Mrs.——, was far more, and better ; sensible, wise and pious, she was one to strengthen and uphold a cause in which she embarked. And the daughters of this mother were obedient to rules, studious and diligent, simple in dress, and conscientious in morals and religion. How does a mother's character appear in the dress, deportment and mind of a daughter. In the midst of plans for the proper training of her children, this excellent mother was removed to another world ; the orphans must journey on in life, no longer watched and guarded by her care. The places which the two elder daughters last year occupied with us, are now filled by others—they must remain at their lonely home, the stay and support of younger children.

On the same day that Mrs. —— first brought her daughters here, a young gentleman from Pennsylvania came with his sister. The personal beauty aud manly bearing of the youth were striking—the sister went home before the close of the school year, to be present at the marriage of this brother, but in the midst of the festivities which followed, a fatal accident rendered a young bride a widow, and the home of your associate and friend has become " the house of mourning."

And far off in the distant Cherokee nation, there is the sound of mourning for a young man taken away in the bloom of life, and amidst prospects of usefulness among the people of his tribe. Educated at Princeton, young Mr. R. had returned to his nation prepared to vindicate their rights, and to exert himself to improve their condition. A few short months have passed since he visited his sisters here—he expressed great delight that they were enjoying advantages for education, and his determination to induce the "*Head men*" of his country to send their daughters to Patapsco. We see, to-day, his sisters in garments of mourning, and in a far distant region in the West there is a new grave over which bereaved parents weep.

Again, one of your number, by a mother's decease, is called home to be the consoler of her father, and the directress of his house. Such are some of the changes in the families of those who last year were here assembled. And what changes may this year witness?

We have, my dear pupils, brought forward these instances, to show you the uncertainty of every situation in this life. While some of you are repining, perchance, that you are to be kept longer at school, the decree may have gone forth that shall suddenly remove you from this place; you may be taken from life, or fortune may change, and your parents be no longer able to meet the expenses of your education. How ought you, then, to improve the advantages here enjoyed, and to lay up in store wisdom to guide you, if left to yourselves. Seek to do your duty to your friends who sent you here, to yourselves, and to the Institution, by improving to the utmost of your power all the means put into your hands for your own benefit.

There are those who love knowledge, who thirst for it, and who would gladly make great efforts to gain the opportunities which you enjoy. The factory girls of New England often study hard in hours allotted to rest, and not unfrequently make great proficiency in literary pursuits. In some parts of our country, especially in New England, the daughters of those who might be called independent in circumstances, often assist in educating themselves, by teaching a portion of the time, and thus strengthening their minds, while they aid their parents. Should there be less zeal for education among the daughters of the South? They are not less gifted in intellect, nor less aspiring in their ambition to attain excellence. The state of society among them is, indeed, somewhat different; woman is considered more helpless. There is a cause for this that will have its influence—the misfortune of being waited upon by those who have nothing else to do. But it is this very helplessness that we would urge you to cast aside. There is a problem to be wrought out, and you, my daughters from the South, are called upon to assist in its solution. It is the use of education to woman in rendering her better fitted for her duties, and more efficient in their discharge. Enlightened in intellect, cultivated in morals, and firm in religious principles, may American women comprehend the high destiny of their country, and whether of the North or the South, may they use their powerful influence to hold fast the ties of union—Sisters of one country, may they never cease to cherish the sisterly bond, nor to do all in their power to soften asperities of sectional feeling which may hereafter rise up among their fathers, brothers, and husbands.

Nov., 1842.

NOTE.

Such was the advice given in 1842;—but women on both sides had their share in sundering the Union—may they now seek to re-unite the country by meek resignation on the part of the conquered, and by a generous and noble sympathy from those who have the means and the opportunity to be magnaminous.

1868.

ADDRESS II.

DIGNITY OF CHARACTER.

The word *dignity* is by most persons falsely appreciated; it is supposed to relate to that which is grand and lofty, and associated with the characters and actions of those who occupy superior stations in society. If we consider dignity as the opposite of *meanness*, we must admit, that while the latter quality is often found among the rich and elevated in station, the former may be seen in the humblest condition in life.

In what, then, does dignity consist? When we behold one occupying an elevated position, surrounded by accompaniments which suggest ideas of refinement and authority, we naturally associate with these circumstances, dignity and elevation of mind. Yet, experience of the world shows, that meanness of spirit may exist in the individual thus surrounded by external grandeur; and that on familiar acquaintance, the character of those occupying high stations may appear mean and undignified; while we often feel respect for the poor and lowly whom we see above mean actions, whose thoughts are noble, though their circumstances are humble.

Approach yonder proud mansion, enter its spacious halls, survey its costly furniture, its works of art, its hoards of rich plate, bespeaking family antiquity and honors. In a tasteful boudoir, reclining on a luxurious couch, and clad in costly robes, is the mistress of the mansion ; from her infancy she has been the pampered child of fortune, she has been taught no lessons of self-denial, she has never felt want, and knows no sympathy for the distresses of others. Accustomed to command with imperial sway the menials who are taught to obey her slightest wish, her own passions have grown with her growth, and strengthened with her strength. Of self-control or self-denial she knows nothing. Material wants and schemes for self-gratification occupy her thoughts ; something to pamper the appetite, some new fashion of dress, some new party of pleasure, some new excitement in which she may forget the *real* worthlessness of her existence ; these may be the desires which occupy her mind ; while "envy, hatred and malice," are indulged by her without compunction or remorse. Does this woman in all her luxurious surroundings and grandeur of position, exhibit true dignity in her character and conduct ?

In the mud-plastered cottage near the great house, is the servant, whose birth may have been contemporaneous with that of her haughty mistress, whose commands even in childhood she was taught to obey with patient and uncomplaining submission, to tremble at her frown, to go and come at her bidding, to be by turns the sport and plaything of her gayer moments, or the victim of her temper and passion.

Day after day, the menial has gone on, striving, though in vain, to satisfy the demands upon her skill, labor and self-devotion, attaching herself with warm affection to one who showed no mercy to her; gentle, uncomplaining, she has submitted to her fate, and striven to perform her duty. Through the long vista of life she sees no amelioration of her lot; but she hears, perhaps from one ignorant as herself, of a friend in heaven who sitteth at the right hand of God making intercession for her, that when her toils are over, she may be received into mansions of everlasting peace; she sees through the light of the Gospel, so clear that the most ignorant are enlightened by its beams, that beyond this vale of tears, there is a land where the weary are at rest, and the wicked cease from troubling. The blessed hopes of everlasting life and peace spring up in her benighted soul; she loves that Saviour who gave himself for her, and piety gives her new resolution to go on, from day to day, laborious and patient, looking for glorious rewards hereafter.

Who would say that there is not in the character of this poor menial, more true dignity than in that of her selfish, worldly and unscrupulous mistress? May such of you as in your future lives will have control over fellow beings whose happiness in God's providence is made dependent on your kindness, sometimes think of the pictures here presented; and may you never be excelled by them in dignity and true nobility of character. Show to them that you, too, can sacrifice your own inclinations, and that you are willing to do it out of regard to their comforts and feelings ;—be not surpassed by them in self-command, or in generosity of spirit.

It is not to be denied, however humiliating may be the admission, that many women live with little regard to true dignity—that their estimate as to what constitutes this is low, and entirely at variance with the Scripture definition of a good woman. If they think of beauty, it is not the beauty of holiness ; if they hunger and thirst, it is not for righteousness ; they do not regard "wisdom as more precious than rubies," or consider it as "an ornament of grace to the head ;" they forget that "favor is deceitful and beauty vain," and that *praise* belongeth only "to the woman that feareth the Lord." Vanity leads many of our sex into fearful snares ; and the love of pleasure and admiration tempt them to stray in forbidden paths. False notions of life often fill the minds of young girls about to leave school. The expressions "coming out into society," "finished education," "entering life," etc., seem to mean something, though what this something is, cannot always be easily defined.

The "*coming out*" of a young lady, or her being permitted to partake freely of fashionable dissipation, is but a poor beginning for a life of duty, trials and cares. It would be far better if, for the foolish notions which too often fill the heads of young girls, could be substituted more just and rational ideas of life. It is true that some parents, with ill-judged kindness make the period of a daughter's leaving school an era of extravagance and dissipation, and instead of seeking to develop good principles and confirm the habits of industry, order and self-restraint which the faithful educator has so carefully labored to cultivate, they seem in haste to change all; and before the daughter shall be called upon to encounter the realities of life, to suffer her to become dazzled with the false glare of pleasure, and rendered unfit for the scenes of duty and trial which await her.

"Poor girl," they may say, "she has been long confined to school, she ought now to be indulged; the troubles of life will come fast enough;" and so she is permitted to destroy her health by dissipation, to lose her innocent simplicity in the search for adventure, and to acquire a fondness for excitement, which will render the quiet scenes of practical life dull and monotonous.

Surely this is ill-judged kindness on the part of the parent. The idea that in "coming out," a young lady must have admirers, and that the greater their numbers the greater her triumph, naturally leads her into folly and flirtations. In her haste to secure beaux she perhaps loses a worthy and devoted admirer, who becoming disgusted with her frivolity and apparent heartlessness, leaves her for one less brilliant, but more worthy of his affection.

Those of you who are expecting soon to complete your school education and who earnestly desire to do right, are ready to ask, "What ought I, as a young lady, entering society, to do?" Accustomed as you have been to regard my counsels and warnings, and hoping my advice may be remembered when you have entered life's busy scenes, I will look into the future, aiding you as far as my experience may go, in discriminating the path of duty before you.

When you cease to be school-girls, your situations and occupations will, of course, be different from what they were in vacations, when you were at home preparing for a return to school. I would ask you, if it is a time for you to plunge into amusements when life opens before you, and you should begin in earnest to act your part in its varied scenes?

Resolve seriously to set yourselves about living according to some method. Consider what you *can* do, what you *ought* to do; and what your friends wish you to do. Observe the cares of your mother, if you enjoy the blessing of such a parent, and begin to share them with her. If she should be feeble, tenderly regard her weaknesses of body or mind; comfort her heart by your sympathy, and sustain her by your prudence and stability of character. Look over the household arrangements; you have perhaps in your school-days been ambitious to keep your small room with taste and neatness; apply your industry and skill to putting in order the different apartments of the house, observing the arrangement of furniture, and looking into domestic operations.

In New England young ladies of education and refinement often take the charge of parlors, and sometimes assist their mothers in doing all the household work. The many factories in the eastern section of our country, offer employment of an easy and profitable kind, so that few females are willing to engage in domestic service when they can get better wages in factories, and live independently as boarders to be waited upon. Thus it happens that those who could hire servants are often obliged to do their own work; to look after their own houses and to prepare the family meals.

But you should see how these things are managed, for I could not otherwise make you comprehend the neatness, comfort, and order which are often seen to prevail in those families in the eastern States, where the mothers and daughters do the household work.

Early on Monday morning all are up; the mother, perhaps, engages in preparing the breakfast, while the daughters commence the family's washing for the week. They have, of course, all been careful not to make unnecessary washing. Everything is life and activity—the cheerful voice of singing from within, mingles with the matin songs of the birds without. On this day, a simple dinner is provided, which requires little time in preparation, but for which labor gives a keen relish. Before the devotee of fashion has arisen from her disturbed and restless couch, the industrious mother and daughters have finished their washing—clothes, white as the driven snow, are hanging upon the lines, and the kitchen and wash room floors are nicely washed. Everything is put in place; our matron and her blooming daughters are dressed for company, and very likely either receive some good neighbor, or go out and take tea sociably with a friend. And such teas! The snow-white table-cloth, the biscuit or rolls scarcely less white, the honey in its rich comb, the delicious butter made by fair hands which are perhaps no less skillful to play upon the piano than to perform domestic labor; the cake of several kinds, the nice preserves, and the exquisite tea;—this tea not put into a tea-pot musty through neglect, nor decocted with water below the boiling point; but made exactly right by the mistress of the house, who esteems herself responsible for her housekeeping, and ranks neatness, care, and economy among her chief duties.

While you listen to my description, you think perhaps of a vulgar mother and coarse-looking, unrefined daughters;—would that I could take you by clairvoyance to some one of the intellectual and agreeable families in New England, where is realized the picture I have drawn of a home of comfort and plenty.

In homes where there are no daughters, or they are sent abroad for education, a young girl as domestic assistant is often received into the family, and in many respects treated as a member of the same. She is sent to the public school until she has obtained a good common English education, rendering in the meantime most useful services to her kind benefactors. She becomes an intelligent and useful woman, and perhaps marries the son of a neighboring farmer ; and in a home of her own, practises those lessons of industry and frugality to which she has been trained. But this may be rather a picture of past times than of the present. The great influx of emigrants in every part of our country renders it more easy to obtain domestic servants, and Bridgets and Noras, with their strong hands and red, brawny arms, are relieving their more delicate mistresses of the burdens they formerly so cheerfully, bore. Whether this is in reality increasing the happiness of society, is doubtful. The feeble, sickly women of our country, drooping and nervous for want of exercise, would indicate the negative.

Most of you, young ladies from the southern States are not under the necessity of performing household labor. It would be a mistaken kindness in you to do the labor, and let the menials live in idleness. But yet it is well for you to know what labor is, that you can feel sympathy for them; besides, your servant may be sick, and humanity may require of you to relieve her from duty, even if you should take upon yourself the burden of her labor. Though not called upon, in general, to servile labor, you are not excused from a life of usefulness. No family can be well ordered, or even comfortable, where the care, as well as the labor, is thrown upon servants. I would hope that you have here learned to respect the virtues of industry and neatness, and with your other accomplishments, have acquired habits of order and system, which in future life will be more important to you than the merely ornamental branches of education.

To woman it belongs to soothe the couch of sickness, to minister to the wants of declining age, to diffuse around the fireside an air of cheerfulness and comfort, to watch over the wants of a household, and to arrange and control in the little empire of home. First, as daughters you should learn to minister to your parents, to anticipate their wishes, to study their happiness, even though it call for the sacrifice of your own enjoyments. This picture may be far different from the one in your fancy, where gay parties with all the excitements of a life of pleasure occupy the foreground. But how absurd for any rational mind to consider the mere accidental circumstances of life as its business or employment. It was said by Hannah More, one of the greatest and best of women of the past generation, that, "from the manner in which girls were brought up, one would suppose that life was a perpetual holiday, and that the great object was to bring them up to shine in its amusements and sports."

Accomplishments should be valued chiefly for their influence in rendering the domestic circle more cheerful and refined; most young ladies seem to consider them as only intended to gain for them the homage of admiration in society. The idea of merely entertaining their parents, brothers or sisters with their accomplishments would seem unreasonable ; a loss of time and trouble ; a very dull affair. How false, how destructive to the happiness of domestic life are such low views of education.

You disregard the happiness of your parents when you fail to do your duty. They are distressed not so much on their own account, as that you act unworthily ; they perceive in you a low standard of character, a mean selfishness, which would seek your own gratification at the expense of others; an exacting spirit which is never satisfied with indulgence, and which ever cries, *give, give,* caring little for the *giver*, but eager for the gifts. May you all be led to consider whether you do not too often give your best friends reason to think you are more anxious for the *favors* you receive from them than to contribute to their happiness, or to render yourselves worthy recipients of their kindness.

Pay attention to all your words and actions at home and abroad. Lavater says : "*Actions, looks, words, steps,* form the alphabet by which you may spell *characters.*" In your intercourse with society, strive to show yourselves prudent, considerate and intelligent. It is expected of those who have had superior advantages of education, that they will exhibit the fruits of a cultivated mind. When you go into society, you may not be *au fait* in all matters of etiquette, and in the current language of the day. But there is to those who are wearied with the trifling and folly of fashionable life, a charm in an unsophisticated mind.

You can, at least, be intelligent listeners if you do not know exactly what to say on all subjects, and can show by your manner that you have mind enough to receive information, when you meet with those who can impart it. One great advantage of some of your studies, especially mathematics, logic, etc., is to teach you the manner of learning, of investigating subjects. You must enter upon life feeling that you are only prepared to begin to learn its duties and its customs. So far from considering that you know everything, you must think you have yet almost everything to learn. With a just sense of your own deficiencies you will appear unassuming and amiable, and behave with more true dignity than the proud, self-conceited woman, who in her own estimate of herself looks down upon others far her superiors in knowledge and worth of character.

The subject on which I address you might well occupy a volume. Dignity of character implies correct and proper conduct in all the circumstances of life. We might apply our remarks to the different situations in which you may be placed in your future lives, to the relations of daughter and sister, wife and mother, mistress of a household, a member of the Church of Christ and of society at large. But our limits forbid this extension of the subject; you must pursue it yourselves; you must make it your own study to learn the path of duty. By following this course, you will not fail to exhibit in your life and conduct, true dignity of character, and the rich fruits of a liberal and Christian education.

1842.

ADDRESS III.

BEAUTY WITHOUT DISCRETION.

"As a jewel of gold in a swine's snout, so is a fair woman without discretion."—PROV. xi. 22.

IN the figurative language of the Bible we have the annunciation of a truth to which I would, at this time, call your attention. You, my daughters, are to be fair women. May you not be of those who in lacking discretion, render beauty a disgrace rather than an appropriate ornament to a casket enshrining a rich jewel within. Beauty by attracting observation renders the want of discretion the more striking.

But let us consider the metaphor we have selected from the "Book of Wisdom." The picture presented is that of a swine, the most disgusting, and the least respectable (if I may so say) of all animals, wallowing in the mire, herding with others as gross as himself, and yet wearing in his unseemly snout a rich jewel.

A fair woman *without discretion* is the object to which this image is compared. We will consider the application of the simile, and in pursuance of this object will inquire what is meant by discretion, the lack of which reduces a beautiful woman to a level with a brutish swine made ridiculous by an ornament, in itself, valuable. But the jewel in the swine's snout does not render him other than he is by nature and habit; it does not take from him those characteristics which degrade him to the lowest rank among the brutes. The contrast between that which is in itself beautiful and lovely with the disgusting object to which it is attached, draws our attention, and what we might without such contrast have passed by unnoticed excites our disgust or contempt.

The author of the memorable sentence chosen for our motto is Solomon; a man of the most polished manners, the most thorough acquaintance with the human heart, and especially the female character, of any individual with whom the page of history has made us acquainted.

When God appeared unto Solomon soon after he had ascended the throne of his father David and directed him to ask whatever he would have, and it should be given to him, the young king of Israel, acknowledging with gratitude the goodness of God as shown towards his father, with filial regard to his memory asked only that the promise made to him by God might be fulfilled in the prosperity of the kingdom; and that he might have wisdom and knowledge to discharge the duties of his high station. God was pleased with this request, and said to Solomon, "because this was in thy heart, and thou hast not asked riches, wealth, or honor, wisdom and knowledge is granted unto thee, and I will give thee riches, wealth and honor, such as none of the kings have had that have been before thee, neither shall any that come after thee have the like."

Solomon had remembered the words of his father, who in the sight of all Israel and the congregation of the Lord, and in the audience of God, had commanded him to obey the voice of God, and to serve him with a perfect heart and a willing mind, saying, "the Lord searcheth all hearts, and understandeth all thoughts; if thou seek him, he will be found of thee, but if thou forsake him, he will cast thee off forever."

The reign of Solomon was brilliant and magnificent, his court was filled by ladies of surpassing beauty and accomplishments; even the great queen of Sheba "came *from far*" to hear his wisdom and to see the grandeur of his court. We cannot, therefore, say that Solomon had not an opportunity of estimating the comparative value of beauty and discretion, nor suppose that in his day there were not some beautiful but indiscreet women, whose actions contrasted with their looks suggested to him the image of the jewel of gold in a swine's snout.

The word discretion is sometimes used as synonymous with judgment and prudence—they are qualities nearly related, inasmuch as they express the various modes of practical wisdom which regulate the conduct of individuals in the affairs of life. Judgment is the more comprehensive term, as it distinguishes between what is right or wrong, in general. Judgment pronounces on general principles, discretion on particular actions; the latter may therefore be regarded as the offspring of the former. Considered critically, we find a difference in the meaning of the terms. A judge may decide upon cases of law or equity with sound judgment, and yet he may act with indiscretion in his own private affairs. Judgment requires knowledge and experience ; discretion requires reflection and consideration. Prudence is often used in relation to property, as a prudent person may be understood to be one who lives within his income, or the expression may denote one who is *careful* in respect to his conduct. Discretion takes a wide survey of circumstances, it looks to the moral fitness of things as well as to the consequences which may result from particular actions ; considers their real propriety and fitness as well as the advantages which may result from them. Prudence is rather a negative virtue; it prevents a person from exposing himself to danger or harm ; discretion enables one to do what is right. Still, the words discreet, judicious, and prudent, are often applied to the same class of actions ; but we perceive on a close analysis a difference in their signification.

Why is it that beauty in our sex is so seldom united with discretion, and that so many beautiful women are like the swine with a jewel of gold in his snout ? The little girl who is handsome is flattered from her cradle—mamma's visitors exclaim, "Oh, what a sweet child! what bright sparkling eyes, what a beautiful complexion, what fine hair and how prettily it curls!" One says, "she will be very handsome when she grows to be a young lady;" another, "she will make many hearts ache." The gentlemen tell the child that she must be their little wife, and that they are already in love with her beauty. She is thus made vain and loses the simplicity of childhood. She thinks that beauty is all she needs to make her beloved; she practises airs and graces before the glass, and becomes silly in her actions, and affected in her manners. She is unwilling to learn to be useful because she thinks she is made to be looked at and admired. When she goes into company she supposes every one is looking at her, and fancies she has an important part to sustain; every curl therefore must be adjusted, every dimple in motion, and every gesture bespeak that she is a beauty. A handsome little girl thus spoiled, may be compared to a *pig* with a jewel in his snout; and she is in a fair way of being like the *swine* through lack of discretion, when she becomes a *fair woman.*

From childhood we must not expect too much. Indeed, the term, "to arrive at years of discretion," implies that a certain degree of maturity is necessary, in order to acquire this virtue. A child may however show, as the bud indicates the flower, a cast of character which leads us to foretell the future woman. Vanity, self-conceit, and imprudence, may be seen in children as well as in those who are older. It becomes of great importance that the guardians of the young should begin early the work of education, carefully observing unfavorable developments, and seeking to counteract them. The period in which indiscretion in girls appears most striking, is that when they begin to think of the society of the other sex, and of forming intimacies with their own. How often do such intimacies lead them into great imprudence and folly. Family secrets are revealed to the beloved friend—every foolish thought of their own hearts is unfolded, and advice of the most improper kind is given, received, and acted upon. But indiscretion in respect to the other sex is often fatal to reputation and peace of mind. There are degrees of folly and guilt in this—there are silly attempts to gain attention, actions intended to be artful, but which deceive no one. In her eagerness to gain admiration, the indiscreet woman often defeats her own objects; for nothing sooner disgusts a man of any refinement than forwardness or indiscretion in a woman. But, again, if a girl *affect* reserve and extreme modesty, the artifice is seen through, and she receives no credit even for the virtues she may possess. There may be indiscreet *looks*, looks that encourage the unprincipled to make advances which true female delicacy and correct principles would indignantly frown upon.

Indiscretion may exist in words. Feelings which should be governed and suppressed may be allowed to appear, and conversation indulged in which would lead to unfavorable inferences respecting a young lady's delicacy and principles. Habits of trifling and flirtation are indiscreet. There are some young women so lost to dignity and sound morality, as to pride themselves on being called flirts: did they know how they really appear to persons of sense, they would blush for their conduct; they would see that their beauty—if beauty they possess—is but the jewel of gold in the swine's snout.

Young women should early acquire a contempt for flattery, and a real dislike of flatterers. They should seek to be able to converse with gentlemen without the flutter of spirits, which results from thoughts of broken hearts, or the desire of admiration. Modesty and simplicity are far more charming than personal beauty, which soon fades; and which, even in its greatest brilliancy, soon ceases to attract where intelligence and discretion are wanting.

When a man of observation goes into society, he soon sees who are the discreet women, and which are those that the sacred writer compares to a swine with a jewel in his nose.

There is a beautiful girl standing amidst an admiring group—you listen to her words, they are silly and unmeaning; her actions are bold, *almost* indelicate; you observe the free air with which she is addressed by the young men who gather round her; and as you gaze, the words of inspiration suggest themselves to your mind, "as a jewel of gold in a swine's snout, so is a fair woman without discretion." You turn disgusted away—you walk in another direction;—and here, apart from the crowd, you meet a pair sauntering in solitary shades, apparently forgetful of the crowd around them. You might hope here to find a discreet female, but when you hear her listening to sentiments of a dangerous tendency;

such as allusions to the pleasures of friendship, unalloyed by the cautions of narrow souls or cold-hearted beings; you hear her consent to hold a correspondence of friendship with him who laughs at the restraints of discretion, and you again think of the jewel in the swine's snout.

Dinah, the daughter of Jacob, was indiscreet in going out to visit the daughters of the land, when her father was sojourning among an idolatrous people. Her indiscretion resulted in her own ruin, and brought great calamities upon her family—involving her brothers in guilt, and her father in sorrow. Let the talents of a female be what they may, without discretion, they, too, are like the jewel in the swine's snout. Of what avail is it to have a penetrating mind which can search into the philosophy of nature, explore the mysteries of cause and effect, or explain the relations of matter and mind, if one does not learn to apply her knowledge to her own conduct, to keep out out of danger, and to direct her own ways with discretion. We should know the geography of our own hearts, the mechanical powers of our own judgments, and be able to analyze our own weaknesses.

It is indeed the true end of knowledge to gain discretion, so that we may act according to the dignity of our nature, and that beauty, if it exist, may not disgrace the possessor by being united with qualities which belong rather to swinish natures than to rational and intellectual beings.

An imprudent girl can scarcely be expected to make a discreet woman—and when we consider the evils which are brought upon the world by mothers who bring up their children without discretion, by wives whose indiscreet conduct causes gloom and contention to hover over the family circle, and by women who give to society a wrong tone and impulse, can we but perceive the importance of the young being early taught to govern by discretion, their looks, words, and actions?

To quote from another, "There are many more shining qualities than discretion, but there are none so useful. It is this which gives value to all the rest, which sets them at work, and turns them to the advantage of the person who is possessed of them. Without it, learning is pedantry, and wit impertinence—nay, virtue itself often looks like weakness. Discretion is like an agent of providence, to guide and direct us in the affairs of human life."

December, 1842.

ADDRESS IV.

TRUTH AND SINCERITY.

"She whose honest freeness will make it her virtue to speak what she thinks, will make it her necessity to think what is good." —*Marstan.*

THE *essential* virtues of a good and estimable character are truth and sincerity. As counterfeit coin or bank notes are without any real worth, so are all affected graces and assumed goodness destitute of any claim to our regard. He who counterfeits money is severely punished by the laws of the land ; the artful and hypocritical are justly chastised by the contempt of the good, and avoided by them, as the honest business-man would shun such as traffic in counterfeit money. But most persons wish to appear good and amiable in the eyes of others. How shall this be accomplished? The answer is plain ; let all strive to render themselves such as they would be esteemed ; *to be* in reality what they would *appear* to be, and then there would be no temptation to deceive, or *put on* the *semblance* of virtue. Shakspeare makes Hamlet say, with honest indignation, "I know not *seems*;" happy those who are free from all hypocrisy and disguise, all *seeming* to be what in reality they are not.

There is much in the conventional forms of society which leads to deceit, and should be guarded against. One can be civil and polite without expressing warmth of feeling when it does not exist; it is not necessary to profess delight in meeting persons for whom we do not feel any particular interest; or to urge such to visit us, or to correspond with us. Are there no young ladies who meet others with enthusiastic professions of regard, and part from them as if they could not endure a separation, when in reality, they can join in a sneer against those intimate friends? and do they never use the very confidence reposed in them against the unsuspecting and incautious? Would that such evidences of duplicity were not but too common even among those whose youth should be a pledge for artlessness and sincerity! The educator, like the physican, must examine cases as they are; unfavorable symptoms cannot be overlooked if we would do our duty to our patients—or our pupils, and, morally speaking, the latter are too often found affected by maladies which require firm and judicious moral treatment.

It is well for the young to resolve to *practise* what is right, without too much anxiety to please others. The boundaries between right and wrong are often obscure. Thus it is right that we should strive to render ourselves agreeable to others, to say and do that which will make them satisfied with themselves and with us, as far as we can do so without being insincere; but there are some who cannot be happy unless they are flattered; praise is the incense which their hearts crave, and unless this is constantly offered, they are restless and dissatisfied; but the appetite for praise grows on what it feeds, and can never be satisfied. If we have a friend, then, who is not happy unless flattered, it is our duty to withhold the poison, and to seek by a sincere and honest treatment to bring her back to a more healthful state of mind. For a time we may be the less agreeable to her; it may be that a lasting prejudice will spring up against us on account of our sincerity, but if so, we should be satisfied that we have done our duty.

Flattery among school-girls is too common a vice. If one desires the love of another, she too often commences by studying her weak points; and in how many are these self-love, fondness for admiration, and an eager desire for preëminence. If the young girl is vain of beauty, the flatterer tells her of her personal attractions, what she has heard such a one say of her eyes, her features, her complexion, or her form. If she is proud of family connections, or fortune, the flattery is of a different kind. The flatterer talks of distinguished persons and the advantages of good family, wonders how such and such ones should presume to place themselves on an equality with those who are entitled to *exclusiveness*, intimates that she is determined to associate with none but those who have certain claims to family distinction; all this, of course, feeds the vanity of her who is thus sought out by one who is so very particular as to her society.

Again, another young lady who has no pretensions to beauty and makes none as to family or fortune, fancies herself highly gifted in intellect; she likes to be told of her talents, and is inclined to love those who praise them, or who report the praises of others.

What a sad picture is that of one rational and responsible being, for selfish purposes, acting on the bad propensities of another, where lying, insincerity and flattery are seen ministering to disgusting vanity or pride!

If you desire true friendship, seek out a virtuous and sensible person, and let your intercourse be marked with honest sincerity. Despise that regard which must be purchased by a sacrifice of truth, or the ministering to the follies and weaknesses of another. One who is truly worthy and noble should avoid a flatterer whose selfish designs may be easily penetrated. When we hear unpleasant truths, we should reflect that those who utter them can have in this no motive but our own good—unless, indeed, we have reason to believe that they desire to humiliate us in our own eyes, or to render us unhappy; in which case, we cannot consider them as our friends; but the poet says:

——"Your defects to know
Make use of every friend and every foe."

It is one of the most sacred duties of friendship, though often a painful one, to point out faults to a beloved friend; and when you have an associate whom you believe to be your friend though not afraid to speak the truth however disagreeable it may be to you to hear it, you cannot too highly value her friendship.

In the book of Wisdom, we find many passages which point out the danger of flattery, the wickedness of hypocrisy and lying.

" A hypocrite with his mouth destroyeth his neighbor."

" My son, if sinners entice thee, consent thou not."

" Surely in vain the net is spread in the sight of any bird."

Among the six things which are enumerated as those which the Lord hateth, and which are an abomination to Him, are, " A heart that deviseth wicked imaginations. A false witness that speaketh lies, and him that soweth discord among his brethren."

" The opening of my lips shall be of right things, and wickedness is an abomination to my lips."

" Reprove not a scorner lest he hate thee; rebuke a wise man and he will love thee."

" The wicked worketh a deceitful work."

" He that speaketh truth sheweth forth righteousness, but a false witness deceit."

" The lip of truth shall be established forever, but a lying tongue is but for a moment."

" Lying lips are an abomination to the Lord, but they that deal truly are his delight."

" He that walketh with wise men shall be wise, but a companion of fools shall be destroyed."

" A faithful witness will not lie, but a false witness will utter lies."

" Go from the presence of a foolish man, when thou perceivest not in him the lips of knowledge."

" Whose hand is covered by deceit."

" Open rebuke is better than secret love."

"Faithful are the words of a friend, but the *kisses* of an enemy are deceitful."

"He that *blesseth* his friend with a loud voice, it shall be counted a curse to him."

We might go on multiplying examples of a similar nature, but these may suffice to show how the Almighty regards flattery and deceit.

Even little girls are sometimes deceitful, and flatter others for their own selfish purposes. But a deceitful child is an unnatural being. What can be expected of such a one when she becomes older, and is surrounded by the temptations of the world!

Flattery is not the only form of insincerity and falsehood. Those who have a lying spirit are constantly tempted to deceit. In the most trifling things they pervert the truth—they appear not to know what truth is.

But we meet with many encouraging examples of those who have reformed in respect to these habits. The influence of education is often powerful in accomplishing such reformation. Every one who perceives in herself a tendency to falsehood, whether in the way of flattery, slander, or for any selfish or evil purpose, should betake herself to serious self-examination; she should say in her heart, "Thou, O God, seest me," and reflect, that though she may deceive men, "God is not mocked," but discerns "the most secret thoughts and intents of the heart."

How solemn the thought that the All-seeing Eye is ever upon us—that there is not a word on our tongue but God knoweth it altogether. We are the temples of the Holy Spirit, and should not pollute them by deceit or guilt, or any other sin.

Each one of you knows what are your secret sins; may you strive earnestly to be delivered from them, not trusting in your own strength, but in His might, who can save you from the enemy of your soul. How earnestly should you all join in the supplication in our school litany, that "God will have mercy upon us; that he will deliver us from all the dangers that beset us—from evil and mischief, from vanity and lies, from the temptations of the world, the flesh, and the devil: from hypocrisy and corrupt examples. That God will bless us, keep us from evil, lead us unto all truth, and bring us to everlasting life."

Short is the period allotted to you to prepare for eternity. How often do you hear of near and dear friends called away by death—none are spared—the little infant, the playful child, the blooming youth, the strong man, the mother in the bosom of her family, the old and grey-headed, all—all become the prey of the destroyer. Yet we go on from day to day, engaged in our worldly pursuits; we see death around us, but we feel secure; we are as anxious about the things of this life as if this were our everlasting home.

And yet we are as passing strangers and pilgrims through a world of trials and temptations. The homes which await us beyond the grave will be mansions of happiness or woe, as we prepare ourselves here for them. God has declared that in heaven "there shall in no wise enter anything that defileth, neither whatsoever worketh abomination, or maketh a lie;" but they are blessed "who do his commandments, that they may have a right to the tree of life."

ADDRESS V.

CHRISTMAS AND NEW YEAR.

The return of the season of festivals which has just passed by, brings with it feelings as various as there are conditions or states of human life. To the child it suggests images of pleasure and mirth ; but often to the minds of those more advanced in life, arise thoughts of departed friends, and of disappointed hopes.

Scarcely have the fading glories of autumn become lost in the desolation of winter, and nature yielded herself wholly to the influence of the season of ice and frosts, when we begin to realize that we are verging towards the ancient, and sacred festival of Christmas. So rapidly has time passed since the last return of this season, that we can scarcely believe another year has fled. On Christmas day, it is customary in most churches to have religious services, and to administer the Holy Sacrament of the Lord's Supper to the piously disposed. This seems the proper mode of observing the anniversary of our Saviour's birth, that the heart comforted by a sense of the goodness and mercy of God, may thereby gain fresh courage for the trials and the toils of life.

When nature is blooming and attractive we love to

be abroad, and watch the changes that diversify the scenery—the flower-bud as it swells upon the stalk and unfolds into a fair blossom ; the foliage in spring gradually changing from a light green to a richer shade, and then, as touched by the fingers of the declining year, exhibiting those gorgeous hues which like the hectic flush on the cheek indicate decay and death. When the flowers have become fruits, and the fruits are fully ripened and garnered for the use of man, then comes the season of contemplation, of reflection, and of moral culture. We are not tempted to rove abroad by balmy air, murmuring brooks, sweet flowers, or warbling birds. Our thoughts naturally turn inwards, and the state of our own hearts becomes an object of reflection. We are led to gather around the fire-side, and to think what treasures of affection and friendship may be ours to fill up the void caused by the absence of those enjoyments which external nature had so bountifully spread before us in her gay and fruitful seasons.

The beginning of the winter season is a favorable time for the young student. His thoughts not tempted to stray abroad by external attractions, are more easily collected and concentrated. The moaning winds as they sweep by his casement, seem to admonish him of the shortness of life, and that he is bound to cultivate those high intellectual powers which assimilate him to angelic natures. He resolves that he will devote himself more than he has yet done, to the work of his own improvement, so that when called to account for the use he has made of his talents, he may not like the unprofitable servant be found to have "hid them in a napkin."

But mental efforts are for a time superseded by the social and religious claims of Christmas and the New Year. High and noble as is our intellectual nature it must acknowledge in other powers of our souls a superior rank. Satan was high in intellect, and so have been thousands who have given their souls to him. There is the greater condemnation to such as *know* their Master's will, and do it not.

The social affections need culture as well as the intellectual faculties, and we may so neglect them that they cease to have an influence over our hearts, or to contribute to our enjoyment. And how much to be pitied is that lone being who neither loves nor is beloved! What avails it how high he may soar in the regions of lofty contemplation or fervid imagination, how deeply his mind may be imbued with ancient lore, how intimate may be his communion with the spirits of philosophers of past ages, or how great may be his delight to wander alone down the stream of history and hold converse with the shades of departed heroes and statesmen! He may indeed enjoy a temporary gratification while forgetting what, and where he is;—but the mind becomes wearied with its flights, and the straining of the mental eye to look after the dim shadows of the past; with its efforts to investigate the truths of science, or attempts to search into the depths of philosophy; or to penetrate the designs and secret motives of the Almighty;—the restless wing of thought droops, and man finds himself on the humble earth surrounded by objects as lowly as himself—is he not greatly to be pitied if here he finds no friend, no companion, to whom he may impart his feelings and from whom he may expect sympathy and affection! He cannot call from their sleep of ages the philosophers and heroes with whom he has delighted to wander in the pages of history, and for whose sake he may have neglected companions who once courted his scoiety and friendship. Alone, he feels how sad is man without sympathy, and without affection. We may be pleased to spend some time in a gallery of portraits; we may admire the skill of the painters, and interest ourselves in the characters successively brought before us; but when we have ceased to look and admire, we turn to the friends who are beside us, and one look of affection, one word of kindness, or one simple loving act, strikes a chord within the soul drawing forth deeper and sweeter tones than art, science, or philosophy can produce.

The returns of Christmas and New Year, these social and religious festivals, have a happy influence in reviving those affections which are often chilled by the world without, and smothered by selfishness within. Children love Christmas and New Year's day, because they are then more especially remembered, and made to feel by the gifts and attentions of the season, that they are beloved. But children who love these days merely for the sake of *gifts*, are selfish indeed; and it is to be feared that too many think more of the presents they receive, than they do of the affection which offers them. We should value a kind look or word dictated by love, more than the most costly offering without affection ; and if those who have nothing else to give, offer their good wishes with the sincerity and warmth of friendship, such as are capable of sympathy will respond to their greetings from the depths of their hearts.

While Christmas calls on all who have friends to manifest for them a kind remembrance—if they are near, to seek their society, if distant, to send some token of their love—it most especially reminds mankind of Him, who gave *Himself* for them. On this day we celebrate the birth of Christ. To Him, therefore, should our thoughts ascend in thanksgiving and adoration. We should, if opportunity presents, go to the Holy Communion, where the professed followers of the Redeemer meet to comply with His dying request: "Do this in remembrance of me." It is here that the Christian gathers new strength to encounter the spiritual enemies who would draw him away from God. Here he not only presents himself, but, in his supplications, all who are near and dear to him. He intercedes with his Saviour that they, too, may enjoy that "bread of life which came down from heaven," and be fitted for a better and happier world by the toils and trials of this.

Going from the worship of God and the communion of the church, the sincere Christian will feel a renewed love for his fellow-beings, those for whom Christ died, and who are loved by Him. A feeling of benevolence, of holy serenity, and of trust in God's mercy and goodness, goes with the pious Christain as he returns from the sanctuary to mingle in the social circle. The merry laugh of childhood, the innocent gaiety of the young, their harmless sports, their songs, and their dances, are not, in his view, opposed to any of the requirements of religion; whose great command it is to "love your neighbor as yourself," to "do unto others as you would they should do to you," and which declares that "love is the fulfilling of the law." The same religion says, "let all anger, and malice, and revenge, be put away from you." Everything, therefore, which tends to promote love and kindness, and to repel malice and anger, is sanctioned by religion, and we need have no fear that we are acting contrary to its dictates when we indulge in innocent enjoyments which tend to sweeten life, and to dispel from it that gloomy acerbity by which the heart of man is too often possessed.

We have remarked that the Christian may indulge in innocent amusements. The question arises as to what may be considered innocent. On this subject there are various opinions; and because amusements in themselves innocent have been perverted, many Christians condemn all as sinful. We would observe that our conduct in this, as in many other cases, should be governed by circumstances. If we were likely to grieve Christian friends by doing that which we consider innocent, we should, nevertheless, from regard to their feelings, refrain from the act, since it would not be sinful to abstain from joining in the amusement.

There are, however, imprudences into which the young are liable to fall when they give way to the social and mirthful feelings—they are then often thrown off their guard, and do that which they afterwards regret.

After the season of holidays, you are now again to pursue your studies, and to engage in a regular routine of duties. There may be among you some who would wish that holidays might last forever. There are young persons who love pleasure better than duty; to whom the desire of improvement is unknown. Unhappy they whose minds are incapable of noble aspirations, who are ignorant of the pure and tranquil enjoyment connected with intellectual cultivation, and the consciousness of moral excellence. We would call upon such to look to their mental diseases, to forsake the follies which confine them to the low condition in which they have hitherto been contented to rest. We will draw two pictures—pictures made with words, but which you can see with your mind's eye, as if delineated on canvas. Let us look at the young person who considers *pleasure* as the chief good: her outward aspect evinces her tastes—for the intellect and the heart are read in the expression of the countenance. The vacant look, the meaningless smile, the withdrawal from the glance of others as though unwilling to have the perverted heart and the empty void of mind exposed to the view of penetrating observation; the indifference with which instruction is received; the evident wandering of the thoughts as seen in the expression of the eye; the listless, dreamy manner which says, louder than words could do, "Would that this lesson," "this address," or "this sermon were over." She who loves pleasure more than moral excellence, thinks not what is best for her, but what she *likes* to do. Let us pause a moment, and consider to what will all this tend. Think of your unpardonable neglect of past advantages—that a little space remains to you in the which to repair your past errors, before launching forth upon the sea of life, where you will need habits of self-control, power over your inclinations, and the knowledge and accomplishments you have now an opportunity of acquiring. Can you not shake off the lethargy in which your soul has been bound, and spurn the trivialities which choke the nobler sentiments of your nature. Say to yourselves, "Old things with me shall pass away, and all shall be new. "*I will be changed*"—resolve this, be firm to your purpose, and your work is done; you have bought your own freedom from that worst of all slavery, the thralldom of the mind. You may yet be able to take your place among the good, the noble-minded, the candidates for a glorious and happy immortality.

Let us turn to the brighter picture.—We see a young person whose object is to do right, to improve all her faculties as due to the author of her existence, and to the earthly parents whose hopes are centered in her. She lives day by day in the full consciousness of her great responsibility as a rational, immortal being. She listens attentively to instruction, her eye kindles as her mind receives light. The sparkling of intellect is vivid and apparent as is the flame upon the hearthstone ; but how infinitely more sublime is the beaming forth of mind than material light! She whom we picture to you may not be beautiful, as some count beauty; she may be plain in features, her complexion destitute of the rosy tint or alabaster whiteness; her eye may not be dazzling black, or "softly, beautifully blue"—but when the light of the soul illumines her countenance, beams forth from her eye and plays over her features, how infinitely superior the charm to that of mere material beauty! The dolls that you left at home in your nurseries had sparkling eyes, regular features, and beautiful white and red complexions ; they were very pretty, you liked to look at them, and to fancy that you loved them, and that they loved you ; but as you grew older, they ceased to interest you. You felt for them no affection, you did not esteem or respect them; but you do not now despise your dolls, they were only effigies, incapable of moral agency, not like yourselves, accountable beings, and to be blamed or approved according to bad or good conduct.

There is a fearful weight of responsibility resting upon each of you, whether you are willing to acknowledge it or not ; whether you choose to keep it out of your thoughts or not, it is the same—your youth will soon pass away. Days will come, should your lives be prolonged, in which you will be called on to care for others, to set good examples to those who may be connected with, or dependent on you; and then, how soon will come the decline of life, and old age! Then all that remains to render you interesting and valuable to others, will be the fragrance of virtue and piety; and all that can give you light for the future, will be the hope of happiness in the world to come founded on a well-spent life.

May these solemn truths inspire you all with ardor to begin anew your journey of life; to do better than you have yet done. May those who have been careless of duty and regardless of instruction, begin in earnest to search after true wisdom, and may those who have felt feeble desires after that holiness, without which none can see the Lord, be stimulated to renewed efforts.

A New Year has come—we have lived to greet its arrival. Where shall we be, and under what circumstances, at its close! A startling question! Varied scenes of trouble lie before us, this is certain, for it is the inevitable doom of man.

"Lord, so teach us to number our days that we may apply our hearts unto wisdom."

Close of 1848, and commencement of a New Year.

ADDRESS VI.

PLEASURE AND DUTY.

We are again assembled, my dear pupils, after a short suspension of duty; and you have already resumed your accustomed occupations. Pleasure has resigned her sway, and duty, less attractive but more honest and sincere, has taken the helm.

Pleasure and duty! how opposite sound these words to the ears of the young, and how different are the emotions with which they regard the one and the other. Most of you have doubtless read the beautiful allegory from the pen of Mrs. Barbauld, where a young girl is accosted by two personages, the one representing Pleasure wreathed with flowers, and radiant with smiles; the other, of a serious aspect, and presenting no attractions. Pleasure, in silvery tones, tells of the delights she will give; but Duty uses no flattery, she acknowledges that her path is not strewn with flowers, but she tells the fair girl of mansions of rest and peace to which this straight and narrow way conducts. The child hesitates, for Pleasure is bright and beautiful, fascinating and enticing; while Duty is stern and unattractive, so inelegant and unfashionable that the heart revolts from her acquaintance. Both hold out their hands to the young girl. Pleasure's sweet and inviting smile wins her heart, and she is about to follow her—when a sudden gust of wind blowing aside the beautiful robe of Pleasure, torn and filthy rags appear beneath: as she tries to conceal them by drawing around her the folds of drapery, the mask with which her features were disguised, falls off, and discloses a haggard and disgusting aspect, marked with the deep furrows of evil passions. The child shudders, draws back her hand, and turns to Duty. For the first time, she now perceives a pleasant smile irradiate her countenance, as she draws closer to her side, and embraces her, and in her companionship in the journey of life, she obtains that which the devotees of Pleasure seek in vain—peace and happiness. Yes, even in sorrow and affliction, she who loves and follows duty, enjoys that sweet peace "which, as the world giveth not, neither can it take away."

Yet it is well, sometimes, to relax from the calls of duty, and try how happy we may be with nothing to do, *but to enjoy.* The change at first is pleasant; our spirits are exhilarated, and our hearts beat with a quickened pulse; but we soon weary of doing nothing. The young do not care to sleep always, though no matin bell call them to duty; nor can they eat always, though every dainty be spread before them. We begin to feel, after an interval of indulgence, that we must exert ourselves even to be happy; we must do something even to secure pleasure. Is it not, then, wise that the efforts which the constitution of our minds impels us to make, should be directed to something useful? Thus, while we are obeying a law of our being, which obliges us to be active, we are doing good here, and laying up treasures in heaven

You have all, I doubt not, in some degree, shared the feelings of one of your teachers, Miss ——, who accompanied me in my late journey to R——; perhaps it was almost the first time in her life that she commenced an undertaking which had not some immediate duty connected with it; and it was so with this, in one sense, since it was in obedience to the dictates of affection for her young friend, just settled in domestic life, that she made the visit. She was going to see, in her own home, one to whom she was devotedly attached, and to meet with others from whom she had received particular marks of esteem. For a day or two, she was no longer the impersonation of serious, sincere and laborious duty, but joyous and almost gay. She ran about the pleasant apartments of her happy young friend, delighted with, and enjoying all. "How pleasant," said she, "if we could always stay here!" After a few days, our friend says again: "It is tiresome to do nothing but visit and see company."

I cannot suppose that you, who are younger, less habituated to be active in well doing, and who have left your homes and their dear inmates to return to school, did not feel regret at leaving them; but yet, I am sure, were the appeal made to your own consciences, you would say that you are, in reality, most truly happy when you are doing what seems to be your duty.

Since we last met, we have passed another anniversary of the birth of our Saviour. Eighteen hundred and forty-three years have passed since Jesus of Nazareth was born in a stable, in the obscure town of Bethlehem, in the Roman province of Judea.

Far in the eastern, Asiatic country, the tradition had spread among the Gentiles, or heathens, that a remarkable personage was to appear on the earth, about that period. The Jewish scriptures, though not received by those nations, had, yet, disseminated among them many religious truths; and the prophecies respecting Christ seem to have been better understood by the magi, or philosophers of the East, than even by the Jewish rabbins, or doctors of divinity. While, therefore, the Jews were reposing in their indifference as to the fulfillment of the prophecies respecting a Saviour, the eastern magi, who were also astrologers or observers of the heavens, being surprised by the appearance of an uncommon celestial body, followed its direction until they came to the city of Jerusalem. They then inquired: "Where is he, who is born King of the Jews, for we, in the East, have seen his star, and are come to worship him." King Herod, a bad and ambitious man, was much troubled at this, and collecting the doctors of divinity, or chief priests and scribes, he demanded of them, where, according to the Scriptures, Christ should be born? The answer was: "In Bethlehem of Judea." Herod was much troubled at these things, and pretending that he himself wished to worship the infant Saviour, desired that the magi would go and search, and when they had found him, send him word. The star went before, and guided them until it stood over the place where the young child was. At this, they rejoiced greatly, and withheld by no infidel scruples, they fell down and worshipped him; after which, according to eastern customs in offering homage to a sovereign, they presented rich gifts, "gold, frankincense, and myrrh." A glorious light from heaven appeared also to some shepherds of Judea, who were watching their flocks by night; and while they were wondering and afraid, the angel of the Lord appeared unto them, and said: "Fear not, oh, shepherds! for behold I bring you good tidings of great joy, which shall be to *all people;* for unto you is born this day a Saviour, which is Christ the Lord; and this shall be a sign unto you, ye shall find the babe wrapped in swaddling bands, lying in a manger." And suddenly there was with the angel a *multitude of the heavenly host*, praising God, and saying: "Glory to God in the highest, peace on earth, and good will towards men!"

Having seen this glorious vision, and heard the chorus of the angels, the shepherds hastened to go and see the wonderful babe of Bethlehem; and they returned, "glori-rifying and praising God for all the things that they had heard and seen as it was told unto them." Well might Mary ponder these things in her heart, and regard herself as highly favored among women, though, instead of a luxurious chamber, she lodged in a stable, and the cradle for her babe was but a manger, "where horned oxen fed."

Shall we not, with the magi, the shepherds, and the host of angels, come to offer our gifts to the Saviour of the world? He requires of us no costly offerings, but a "broken and contrite heart he will not despise." He asks only our love, gratitude, and devotion, for the salvation he has procured for us. He has purchased our redemption with his own blood; he offers us pardon for our sins, and that peace which he left with his disciples; he offers us those mansions in heaven which he went to prepare for us; he only asks that we will go to him for the charter of our freedom from sin and death. He stands with open arms; will we not go to him, will we not accept his offer of mercy and salvation!

Since our separation, we have all parted with a friend who has been with us, daily, since the commencement of the past year; who has seen us, by turns, happy and dejected; and who, though he has seen us disappointed, has, every day, whispered of something better on the morrow. Though we may have been indifferent to this friend, and often wished him gone, still we could not bid farewell without emotion. We know that he has kept a strict account of what we have been doing; and his tablets are now registered at that tribunal before which we are to all appear in judgment.

The year 1843 is this friend, now passed into eternity, to give evidence either for or against us. Have we well treated its successive portions of time, its 365 days;—have the twenty-four hours of each day no record against us, of trifling actions, idle words, and evil thoughts? Even one little minute may rise up against some of us, and say: "I heard you, as I was passing, speaking words to blast the name and character of another; the blush upon your cheek proclaimed that you were conscious of the falsehood you uttered, and a dark spot which I saw as I looked through the window of your heart, betrayed the stain of envy upon it." Another minute may say: "As I was passing, I saw you, at the hour of devotion, bending low at the name of Jesus. I was happy, for I thought my testimony would be in your favor; but I saw cold unbelief in your heart, and passed on to give my account." Still, another minute proclaims its message: "I saw you bending in prayer; your lips murmured the name of God, and all around you supposed you worshipped him; but it was all hypocrisy, God was not in your thoughts; at His bar you must answer for such profanation."

And are *minutes*, then, able by their testimony to fix our everlasting destiny? Alas! of what may not even one passing minute have to accuse man! 1,440 of these winged messengers to eternity, look in upon us in one day; 535,600 of these witnesses, either for or against us, have passed on to the bar of God since the last year dawned upon us. New minutes are now coming to take their rapid observation of our thoughts, words, and actions; let us make friends of them as they pass, so that the coming year may depart freighted with friendly messengers to the throne of our final Judge.

With respect to earthly happiness, it is vain to disguise

the fact that we have not much to expect; we should not, therefore, be too anxious to know our future fate. The pages of time, as they are successively unrolled, must present to all human beings some dark passages, and in many cases there may be little light to relieve the picture.

But if we raise our eyes, we may see in heaven a star of hope ; let us follow its guidance, and we shall be led to those regions of eternal happiness, "which eye hath not seen, nor ear heard, neither hath it entered into the heart of man to conceive."

JANUARY, 1844.

ADDRESS VII.

RELATION OF THE PRESENT TO THE FUTURE.

How little do we realize, as day after day speeds on and finds us in one place, that the period will come when all around us will be changed; when familiar faces will be no more seen; and that many loved ones now with us will become as strangers, travelling far distant from us in life's pilgrimage. They may be called from earth without our being near to bid farewell, or to cheer with our sympathies and prayers the fleeting spirit in its fearful journey to eternity!

If such thoughts sometimes occurred to the young as they mingle with their school companions, how differently would they, often, conduct towards them. If the pupil realized the separation from a teacher, and that the time would come when the voice of that faithful and anxious friend would be no more heard, and when that countenance would be lost forever, how differently might her instructions and admonitions be received!

But we cannot live in the future. It is the law of our nature to feel as if to-morrow would be as this day. Thus in sorrow and adversity, we despond of relief; and in prosperity, we think not of evil days to come. Still, there are principles implanted in our hearts, which lead us to make use of the present, in reference to the future. Reflection and reason are ever ready to suggest the importance of making preparations for the changes which we know await us, and the more the character is under their influence, the more will be the effort to act in reference to a future which may seem distant, but which, if we live, will surely come, and come, quickly, too. The school-girl is tempted by her love of ease and present enjoyment to pass lightly over the duties assigned her. She is more pleased to talk and amuse herself with her young companions than to study. Habits of industry and order, of self-restraint, and of untiring diligence are not agreeable to her inclinations ; present gratifications invite, and the *future* the *uncertain future* has little influence. The one is here, the other *far off* ;—is it strange that the young are carried away by temptations, and yield themselves up to the alluring present ?

But *the future*, the *inexorable* future, comes, and demands "what hast *thou* laid up for me ? Thou knowest that time was given thee to prepare for me. So I come to demand an account of thy stewardship ;—where are the *talents* that thou hast received ?"

How solemn this inquiry ! yet there is no getting away from it. The *future* will come, in some way. The grave itself cannot avert its claims, but in those dread regions which lie beyond, the question will come from the judgment-seat of God, "What preparation hast thou made for the eternity on which thou hast entered ?" Will the answer, "I could not school my heart to the love of religion, I could not incline myself to follow the footsteps and commands of Jesus"—will this answer be sufficient at the bar of God? "*Inasmuch as ye did it not,*" ye shall be condemned.

From the first dawnings of reason, to the last day of life, we should keep the *future* steadily in view. The situation *next before us*, or for which we seem, at present, destined, should engage our attention; and our effort should be to prepare for it. The daughter at school should study how she may best conduce to the happiness and comfort of her parents, and that of the family circle—she should consider what defect there may be in her character, disposition, and habits, which would annoy, or in any way affect, unpleasantly, that circle which she will soon join, and which she should desire to enliven and make glad. Those who are looking forward to become instructors and guides of others, should consider the many qualities of heart, the principles and habits, as well as the intellectual attainments, which will be required in that responsible relation. All should inquire and learn, as far as possible, what preparation will be suitable for the journey of life before them; and inasmuch as they know not the paths by which they may be led, the companions who will journey with them, the moral climates, whether *warm* with affection or *cold* with distrust or dislike, through which they may pass, they should lay up *everything* which may become necessary or useful, so far as they have the opportunity to make acquisitions. In one part of the journey of life, habits, qualifications of heart and intellect may be called into exercise, which, in another stage, may seem scarcely needed; while under other circumstances, new virtues or attainments may be necessary, to comfort, success, or respectability. *Education* is designed to furnish the young with a rich variety of resources, which may be available in the various conditions of this uncertain life.

A wife protected by a fond and indulgent husband who has the means of supplying her not only with the comforts, but the elegances of life, has little need for those sterner and more masculine qualities, which would be necessary under a change of circumstances. Should she become a widow, charged with business responsibilities, obliged perhaps to appeal to the laws, in order to maintain her own rights and the rights of her children, exposed to impositions, and frauds which would take from her family all their means of support, she would then require firmness of purpose and decision of character, in order to keep together the fortune bequeathed to her and her fatherless children; or, if fortune be wanting, she would require industry and ability to labor for their support. Is it not, then, desirable that a woman shall possess some qualifications for business, a head to calculate, and judgment to discriminate?

Education, while bestowing feminine accomplishments, cultivating the graces of mind and person, and fitting the young lady for polite and elegant society and to be an interesting and lovely companion, should also strengthen the character of the future woman, so that she may be capable of acting any part in life which the Providence of God may assign her. In connection with these reflections, I would, my dear pupils, call your attention to the importance of your prolonging the period of your school education, when the circumstances and kindness of your parents, or your own resources, enable you to do so. Unfortunately for the welfare and intelligence of future women, young girls are often anxious to abridge even the short time allotted for school education. The love of change, the idea of pleasures to be derived from society, or a fondness for home, are strong inducements acting upon the mind and influencing it to decide against a continuance in school, when parental indulgence leaves the choice to the pupil herself. But think of the future ; not the few months, or the one or two years immediately before you, for in these you might not feel the want of the advantages you would sacrifice ; but think of future life, and of the calls it may involve of rich stores of knowledge, which may be applied to varying circumstances; and think how important that your characters shall have acquired some strength and solidity before engaging in those scenes of life, where temptations and trials too often prove fatal to happiness, if not to reputation and virtue.

When the proper period comes for the termination of your academic life, you have then to begin a new set of duties, to put in practice lessons you have been learning—you will commence a new school—and may you go on improving while life shall last, fitting yourselves for a never-ending state of happiness, and for the society of pure and elevated intelligences in a higher sphere of existence.

1848.

ADDRESS VIII.

STABILITY OF MORAL PRINCIPLE THE ONLY SECURITY FOR THE YOUNG IN THEIR INTERCOURSE WITH THE WORLD.

In addressing my pupils it is proper that present scenes and duties should often furnish the themes of discourse ; but these must not be permitted to occupy our chief attention ; we should sometimes look forward to the future, that we may keep in view the great object of forming your character for the coming duties of life, that we may best learn the precautions which should be taken against the dangers and temptations of the world, and what securities can be furnished for the right fulfillment of duties.

The great mistake of the young, and too often of those who are intrusted with their education, is that of entertaining false views of the qualifications to act, well, a part in the complex, and ever-changing scenes of life.

What are these qualifications ? Notwithstanding all the importance that may be attached by your parents and teachers to the *learning of schools*, or knowledge of books and of things, and to the possession of certain accomplishments, yet none of these is the first and great requisite for a faithful discharge of the duties of life ;—this is *principle*, correct, firm, moral principle, based on religion and having the love and fear of

God for its end and aim. "The fear of the Lord is the beginning of wisdom." Those who have not this fear, have not begun to be wise, however great their other attainments may be.

There are few parents who do not begin early to teach their children their obligations to love and fear God; but such is the imperfection, the sinfulness of human nature, that the pious lessons of parents are often counteracted by examples in direct variance with their own instructions. A parent, perhaps, requires a child to learn the ten commandments, and to repeat them as the solemn requirements of God. The child learns first that he shall not have any God before the Lord, Jehovah; but he sees his parents making a god of riches, of fashion, or of worldly honor, and as example is more powerful than precept, he is led away from the strict application of the words; and seeing the very first commandment set at naught by those to whom he looks up for direction, he is not surprised at observing the whole decalogue disregarded and disobeyed.

Even the most pious and conscientious parents often fail in their duty of practising what they teach, and thus become stumbling-blocks to their children, instead of lights to guide them in the path of virtue and holiness. If it be so with parents who are striving "to live an uncorrupt life," "to speak truth from the heart," and "do the thing which is right," how must it be with those who think little of duty, and who are engrossed wholly with the cares and projects of a worldly career?

It is not, then, strange that children with sinful hearts and propensities to evil, witnessing the little regard to principles of truth and virtue in those around them, should increase in years without growing in grace and in the knowledge of God. The circumstances by which they are surrounded are calculated to obscure in their minds the pure light of truth, and to gild with a false lustre much which is worthless when unaccompanied with the substantial elements of virtue.

You are urged on in your studies, and think, perhaps, that the great point is, to become good scholars ; that in order to appear respectable in life, you must acquire knowledge, and be familiar with such accomplishments as are common to well-educated and refined ladies. Educational institutions that send out the best scholars, usually gain most celebrity, while little popularity may be attached to a school on account of its influence in rendering its pupils moral, virtuous, and pious. How unfortunate that parents, in general, so greatly err, as to the true and permanent interests of their children ! Teachers who are influenced by *worldly* motives only, will, of course, devote their chief efforts to what their interests prompts; and perhaps urged by the necessities of their condition to cater to a corrupt popular estimate, they pass by the great essentials of education, and devote themselves wholly to what will yield them the greatest amount of present applause and profit. The attainments of a pupil in various branches of literature, or in elegant accomplishments, may be striking, and elicit admiration, but improvement in her disposition and principles is not discovered at once; this is to be unfolded in the varying scenes and circumstances of future life. To know, in after years, of one who was a pupil here, that she is a good and useful woman, filling with dignity and fidelity the duties of her station—this will be a reward for the cares and toils of education: may this indeed be mine as respects those who are now before me.

The excellent Hannah More remarked, that from seeing the manner in which girls were educated, one would think that life was a succession of holidays, and that the great object was to fit them for the games, shows, and amusements with which it was to be occupied. But let us look at life as it is, not as the wild imagination of the young may paint in glowing hues which fade into sombre shades before the touch of truth and reality. According to the customs of fashionable society, a young girl on leaving school is "*brought out*," or "finished," as by the common absurd phraseology. She is a young lady, passed from the bud to the blossom; and she must now forget much that she has been learning, and learn new lessons in the school of the world. She considers herself a candidate for admiration, and expects the homage of flattery; a feverish anxiety for attention in society naturally takes possession of her mind, she becomes one among the giddy crowd who throng the temple of pleasure, and on the altar of their idols, fashion and vanity, offer the sacrifice of health and of their heart's best affections. The *débutante* having looked forward with eagerness to her introduction to society, very naturally imagines that others partake of her own feelings, and that such an important event must cause a great sensation in the world—or at least in her own circle, which she imagines to be the first and most important in the world. She scans her own appearance with anxious care; regards with scrutinizing looks her complexion, features and form; her mode of walking, standing, sitting, and dancing are subjects of deep concern to herself and perhaps her parents. The latter, perhaps, blindly overlooking the realities of life, which it would seem experience might have taught them, regard with undue interest their daughter's *entrée* into society, and the impressions which her *coming out* may produce. In all this anxiety to discern external attractions, and fears lest they may be counterbalanced by defects, is there no concern for the soul, no inspection of the heart, no dread of evil passions taking root there, and deformities which may offend the eye of the all-seeing God? Such questions addressed to worldly parents and unreflecting daughters, might be met with a smile of contempt; as if the wisdom of this world were enough, and to be scrupulous in respect to the means of gaining its favor or its pleasures, were to throw away the real, seen, and known advantages, for imaginary, or, at least, far distant benefits. The devotees of the world, however they may profess to *believe*, are practical *atheists*, denying by their conduct that there is a God who watches over the actions of men, and who will judge them not only for the deeds done in the body, but for the thoughts and intents of the heart. Let us trace the young *débutante* through her flowery path of pleasure for a season or two, to satisfy ourselves whether her expectations even for this period are answered.

We know full well that nothing is more illusive than the idea of the great interest which the world takes in the affairs of a particular individual, and that one, a young girl, with merely youth and youthful attractions to recommend her to notice. For the want of something better to talk about in fashionable circles, the appearance of a new candidate for admiration may be made a subject of conversation; but will she receive unqualified praise? If beautiful, she may be condemned as vain; if graceful, as affected in manners; if frank and ingenuous, she will likely be called imprudent; and if cautious, artful. If, to be agreeable to the many, she talk on common-place topics, she may pass for one who has a shallow intellect; if she introduce into fashionable circles, literary or religious subjects, she will probably be shunned as pedantic or bigoted. If she should have admirers, she will be called a flirt; if she should have none, she will be pitied for her supposed disappointment and mortification. If the young lady who has anticipated so much from her introduction into the world of fashion, or what is called society, possess sensibility and principle she will soon perceive that there is a competition going on there, in its nature calculated to chill the better feelings of the soul; that under the mask of affected benevolence, and desire of promoting mutual happiness by bringing to the common stock, pleasure and enjoyment, are concealed frightful passions, "envy, hatred, and malice, and all uncharitableness," from which we daily pray to be delivered. After the labor of so many years, such great expense of time and money to gain accomplishments that may secure triumph and admiration, after the toil and anxiety of preparing the person for the public, the young lady perhaps finds herself receiving far less attention than some one whom she regards as her inferior; innocent, that one may be, of any intentional wrong to her, but mortification will naturally give rise to jealousy, which begets *hatred*.

Allowing, however, that our young lady is decidedly *the belle* of a short season or two, that she has had a triumphant *entrée* into the highest circle, is regarded as the brightest star in the constellation of fashion, can we suppose that even for that brief period she is happy? If she possess penetration, she will see how heartless and vain are the homage and admiration of those, who, like the butterfly flit from flower to flower, selfishly seeking pleasure and amusement, wholly indifferent as to the effects of their heartless attention upon the future happiness of those whom they may choose to flatter. For it must be remembered that in the world of fashion and folly, are seldom found men of true sensibility and scrupulous morals. The game that is there going on, forbids such from becoming initiated in the mysteries of "*high life*," where weak principles are tested by the artful and designing, where fortune attracts, and where modest

merit, unaccompanied by wealth or some *prestige* which is an equivalent for wealth, can find no place. We will suppose our young lady has become quite accustomed to fashionable life; she has gained her place among its votaries —but what has she not lost! Late hours, imprudence in dress, exposure to the impure atmosphere of gaslights and crowded assemblies, and the dainties of luxurious banquets, at length undermine her health. The freshness of youth has faded, her spirits are no longer buoyant; she has grasped the thorn, but the rose has withered. And the warmth of affection, the simplicity of heart and the conscientiousness of principle which were seen in the school-girl, are they, too, lost! We fear so, and yet they may have only been blighted; a timely escape from the ways of folly, and a return to healthful influences, may revive the affections, and rouse the conscience.

In that career, so deleterious both to the physical and moral nature, the aspirant for fashionable distinction before becoming a victim to the world, may be early arrested by the voice of conscience and withdraw herself from evil influences, while she has yet the power of regaining in some degree what she has lost;—before she shall have suffered the chagrin of being considered *passée*, neglected by the world for which she has sacrificed herself. How pitiable the woman of the world, whose seared heart and vitiated taste render her incapable of enjoyments which spring from intellectual pursuits, or the exercise of the affections! If single, she will be forlorn and neglected; if a wife and mother, how much to be commiserated are those who are dependent for happiness or virtue on her faithfulness or conscientiousness.

And now, my dear pupils, do any of you think you would ever wish to encounter all these evils for the distinction of being a belle in fashionable society? Yet you hear too much said even among those who should beware of giving you false impressions, about "*introduction into society*," or in vulgar parlance, as we sometimes hear, "turning out"—or of "*finishing your education*." But why talk of finishing, when the education can never be finished! Even the angels and the spirits of the just in heaven are continually progressing in knowledge and virtue. The period of school education must terminate; but so far from considering this termination as the era in which reflection, labor, and self-denial are to cease, it should be regarded as that period which calls upon the young to lay aside childish things, to assume new responsibilities, and engage in new duties—to begin, in earnest, to contribute to the happiness and comfort of those who have been laboring and caring for them, and to act their part in the drama of life, as those who must give account hereafter, before the great Judge of all.

1844.

ADDRESS IX.

CHANGE.

CHANGE is inscribed on everything around us. Physical nature is constantly in a state of transition; nothing here is fixed, nothing is permanent. The earth itself is continually in motion—on its axis, around the sun, and carried with the system to which it belongs around some unknown centre. The solid rocks upon the earth gradually decay and crumble into dust—their remains enter into the composition of plants, which in their turn, become constituent parts of animals. Again, the decomposition of animal substances furnishes the nourishment of plants; and from gases evolved from both plants and animals, minerals are formed. The anthracite coal we burn, which is considered a mineral substance, is formed from the remains of vegetables. The vast mines of bituminous coal of our country bear indubitable marks of having once been forests of trees; while the beds of peat coal found so extensively in England and Ireland, and some other parts of the world, are well known to be of vegetable origin.

Observe an acorn; take it up in your hands and examine its structure—it is a little brown seed; strip it of its outer covering; there is a softer substance which seems on examining to be composed of two parts joined together, and inclosing a minute filament; this is an oak tree! It contains within its tiny dimensions the vast roots of that monarch of the forest, with its trunk, branches and foliage; and, moreover, the germs of future generations of plants! From this small seed, time, under favoring circumstances, will develop the perfect, full-grown, majestic tree; and other trees in succession, while the earth endures.

Behold the little infant reposing in its cradle, unconscious of its own existence, and enjoying a mere animal life; the most helpless and imbecile of all young creatures. But what mighty intellectual energies slumber within that tiny form; what noble moral qualities!—and alas, it may be, what deep depravity lies there! Time, time, moving on with rapid strides, touches all things in his progress; and as he touches, a *change* comes over them.

But let us come nearer to ourselves, let us note the changes which we have experienced in our persons, our minds, and in our condition. The period of our helpless infancy and early childhood is as dark to our memory as the years beyond the flood. The germ of thought in the infant mind is gradually developed, like the unfolding embryo of a plant. Emotions of love, anger, grief, and joy break in upon the animal existence;—reason and reflection come later; and conscience is last to assert its claims to direct the thoughts and actions of a being destined to immortality. First, is the physical nature; then appear the passions; next, the reasoning powers; and lastly, the *morale* or that higher development of mind which proves man to be a free moral agent, with a guide inherent in himself, which, if duly regarded, may conduct him through this vale of tears to regions of immortal blessedness.

Slowly does conscience work its way through the incumbent weight of appetites and passions—and often are the hearts of the parent and educator saddened at the little progress which the moral emotion seems to make in the mind of the child, or the pupil. Some children seem early to be conscientious; they have a dread of committing sin, and a desire to know their duty; others appear to be wholly governed by their animal nature, or their passions, and to care little for what is right or wrong, provided they are gratified in their desires.

Man has a middle nature, he is a connecting link between angel and brute. In proportion as he allows himself to be controlled by his appetites and passions, he is assimilated to the lower order; the more he obeys the dictates of conscience, the higher he rises in the scale of being and the nearer he approaches to angelic perfection. It is hard to burst the bonds of sinful and depraved appetites and passions; but if we would rise to the dignity of which our nature is capable, we must make the most powerful efforts, and seize hold of every aid which may be within our grasp to assist us in the great conflict.

The young are sent abroad to school that they may learn to live a new life. The scenes of their early childhood are the scenes of the gratification of their love of animal indulgences ; for, as the infant gradually develops into the maturer child, and the child approaches the years of adolescence or youth, the change is so imperceptible, that in many cases, a corresponding change in respect to fewer indulgences, and more rigid demands of exertion and self-sacrifice is not made by the parents; until, suddenly, the truth flashes upon their minds that their child will soon arrive at the age of manhood or of womanhood, wholly unfurnished with habits of self-government or restraint. The *new life* which he must immediately commence, preparatory to his entrance into the world, can better be begun in new scenes, and under new circumstances; and the child is sent away to be trained for the stern duties which await him in life, to be taught to govern his inclinations and control his passions, and to give the higher nature within him an opportunity of expanding and strengthening under more favorable circumstances.

It is not, therefore, a cause of surprise to see pupils at first discontented and uneasy—the same self-indulgence allowed them at home is not here permitted. The morning sleep, so sweet to the young that when not disturbed it is often prolonged to a very late hour, must be interrupted—the kind mother or indulgent nurse does not in the gentlest tones of entreaty beg that the darling will open her eyes to the morning light and favor the household with the beams of her sweet countenance, but the loud and commanding tones of the rising-bell, proclaim that the rules must be obeyed, that Patapsco expects her daughters to do their duty. Conscience doubtless whispered to the dilatory girl, when her faithful nurse was coaxing, or her fond mother entreating, that she ought to rouse herself and shake off the drowsiness which claimed such unreasonable indulgence ; but habit was too strong, it overcame the feeble struggles of conscience;—but give to this faculty a fair opportunity of gaining strength, and you will find yourselves more and more able by its power to fortify yourselves against temptations.

Another indulgence which children often enjoy at home, is that of luxurious living. The first thing in the care of the infant is to cause it to receive nourishment ; the child as it becomes older is fed on what it likes, and its tastes are consulted. Habits of sensual gratification are thus formed, which must in more mature life be corrected, or there can be no dignity of character. Health and reputation are in danger of being sacrificed where the animal nature is allowed to preponderate over the intellectual and moral. It is hard for the pampered children of indulgence to change their habits of luxurious living, and to conform to the simplicity and regularity so essential in an educational establishment. Yet you can bear witness that early rising, and regular and simple meals, promote health of body and activity of mind. You have experienced how sweet is the consciousness of doing your duty.

That when you first entered upon this life of duty and discipline you found it hard and often disagreeable, we can well imagine; but every day it becomes to you easier—conscience, which before was weak and inactive, begins to wax stronger. You feel more self-respect, a greater approbation of yourselves.

If we are injured we cannot be miserable while conscious of our own innocence, and that we have no cause to conceal or blush for our conduct. It is far better to suffer wrong, than to do wrong ; and though we may not always avoid being injured, we can avoid being, ourselves, guilty, for, in respect to moral goodness, we can in a degree become what we desire. God has made us free agents, and we can blame ourselves only for our own misdeeds.

Since we met together to commence the duties of the session, the time has passed rapidly away ; constant occupation has accelerated the flight of days, weeks, and months.

The changing aspect of the physical world is a constant admonition to us. In spring, we are pleased with the promises of nature, and soon the vegetable world is in full vigor and activity. Flowers everywhere surround us ; they come back, the old friends and acquaintances of former years ; and the woods and turfy lawns are enamelled with beds of violets, claytonias, and anemones ; the gardens are ornamented with the crocus, daffodil, and hyacinth ; the bright fleur-de-lis, lifts its head as if to ask our welcome, and roses blush on all sides, loading with their fragrance the passing gale. As the season advances, new troops of flowers come forward in forest, wood, and dell, and the gardens and shrubbery present new attractions; but as the blossoms of the spring pass away, so quickly fades the summer bloom, and autumnal flowers of richer hues, but less delicate texture and less fragrant odors, take their place. But the frost-king watches with envious gaze the remaining beauties of autumn, and soon snatches them from the sombre landscape.

The fading beauties of autumn are dear to our hearts; we love its pensive hours and its sad associations, as we love to linger around the couch of departed friends, who must soon leave us to find perennial spring beyond these changing skies.

As the glowing hues of autumn are the precursor of dissolution, so do we know that the hectic flush upon the cheek of a dear invalid is as the fading glories of the autumnal foliage, before it returns to the dust from whence it was formed.

But to the good there is no terror in the dissolution of the bodily tenement; death seems a friendly messenger to those who think upon it as the entrance into a nobler and happier state of existence. The seasons have their changes; moral beings have theirs also; how is it with *yourselves?* Are you becoming more assimilated to angelic perfection; better fitted for a heavenly home, as you advance farther on in life's journey? If so, no matter how soon you may be called—you are ready to go.

ADDRESS X.

A MODEL CHARACTER.

While we regard the formation of the moral character as of the first importance in education, there are other requisites which should not be disregarded. And yet, the young are liable to so many faults of disposition, so often perverse and wanting in the first principles of integrity and honor, that in conducting their education, we are in danger of neglecting these lesser matters, which, in their intercourse with the world, are to constitute, in a degree, their respectability and success in life. We will now consider our young lady as having formed her character, as to morality and religion. She reverences her Maker and His laws, she has resolved to follow Christ in the ordinances of His appointment ; she is truthful and honorable ; careful not to offend others, or injure the feelings of any by neglect, by a haughty bearing, or by speaking unkindly ; she is a peace-maker, and would do all in her power to reconcile those who are at variance, never repeating words which might wound the feelings of another, except for the high and noble object of doing good to that person, by showing a fault to be corrected, or an error to be abandoned. We will give to our young lady these qualities of heart, and add thereto a high cultivation of intellect, a good literary education. What parent would not be happy in such a daughter; what educator would not rejoice in such a specimen of his work!

But the pure gold needs shaping and polishing that it may become ornamental. So our good young lady must not be neglected, as to her *shape*, and polish. Nature has given to each individual a peculiar form and countenance, but each one may do much towards modifying her shape, complexion, and even features. Habits of stooping injure the figure, and impair the digestive organs. The spine becomes curved when it is habitually kept in a crooked position. The shoulders are brought forward and the lungs, and other vital organs, are impaired by continual stooping. When you sew, write, draw, or practice the harp or piano, you should be careful not to bend over, or hold your figure in a constrained position. When you stand, let it be with your chest expanded, shoulders back, and drawn down rather than pushed up at the expense of shortening the neck. Many ladies, with no more than ordinary forms, are called elegant, because they know how to *carry themselves*, and to make the best of their persons. If girls would practice the direction given to soldiers to make them straight, and show their figure to advantage, we should not have so many crooked, awkward-looking women as the present age exhibits. Proper physical exercises are too much neglected, and there is the more danger of this where the mind is directed to mental improvement. Here, you have dancing and calisthenic lessons, the great use of which is to improve the physique in health and grace. As to the mere learning to dance as an accomplishment in society, there is much to be said against this, as well as something in its favor. And I will here add, that though you may be taught fashionable dances, it is not supposed that you are to exhibit yourselves in them at public places. Men of sense regard with severity, young ladies who give themselves up to the fascinations of these dances. The queen of England forbids them at her court; they are not danced even in Paris, with the freedom used in this country. Many attempt them without knowing how they should be performed; and exhibitions, offensive to delicacy, are often seen at dancing parties; the performers, themselves, may be quite unconscious of the appearance they present, or the unfavorable impressions others may form of them.

Remember that the form can be affected by habits of stooping, and ungraceful attitudes may become habitual. The teeth are injured by too much indulgence in eating confectionery; the complexion, by the free use of rich or gross food, and by neglect of proper exercise. Is not the very expression of the countenance greatly modified by the habitual temper and disposition?

A peevish temper shows itself in a morose expression; a haughty disposition by harsh cast of countenance; while a mean and insincere character appears in the downcast and stealthy looks which seem to fear observation. Would you be handsome? The old saw that "handsome is that handsome does," has much truth in it, even in its literal sense. Would you have a good form? Hold yourselves upright, and do not act as if you were afraid to show yourself as you are; but be erect in your carriage, as you would be *upright* in your actions. If you would be called "sweet," a term coveted by young girls, you must be amiable, for a sour disposition cannot make a sweet face.

Dress is an important subject to our sex at any age; and at yours, especially, assumes a serious aspect. "What shall I wear?" is the great question. And yet, others, in reality, mind much less about our dress than we think for. A simple dress is always respectable; it should be neat; and may be genteel and fashionable. When the hair is luxuriant, as is usually the case with the young who are healthy, it is not well to load it with ribbons or ornaments of any kind.

Dress should be adapted to the occasion. In travelling, custom exacts a strict regard to certain rules. There are few who do not know that it is exceedingly improper to appear with ornaments, in travelling in public conveyances—as stage coaches, railroad cars, steamboats, etc. At hotels, it is better not to appear with an elaborate toilet; such dress gives the impression of persons who see little society at home, and put on their best attire in order to attract the notice of strangers. Americans have been ridiculed by foreigners for this showing off at the *tables-d'hôte*.

In Europe, with few exceptions, meals are taken by travellers in their private apartments—an unsocial custom certainly, but better than in travelling to be obliged to dress magnificently for a hotel dinner. I am not now to give you a treatise on dress, but would lead you to reflect on some principles respecting it, which are too often lost sight of by a young person on her entrance into the world.

But we are supposing a model-young-lady;—she has been improved by intellectual culture, possesses an elevated moral character crowned by consistent piety. She has been instructed to take care of herself, and make the most of the personal advantages God has given her. She knows how to walk, to turn her toes out at a proper and graceful angle, to hold herself straight, and to make the most of her figure—so that, if tall, she does not seem ashamed to acknowledge it; or, if short, she may show that she can, notwithstanding, hold her head up. And she must be amiable, sweet tempered, obliging, so that upon her countenance rests, habitually, a sweet expression, not put on for effect, but an emanation of the spirit within. She is not afraid to look others full in the face, because she is conscious of no deceit, no meanness, no wrong to any.

We will now send our model-young-lady away from these quiet shades. We are to suppose that after the best of maternal teachings and examples, she has been carefully educated.—She must go out into the world attired in modest garments, gracefully worn.

Our model-young-lady knows how to take care of herself, and her belongings; she can pack her trunks, and take care of her keys; she can be ready, at a short warning, to accompany her friends on excursions of pleasure, or a tour to Europe. She is like a pleasant sun-light in the family circle, and diffuses happiness around her. Her manners are gentle and refined; and yet she has energy and decision of character, so that in emergencies of danger or difficulty she may be relied on for presence of mind. She knows how to talk, and how to listen to others.

She has learned how to behave at table, does not use her knife when she should use her fork, is polite, and, when proper, can be helpful to those who are near her. She does not scream in public places, or private houses, to show that she is no longer a school-girl. No, she is capable of judging as to propriety, and acts at all times in conformity with the present situation.

Does our model-young-lady need anything more than she is now furnished with to make her the favorite of society? Will she not be sought for in marriage by admirers, and cherished as the beloved of her own sex? Alas—we have neglected to endow her with wealth! She is not rich—and so, perhaps, the world may pass her by; while the glittering charms of fortune bring suitors to the feet of those who may have neither charms of person nor of intellect to boast of, the real gem is neglected. But our model-young-lady was early taught the potency of wealth to gain the friendship of the world, and instructed to set a just estimate upon this friendship. She does not consider marriage as necessary to her happiness or respectability in life. If in the intercourse of society she has been approached with appearances of particular regard by one to whom she might have become attached, had she believed him in earnest in his addresses, she has strengthened her resolution to keep her own heart, remembering what she had often been told by one who had watched over her education with maternal care, "Young ladies with fortunes have more *suitors* than *lovers;* those without fortunes may have *lovers who are not suitors.*"

Our model-young-lady is prepared to fill that station in life to which she may be called—if necessary, she can be a governess, and introduce into families who have more wealth than education, a higher standard of character. She is a blessing wherever she goes;—she is not afraid of being an *old maid:* she makes the most of herself and her condition, and God will bless her in this world and fit her for a better;—by trials if they are needful, for whom He loveth He chasteneth.

ADDRESS XI.

WISDOM.

Wisdom is the principal thing; therefore, get wisdom, and with all thy gettings, get understanding.—ECCLESIASTES, chap. iv. 7.

WHEN you entered this school, you were severally examined as to your progress in learning, and classed according to your attainments in different branches of study, as languages, geography, arithmetic, philosophy, chemistry, etc. It is probable that most of you have thought your sole business at school is with these varied branches, or the accomplishments of music, drawing, etc. But suppose, instead of examining you as to your progress in various scholastic studies, you had been questioned as to your proficiency in *self-government*, truthfulness, and piety, what answers could you have given?

To commence with *self-government*, suppose you had been questioned whether you had yet learned this art—whether you knew how to control yourselves, so as to do those things which are right, and to exclude from your minds all evil, vain, and improper thoughts, could you have answered, "I am perfectly acquainted with the art of self-government; my conduct is always the result of reason ; I have no need of trying any more to learn how to control my feelings ?"

Would not conscience, the rather, have prompted you to say, "I do not yet understand self-government ; I must make that one of my studies ?" You might have remembered with sorrow and penitence, the tears you had caused a tender mother or friend, by anger, obstinacy, or some other evil passion which had led you to behave contemptuously, or unkindly, towards those who were devoted to your happiness. Perhaps, even while you were preparing to leave home to come to school, you evinced displeasure because all your wishes were not gratified. You may have wanted some article of dress that your parents thought beyond their means, or unnecessary for you, and you may have appeared unamiably on account of their refusal. You may have wished to learn some accomplishment, thought too expensive, or not required for your condition in life ; the refusal to accede to your wishes may have excited resentful feelings, and unpleasant words, or unkind looks on your part, may have wounded your kindest and best friends—those who may be making great sacrifices to give you the advantages of education. Consider, each one of you, whether you have been thus guilty in any degree, and in your next letters to your parents ask their forgiveness, not neglecting to humble yourselves before God for your faults, and join yourselves to the class for LEARNING SELF-GOVERNMENT. Consider whether you are making any advances in this science. If you find yourselves easy to be provoked with your companions, or forward, and impertinent to your teachers, you need not flatter yourselves that you are improving. It is when you are able to subdue the rising temper, to command your looks from expressing anger or contempt, and your tongue from uttering harsh words, though your spirit be agitated within, that you can truly feel conscious of possessing the power of self-government. We cannot expect to pass through this rough world without meeting with much to disturb our peace of mind, and equanimity of temper.

In proportion as we can govern ourselves, we may influence others. It is not easy to be calm when assailed by anger and injustice; but it is the part of wisdom to keep down our own passions, that we may, at least, be sane, though others be unreasonable. What an advantage is afforded by equanimity of temper! The master or mistress who gives way to violent passion loses the respect of the servant who may be property by legal right, but whose mind cannot be fettered, and who will at heart give honor only where honor is due.

One of the branches of wisdom we consider is the power of self-government. Another branch of wisdom is *truthfulness*, without which there can be no dignity or worth of character. And here self-examination is necessary; for truth lies deep in the heart, if there at all. You must learn to know and respect her in her humblest guise, as well as in her Sunday garb. Truthfulness either does, or does not, belong to a character. Without it there is an empty void in that region of the heart from which proceeds all that is good and estimable.

It might seem that where truthfulness is wanting it would be useless to attempt to improve a character; and indeed it is a most discouraging labor to attempt to imbue with good desires a heart where there is not a firm sub-stratum of truthfulness. But the educator must not be discouraged by obstacles. And the young, thank God, are not yet so hardened in evil, that we may not hope much from cultivation. But you must aid me in this work. You would all shrink from being called insincere, hypocritical, and false; but you must look closely into your words and actions, and not try to deceive yourselves as well as others.

We have a straight and narrow way before us, in considering what truthfulness is. We will first examine our subject negatively. One is not truthful who attempts in any way to deceive others, or to give false impressions; in the class-room, to pretend to know a lesson that is not learned; in social intercourse, to affect friendship which is not felt; in chapel, to seem to worship God, because it is reputable to do so. To attempt to enumerate all the artifices and deceits which even the young may be guilty of, in trying to assume virtues which they do not possess, and hiding their real faults, would present a fearful list; we pass them by, urging upon you all, that self-examination which constitutes the vital point of character.

We will suppose you are intent on gaining wisdom,

and have entered into the *truth-class;* if you have done this with full purpose of heart, we shall have courage in proceeding to help your efforts. You are to begin by hating all kinds of deception, and resolving to be truthful and sincere, let consequences be what they may. In the various relations in life, nothing so soon destroys peace, harmony, and confidence, as the discovering that around and about us, is a false and deceitful spirit. Many a woman has rendered herself odious in the eyes of her husband by petty concealments, or false pretences, even in trifling matters. "If she will violate truth in small things," he may reason, "what can I expect in more important matters?" Women are, it is true, dependent, and such a state may lead to hypocrisy. In some families, a mother has been known to use artifice, in order to supply her daughters with articles of dress, or indulgences which the father was unwilling or unable to afford them; what can be expected of such daughters!

It requires moral courage to be able at all times to speak the truth; but you should fortify your minds on this point by reflecting on the denunciations of Scripture against lying and deceit; you should fear the reproaches of your conscience—or still more the hardening of this conscience, so that it would cease its warnings. If, when you are young, you allow yourselves to indulge in artifice, you may be assured the vice will grow upon you as you advance in life; what you perhaps did merely to amuse others, or gratify what you thought a harmless vanity, you will do to serve the purposes of self-interest, until you will become confirmed in habits of lying and dishonesty. As virtues cling together and are found in companies, so it is with vices; and one who does not speak the truth will become familiar with other sins.

A noble dignity of purpose will serve to keep you in straight paths; admitting no thought of concealing your conduct, you will be careful to have your actions such as you would not blush to have exposed. Walking on in life with an upright and sincere mind, you can have nothing to fear. Poverty is not disgrace, persecution is not infamy; and no affliction can be truly a misfortune to the good, those who fear not to look others in the face, and who walk uprightly through the varying scenes of this transitory life. How comforting to be able to feel self-respect—but how miserable one who is conscious that if his real character were known, he would be despised; who knows that he has deceived and betrayed those who trusted in him, and that truth is a stranger to his heart.

Wisdom is the principal thing. You perceive that you must learn self-government and truth as important branches of this great science, and will join the class which we hope to form for learning and practising them.

We include honesty with truth, because they usually go together. The dishonest person will lie to conceal his guilt, and the liar will not, generally, scruple to take that which belongs to others. If you have fault-marks, do not attempt to get rid of them by palliating or excusing what you have done; excuses are too often lies, or lead to them. If you have failed to write letters to your friends when you should have done so, do not say you have had no time, or try to invent excuses. Do not make false professions of friendship, or, by flattery, minister to the weaknesses of others. Though in the common intercourse in life, politeness requires a certain degree of respect to all, yet with this there may, and should be, sincerity. You should never urge persons to visit you unless you desire it, and never promise to write letters unless you intend to fulfill your engagement. As pupils at school, in letters to friends at home, say nothing but truth; do not make a serious matter of a slight indisposition, or cause alarm by needless complaints; study truth, and with all your study, gain habits of truth.

Piety is a branch of wisdom; and this must be sought for as for hid treasure. If brought up from childhood in the fear of God, happy are you; if you have this great thing to learn, you have no time to lose, for life is uncertain, and this is the preparation required for the world of spirits, to which we are hastening. If your hearts are not yet anchored surely upon a firm religious hope, put yourselves in a *class* with those of your companions who are seeking to find God, and to love and serve Him.

When you meet with Christians, to worship God, are your hearts filled with a sense of His greatness and goodness, and of your own unworthiness?

Would that when assembled for religious worship, there were among us, no vacant, careless looks, no appearance of restlessness or inattention, indicating indifference to the solemn duties in which all profess to engage.

Those who love God delight in His service, they love his words, his Sabbaths and ordinances; if you feared Him, you would never dare to trifle when his presence is invoked. When a room-mate kneels down to offer her prayers to her Father in heaven you should feel a solemn sense of the presence of God, and abstain from anything that might disturb her devotions.

Example is powerful; a pious pupil may do much towards influencing others; one who would trifle with religion and religious subjects, cannot fail of doing much harm to the consciences of others; things that they would not have dared to think, much less to do, may become familiar, till they cease to feel compunctions of conscience. Consider these things, your influence over each other, the importance of habit, and of your joining yourselves to a *class* for learning to think and act right.

1843.

ADDRESS XII.

OPENING OF A SUMMER SESSION.

By the good providence of God, we are here assembled, my dear pupils and co-laborers, after a period of separation, to renew our efforts in gaining or imparting knowledge. Yet, ere we become absorbed in present duties, it is well to suspend our attention on the immediate objects before us, that we may look back upon the past, and forward to the future; that we may consider the principles by which we should be guided in our connection with each other, and the bearing which this connection may have upon our future destiny, not only in this world, but in that hereafter, which stretches into an illimitable eternity.

The Institution with which we are connected, has received attention from the public, and been favored with success. A combination of happy circumstances has tended to give it elevation and permanency of character. Among these circumstances, I would mention the favor it has received from the State legislature, which, by its liberality, enabled the Trustees to carry out their own views in respect to building, by giving the necessary conveniences, and adopting that classic style of architecture, so well suited to the locality. The State has distinguished this Institute with especial favor. We are bound to do all in our power to honor Maryland by the high character and utility of our Institution. The first and highest honor to any community is good literary institutions. These are the pride and glory of the New England States; with their granite mountains and barren rocks, their frigid climate and hard soil, what would these States become without their excellent schools and colleges? There is nothing in the air of New England more invigorating to the intellect than the pure breezes of our Patapsco, with its hundred hills covered with the ancient forest-trees, verdant with the carpeting of nature or rich with waving grain, presenting rare scenes of grandeur and beauty.

We, my dear pupils and honored associates, are bound to do all in our power to establish this institution on a firm and permanent basis, so that at home and abroad it shall command respect and confidence, and we shall in so doing, add something to the dignity of the State to which it owes its existence;—and, if from this place shall go forth a future generation of women superior to the frivolities of fashion, trained to habits of industry, order, economy, and piety, enlightened in intellect and fitted to be companions and advisers to the future legislators and citizens of this and other States, then should we well repay the fostering care of Maryland and prove useful to her in promoting the best and highest interests of our common country, and united republic.

We will, *en passant*, make some remarks upon the system of education here pursued, and the principles by which the government of our Institution is administered. Our *monitorial* system is an important feature in our discipline. This differs entirely from what is popularly called the "*monitorial system*," where one pupil is employed to teach another. In our system, every pupil who is of sufficient age and judgment to be intrusted with the office, is, by turns, monitor for a day. Her duty consists in enforcing the rules of the school, and in reporting all breaches of such rules. These rules are the guide of the monitor, nothing is left to her caprice, prejudice, or partiality; if her most intimate friend be found guilty of a breach of rule, her duty is clear, a fault-mark must be given, or she will be found unfaithful to her trust. If, through prejudice, a monitor gives a fault-mark when it is not deserved, the injured party has the privilege of appealing to the presiding teacher, and if dissatisfied with her decision, to the Principal; and it would be disgraceful to a monitor to be found to have abused her power, and the confidence reposed in her. In thus employing monitors, we recognize an important principle of morality, differing essentially from the code of honor which is often proudly vaunted by young men, but which is, undoubtedly, the baneful source of most of the rebellions, expulsions, and other evils which disgrace male institutions. This code of honor prescribes that no student shall expose another to the officers of an Institution, let the nature of his offences be what they may.

Such a principle carried out in society, would shield from detection and punishment, the thief, the incendiary, and the murderer. Baneful indeed is this principle in its effects; it is the opposite of that true moral courage which is fearless in exposing evil when such exposure is necessary to the well-being of an individual or a community.

We would discriminate between the fulfillment of duty in reporting breaches of established rules, or the exposure by one pupil of what is imprudent or wrong in another through a desire of preventing evil and producing good, and that impertinent tale-bearing by which one pupil would degrade another in order to raise herself, or with the view of obtaining the favor of her superiors. It requires little penetration to see through such motives when they exist, and the pupil acting under their influence would ever meet with repulse and disgrace among teachers who are judges of character, and are, themselves, influenced by high and honorable sentiments. An espionage upon the actions of another with the secret intention of injury to the individual, should never be confounded with the exposure of an evil, which, if persisted in, would be the cause of disgrace to an institution and injury to its individual members ; to conceal this, would be like seeing poison mingled with food without giving notice of it, or a fire consuming our neighbor's house without sounding an alarm. What would be our surprise should an individual defend such a course on the ground that tale-bearing was dishonorable ! It is by going back to first principles, that we may, in morals, keep in the straight path of duty. First principles in morality are, in the conduct of life, as the axioms in mathematics, to which, as we proceed in demonstrations, we are obliged continually to refer.

To "*do right*" should ever be our motto, and when we know what is right we should pursue it, even though the path may be beset with difficulties. Yet, in reality, the right way is not only the shortest, but in general the most easy and pleasant. If any should doubt whether the faithful discharge of the office of monitor has a tendency to lead the young to mean espionage or to low talebearing, may the dignified deportment and open frankness of the pupils of this institution ever repel the suggestion. Observe closely whether such as are most fearless in the discharge of monitorial duty, or rather such as have most moral courage, are those who are given to "evil speaking, lying and slandering." Would you choose for your friend and companion, one who would be true and honest—who would be fearless to tell you of your faults, when it became her duty to do so—select the faithful and impartial monitor who will do what is right, even though duty might require her to give evidence against her dearest friend.

When the monitor lays aside her office and is no longer bound to report breaches of duty in her fellow pupils, she may still aid in promoting good order by her advice and example. Having experienced the pain caused by the task of reporting offences, she will naturally be careful not to subject other monitors to the same trial.

Some of you, after a season of relaxation, return to accustomed scenes and pursuits, others come as strangers to an institution, many of whose rules, customs and modes of pursuing studies may appear new and strange. From former pupils we may reasonably expect a strict attention to all duties that from experience you know will be required; we may expect to find in you a reasonable degree of improvement in mind, manners and morals; knowing as you do the rules of the institution, and feeling as we would hope an interest in its prosperity, we may look to you to aid in establishing good order. Receive the strangers who have come to us from so many distant homes as friends, and by your kindness and attention gladden their hearts, so often saddened by thoughts of the friends they have left.

Each school session, each day and year, should be made "a critic on the last," and where you can perceive you have erred in the past time, be the more watchful for the future. Has your fault been that of indolence, of wasting in frivolous thought, or dull inactivity of mind, the precious hours which when past can never be recalled? Has it been that of irregularity in your duties? Have you indulged yourself in anger, impatience, and a spirit of contradiction? Have you suffered yourself to be led from the straight and narrow path of prudence and duty to follow bad examples, or allowed yourself to be influenced by those whom you should have had resolution to resist? And, finally, do you perceive in reviewing the past that you have often left undone what you should have done, and have done what you should not have done? Pray to your Father in heaven to enable you in the future to avoid what is evil and to do your duty better than you have done. To those who have come as strangers among us, I would address words of encouragement and advice. Many things now appear to you strange, and what is strange is often unpleasant. So much are we the creatures of habit, that even if a change be for the better, we are often slow to perceive it. It is said of one who had been imprisoned all his life with no light in his dungeon but through one little hole in the wall, that, when about to be taken from prison, he thought he could never see without the help of that aperture; and he found to his astonishment that the wall was but an impediment to his vision. What may now appear as disagreeable tasks to you, will, in time, become pleasant. To find that you are becoming better, wiser, and more able to take care of yourselves, will be an ample reward for any efforts you may make. You will become more robust and healthy by physical exercise, and your minds will be invigorated by study. The fact of your being here shows that your parents approve of the regulations and discipline of the school; and the fact that you have been received here proves that we suppose you are willing to conform to them. It is hoped and expected that you will here so improve yourselves, that hereafter you will be the pride and joy of your friends and an honor to the institution in which you will have been educated.

To you, my associates and friends, the teachers of this institution, I would make a few remarks. If, in a multitude of counsellors there is safety, there is also danger in *divided counsels*, and that which is the duty of many, may be neglected by all. By the influence of Christian principles, we may hope for union among ourselves, and by a proper division of labor, each one may know her own peculiar sphere of action. Yet the mere discharge of duty, without a feeling of interest in the success of what is done, would be to fail wholly in the spirit while fulfilling the letter of the law.

Some of you have been long associated with me ; first as pupils, and then as teachers. The work in which we are engaged is important, calling for dignity of character, self-command, and self-sacrifices. While so many of our sex live for their own enjoyment, or confine their efforts to the little domestic circle which bounds their sympathies, we live for the public ; to us are allotted trials and difficulties peculiar to our profession. We bring forward pupils in various sciences and accomplishments ; We delight in seeing them go on from one degree of improvement to another, but while we are beholding and enjoying the work we are permitted to bring to some degree of perfection, the objects of our care are taken from us ; the blossoms which had expanded under our culture are removed to other bowers;—others have entered into our labors. It is for this we toil, sure that the greatest success must be followed by the greatest trial when the time arrives for us to give back to parental love those, who, for this very purpose, were intrusted to us. To those who have been long associated with me in the work of education, I can only ask that you will continue the same faithful assistants and devoted friends that you have hitherto been. Your greater experience has, indeed, rendered your services the more valuable, and I can only pray that your life and health may be precious in the sight of the Lord, and that our labors of love may be still blessed as we have reason to believe they have been. But all who have walked with us are not here; some, in a new sphere of life, are occupied with domestic cares; others have been called to labor elsewhere, in promoting the interests of education. Death, too, has claimed his victims among our number, for what human circle does not the destroyer enter!

It may be proper here to make some remarks on the relations between teacher and pupils. It is desirable that teachers should be familiarly acquainted with the pupils, that they should mingle with them in their hours of recreation, and be to them as friends, elder sisters, or mothers. But while the teachers are willing, in their social intercourse, to lay aside restraint and ceremony, the pupils, bearing in mind the difference in their relative positions, should avoid too great familiarity of manners, or the doing or saying aught which might require reproof or admonition. A respectful manner towards all the officers of an institution should ever mark the deportment of a pupil; and if she wishes to be beloved, she should be frank and affectionate in her intercourse with them, considering that if they appear cold and formal, this may be the effect of outward influences, and no indication of want of sensibility or warmth of affection.

1844.

ADDRESS XIII.

THE DRAMA OF LIFE.

TO PUPILS AND TEACHERS.

The commencement of a new era is a favorable time for reflection, and for forming good resolutions as to the manner in which we will perform our parts in the drama opening before us. The drama of life is an expressive term, and its various portions may properly be considered as the acts and scenes of which this drama is made up. Following this analogy, we may regard ourselves and others, as the actors in this drama. There is much of pantomime in life ; the going about with looks of care or distress, the sullen air, the pouting lip and contemptuous manner, deep sorrow, and despair; gaiety, imprudence, and levity, all may be seen in the looks and manners of mankind.

God, in his all-wise providence, has brought us together for a brief space of time, to perform in this place, acts in the drama of our lives. But the analogy between theatrical representations and the stage of life, fails in one important respect, the former is imitation, the latter reality ; the one having no bearing upon futurity, the other a preparation for a future state of happiness or misery. Thus, though in a play or drama, we might choose our part without reference to actual virtue or vice (so the murderer on the stage may be an amiable man, free from murderous thoughts); in real life, we act according to the principles of our nature, whether they be good or bad.

What scene in life can present greater interest than the one now before us?—A large assemblage of young persons gathered together from different sections of our country, meeting here for education under the care of one late a stranger to them, and surrounded by new faces, under new relations, subjected to new duties and restraints, and expected to make new and great efforts in the accomplishment of the objects for which they have left parents and home. In order to fulfill entirely the obligations which rest upon you, it would seem necessary that the child should be transformed to the woman, and the thoughtless girl become reflecting, and anxious to know her duty.

It has been appointed by Providence that I should have much to do with the education of the young. Successive groups of fair girls, for many years, have been congregated to receive instruction here. I was early impressed with the idea, that though, in many cases, parents might value most the literary improvement of their daughters, my own greatest obligation consisted in the right use of the moral and religious influence which my relations to them gave me; and thus it was, that I was often led to lay aside books, and talk to my pupils of their future destinations in life, of the formation of character, comprehending not merely literary attainments and accomplishments, but moral principles, and the cultivation of the heart with its noblest affections. While the various literary branches in which these pupils were instructed were important to them in regard to a respectable appearance in society, those moral and religious lessons, we may believe, have proved useful to them at almost every hour of their existence. Were there time now to narrate to you their various fortunes, we should here present you with one who was cut off in the bloom of life, and whose earthly remains have long since mouldered in the dust; of another, who was early deprived of parents and fortune, and thrown upon the cold charities of the world; of another, who was flattered and betrayed, and finally sunk to degradation and ruin; of another, too proud to acknowledge her interest in one who had flattered her for his own amusement, and whose heart became chilled by the setting back of the cold current of unrequited affection.—Again, I could show you one, who, after many fearful alternations of hopes and fears, during, perhaps, years of suspense, having at length gained the prize which her trusting heart had deemed so rich and precious, is doomed to suffer the caprices and unkindness of an unprincipled and tyrannical husband. But these, you may say, are extreme cases;—those women were peculiarly unfortunate, and though such examples may be met with, they are exceptions to what is to be generally expected in life. We will, then, take other cases, the very best as regards worldly happiness and prosperity that can be found. I could point you to those whose ambition and affection have been gratified, who have passed from the care of kind parents to the protection of affectionate and devoted husbands;—but who is not called to mourn the loss of near friends, to witness the footsteps of death in the domestic circle? Those who have become mothers, even under the most favorable circumstances of health, and surrounded by all the attentions of love and kindness, have been made to taste the bitterness of the fearful curse pronounced by the Almighty on our first mother. And what maternal watchings and anxieties follow the gift of a feeble child of earth, exposed to innumerable ills, dearer to the mother's heart than her own life, and yet holding its frail existence upon the most uncertain tenure.

Such is woman's life! if she form no new domestic ties, she sees, one by one, her early friends become engrossed with their families, while her parents and other near relatives, one after another, drop into the grave; she at length, feels herself solitary and alone, in a world where there are none to care for her; if she enter into the marriage state, she multiplies her chances of unhappiness, increases her cares, and becomes compelled to forget herself in her sacrifices for others; and often, too, without a return of gratitude and love from those for whom she has made the sacrifice.

Those of you who have mothers should think of this; the very term mother, is one which involves the idea of suffering, anxiety, and love. The Scriptures make the love of a mother the highest standard of human affection, and they compare, too, the highest degree of suffering to the mother's pains. You that are daughters, and may yourselves be mothers, be kind and attentive towards them who have suffered so much for you. We sometimes witness the sad exhibition of a daughter disrespectful and disobedient to her mother; the same daughter may restrain her temper in the presence of her father, perhaps caress and flatter him, selfishly calculating the value of her influence over one on whom she depends for the gratification of her wishes. The daughter sees her mother under disadvantages, she is a witness to her weaknesses of temper, and provocations to fretfulness or passion in the petty trials of every-day life. The father at the domestic fireside is a visitor, whose comfort and accommodation are to be especially cared for;—not aware of the importance of trifles in domestic arrangements, the husband may seem amused at annoyances which disturb her who feels responsible for the order of the household, and which, if she were indifferent to them, might soon render his home uncomfortable. Should a good daughter join in wondering that "mother makes so much of trifles,"—or, should she not with tender sympathy, seek to remove the thorns which spring up in her pathway?

We have entered the sacred precincts of home. We have alluded to the duties and trials of domestic life, because in the formation of your character, it is important that the serious obligations which rest upon you as daughters, and may be incurred as wives, should be considered.

There is danger while cultivating accomplishments that the young will imbibe false notions of future life. Thus many girls are accustomed to regard proficiency in music, French, drawing, etc., as of the greatest consequence; and are led to act as if the concerns of the soul and eternity were light in comparison to the acquisition of elegant accomplishments. But in many cases, too great anxiety to become accomplished proves an obstacle to proficiency; if young ladies would cease to regard their playing and singing as of infinite importance, they would not feel such a trembling anxiety lest they may not answer expectations, but do the best they can without the agitation and fear which defeat their own hopes and the wishes of their friends.

The cultivation of taste and refinement belongs to a state of civilization. The fine arts afford pleasure, and tend to elevate the mind; they add to the innocent enjoyment of life, but should not be made to take the place of necessary virtues and useful occupations. Education should be conducted with reference to the good of the subjects of it both in this life and that which is to come.

My associate teachers, these young persons committed to our care have a brief space allowed them, in the which to prepare for future life in this world, and their destiny for eternity will also be greatly affected by the impressions received and the habits here formed.

A home school for the young should be, as far as possible, the abode of piety without severity or superstition; of elevated morality, and of all that is "lovely and of good report." All its officers and teachers should be examples of sincerity, faithfulness, and gentleness; while their duty obliges them to enforce discipline, they should show themselves long suffering and forbearing. Upon the characters and conduct of the teachers, in a large institution, must its prosperity and usefulness in a degree depend. The Principal, who cannot be ubiquitous, is represented by the officers, and teachers employed, and must rely on their faithfulness and ability; the relations between them are of a sacred character, and as they should never be lightly entered into, they should not, for slight causes, be dissolved.

The relations of the different teachers towards each other demand serious consideration. Engaged in the same calling, separated alike from home and kindred, they should be friends to each other, regarding it as a duty to cultivate each other's acquaintance, and as much as possible to seek each other's society. It is not well for a teacher to separate herself too much from the family of the Principal, and when not engaged in school duties, to live chiefly in imagination with absent friends, neglecting efforts to promote the happiness of those around her; in short, to render herself a cipher in the social circle to which she should seek to give light and warmth. Teachers should sympathize with each other, and be ready to give mutual assistance or advice when needed

Watching over the interest of the school with anxious care, a teacher should not hesitate to caution or admonish another teacher, who might, through inadvertence, or a want of reflection, do that which would be injurious in its effects on the prosperity or reputation of the Institution. As in a well-ordered, conscientious family, each member is studious of the general good, so in a school-family should those who are employed as its guardians, regard with deep interest the welfare of the same. We have mentioned duties and obligations, let us acknowledge that mere morality is of itself insufficient to keep us free from error in conduct and thought, but that the source of all good is to be found in religion. We may be deceived in ourselves, we may be deceived in, and deceive each other, but if we study the word of God, and look to that as the pole-star to direct our way through the devious mazes of life, we shall not go far astray, or wandering, we shall soon return to the "strait and narrow way which leadeth unto life eternal."

The Apostle Paul, being about to visit the church at Corinth, said: "I fear lest, when I come, I shall not find you such as I would; lest there be debates, envyings, wrath, strifes, back-bitings, whisperings, swellings, tumults," and he closes his epistle with this touching and solemn benediction: "Finally, brethren, farewell; be perfect, be of good comfort, be of one mind, live in peace, and the God of love and peace shall be with you."

How expressive the words of that farewell, and let us all, the "teachers and the taught," appropriate to ourselves the precious advice. "Be perfect, be of good comfort, be of one mind, live in peace," and then shall the God of love and peace be with us both now and forever.

1844.

ADDRESS XIV.

ON THE CLOSE OF A SCHOOL-SESSION IN AUTUMN.*

TO PUPILS AND TEACHERS.

When we assembled at the opening of the session the spring was giving its promise; we had before us its beautiful flowers, and were looking forward to the ripened fruits of summer. Then, to us, the end of the term, was in the far-off distance; we thought perhaps there was much time for many things. But that distant period has come, the opportunity for improvement has gone by, whether improved or not; it waited not for us. We look now abroad upon nature, and behold a change has come over the landscape. The bright green of spring has passed away, its verdant foliage and bright flowers have disappeared. The changes have been gradual; from the beauty and cheerfulness of spring we passed into the fervid and glowing summer; though often oppressed by its heat and lassitude, we were comforted by rich and cooling fruits, fresh water, the ice of the preceding winter,

* Soon after this period, the two sessions in a year were merged into one which closed in summer—the new school-year commencing in September after an interval of some weeks.

laid up for that season, and the refreshing breezes from the surrounding hills which played among our groves. How beautiful is the succession of the seasons, and how do they, as they proceed onward in their ever-varying, ever-uniform march, testify to the wisdom and goodness of the Creator!

Summer has given place to autumn, the sober season for meditation and self-examination. At this period nature without, and the peculiar circumstances of our relations in view of a coming change, call us to reflection.

At the opening of the session, you looked forward to its close, as to an eminence you were to ascend; you have now nearly reached it, and can look back upon the road through which you have passed; you knew not who would be the companions of your way, whom you should love best, who would do most towards rendering your journey pleasant; what opportunities you might have for doing good to others, or of benefiting yourselves; your future trials, your temptations, and your pleasures were then unknown to you. Quiet and retired as may be your lives here, and devoid of thrilling and romantic incidents, such as would give interest to the pages of a novel; still you have opportunities to learn lessons of human nature, which will never be forgotten. A school is a little world, a miniature picture of life. The passions which agitate the breasts of men and women in the great world, are here seen, and with far less disguise than in the active scenes of life in the world without; vanity shows off her airs to attract attention, pride assumes her cold indifference, and haughtiness her contempt ; ambition incites to efforts for the sake of gaining superiority over others ; flattery uses her blandishments, and deception, even among the young, shows the depraved nature of a fallen race.

Falsehood and insincerity are witnessed even among children, and in short, few of the passions, prejudices, follies, and vices of mankind, may not be seen, in a germinating or mature state, among the members of a school.

For this reason it is, that the careful educator must be ever busy, ever watchful to eradicate the weeds which spring up in his garden of young plants ;—our weekly journals of the board of officers and teachers show so many records of lesser faults and errors, because we think it wise to crush the evils in the bud, to eradicate the small weeds before they shall become firmly rooted.

On entering this place to become the inmate of a new home, as you looked around, you saw pleasant and open countenances, which seemed as an index of all that is amiable and lovely in character ; you said to yourselves of some particular one, "Surely I can love and trust her ;" you became intimate, told all your little secrets, and heard in return those of your friend ; but soon some cause of envy or jealousy separated you, and cold indifference, or open enmity took the place of the warm friendship at first professed.

You saw, perhaps, on your arrival among so many strangers, one who impressed you with no sudden admiration, whose countenance might have appeared uninteresting—you felt, at first, no sympathy kindling your affections into a glow; day after day, you met the same face without, perhaps, any change of feeling; but by and by, an occasion was offered for you to do some little kindness, to show some civility to the uninteresting stranger; you marked the beaming of her countenance, and her look of grateful acknowledgment for the trifling favor, and then you wished, perchance, it had been greater, and resolved that hereafter you would pay more attention to one who seemed to have a sensitive and grateful heart. By degrees you became acquainted, and a firm and enduring friendship sprung up between you, which you now hope may continue through future years. Such is human life, often disappointing us when we had hoped most, and offering flowers and fruits from an apparently barren soil. Such is the history of many of the most important events of our lives; from the most unpromising beginnings proceed the most interesting results; while from the most specious hopes and promises we often reap only disappointment or disgust.

The views which young persons gain of human life from morbid poetry and tales of fiction are illusory, and lead to an entire misconception of the duties and realities of life. They usually give to the morally good, personal attractions, and represent the bad, as repulsive in look and manner; but this, in reality, is far from being the case. The very effect of personal beauty is to render its possessor vain, imperious and selfish; and nothing but good training, and the special care of God's Providence can preserve from these faults, a young person in a high degree gifted with external attractions; while the consciousness of a plain and unattractive person, often begets humility and meekness, resulting in excellence of character, and loveliness of soul.

But after all, what is beauty? It is regarded as the outward and visible sign of inward graces and virtues. Regular features, a clear complexion, sparkling eyes, and rosy cheeks and lips may be pretty to look upon, but unless the countenance be lighted up by an agreeable or intelligent expression, it can never excite permanent and deep emotions, but like a waxen beauty, or a scentless flower, it will be regarded with indifference.

But according to our test of beauty, as being the outward and visible sign of inward loveliness, we admit that there are those who possess those outward signs, whose expression of countenance and graceful motion inspire the expectation that the gem within such a casket must be rich and precious; yet we may be deceived—and how great is the disappointment, to find where we expected moral worth and internal beauty answering to the external, that all is hollow and void, or deformity and ugliness. And how does the most beautiful countenance cease to please, nay, excite disgust and loathing, when associated with unamiable and hateful qualities of soul! If the inward beauty be possessed, it will make itself known and loved; but no outward appearances can long deceive, where the reality is wanting. The sign fails; the casket attracted, but was found worthless, enshrining nothing precious within. Where we looked to find a rich gem, is but paste set in tinsel.

All, doubtless, wish to be beloved, but all do not use the proper means to gain, and secure affection; you here see many young girls like yourselves; your own characters, your faults and follies are reflected in those around you. In studying others, you learn to know yourselves; happy, if by means of such knowledge, you learn to govern yourselves. The session is now approaching its termination; a few short days, and it will be numbered with *past time*, with "the days beyond the flood," it will be no more in your possession than time which was never yours—yet once, it was yours; each day, with its hours and minutes, was yours to spend as you liked, to be made a friend to carry into eternity a good report, or an enemy to bring accusations against you in the day of judgment. How little, perhaps, have many of you reflected, as time fled, that it would bear with it, reports for, or against you—at the bar of God. Although no regret for time misimproved can bring it back, yet such regret may render you hereafter more careful to seize the fleeting moments, and enstamp upon them a mark of inestimable value. We know not how long we may have moments to spend. Every closing day and week is an emblem to remind us of the end of life; and how much more so, the termination of a school session constituting so large a portion of that period of youth devoted to education! Have its advantages been neglected—has a feeling of repining for home prevented attention to the interests and objects for which you left that home?

Who will be most likely to carry happiness, and a fund of cheerfulness and satisfaction into the domestic circle of home—those who, when at school, were ever complaining and discontented, so that they could lay up no stores of knowledge, could improve in no accomplishment, to please and enliven home, when they should return to it; or those who resolutely dismissed from their minds thoughts which would impede their progress, and diligently improved the advantages for which they left parents and home. This question carries with it a response which must be felt deeply by those who are conscious of time misspent, and instructions slighted. Those who have faithfully studied, who have made each hour perform its own work, have done all they could, and are ready to show forth the fruits of their industry and application at the approaching examination. Thus may it be with us all, at the end of life—may we be found prepared for the *great examination* before the "Searcher of all hearts," and the "Judge of all men."

May the teachers and officers here collected for the instruction and care of the young, ever bear in mind their great accountability as the assistants and representatives of the Principal. Great conscientiousness is required in the faithful performance of your duties. Constituting as we do one large family, there should be harmony and unity of purpose among us. Such an establishment as this differs greatly in organization from a college, where the different officers are appointed by trustees, and accountable to them ; where the President is but a nominal head, with but his own share of accountability in respect to students. Here the Principal bears the whole weight of pecuniary responsibility, and is as a parent in a large family. Suppose a teacher, regarding only her own interests or feelings, works solely for her own purposes. If she differ in opinion from the Principal, that she secretly sets in motion projects to bring about what she thinks is best, even against what she knows would be disapproved of by her employer—that she introduces disunion and distrust into a community which should be the abode of peace and confidence.—Suppose she should do this under the specious pretence that some good was to be attained by that secret combination, that her difference in opinion from the Principal made such a mode of proceeding proper and right; the sophistry of such reasoning is obvious. We are not to "do evil that good may come." Far better would it be to withdraw from a connection which involves trust and obedience the teacher is not willing to give. The association is voluntary on both sides, and should exist no longer than there is mutual good will and confidence.

We have supposed what we trust may not take place among us. The confidence reposed in you, my associates and friends, is truly great ; I am accountable for your acts, for your influence on the character of our pupils. It is because you are considered worthy of esteem and confidence that you are called to aid in carrying forward plans for the proper training of the young. To your keeping is committed in a degree my own happiness and reputation; any great mistakes on your part would disturb my peace of mind, and injure the reputation of the institution whose interests you are bound to promote. It is only as mutual friends that we can go forward in our work. What pure and elevated happiness might be enjoyed in a community like ours, where the pupils were all amiable and gentle, only desiring that the path to learning might be pointed out to them, that they might eagerly walk therein; where those who teach were all affectionate towards each other, devoted to their office, and united in efforts to sustain their Principal in her duties, sympathizing in her cares, and scrupulously guarding her reputation from the attacks of malevolence, who regarding this as their home, look to the honor and prosperity of the Institute, in minute, as well as important matters, by whom education is considered as a noble profession fitted to bring forth the very best faculties of the soul, while exerting them for the good of others!

Such should be the relations subsisting between those engaged in training the young to habits of virtue, and to a faithful fullfilment of their duties; such should be the teacher's estimate of her own high calling.

The example and influence of teachers are of great importance; dress, manners, conversation, government of temper, and religious habits, all are to be considered by teachers with reference to their office, and the influence they may have over others—ever bearing in mind that the results of their labor are not for this life only, but are destined to modify and influence the condition of souls in a future existence.

Dignified, prudent, and discreet should be the conduct of those who instruct others—noble and elevating should be their sentiments and aspirations; and if they be found faithful in the duties of their calling, their reward will, in this life, be a happy consciousness of great good performed, and cheering hopes of "rest" hereafter.

Close of school year for 1844.

ADDRESS XV.

TEMPLES DEDICATED TO IMPROVEMENT—ALLEGORICAL.

VARIOUS are the characters and the conditions in life of those now before me, and known to each the peculiar circumstances which may affect that character and condition, in a manner perhaps unperceived by the world, and seen only by the Omniscient eye of God. He alone knoweth what is to be your lot in a world of trial and suffering where all must undergo the ills of life, falling upon the queen in her palace, not less heavily than upon the peasant in her cottage. Wealth may alleviate suffering, but it cannot prevent sickness and death, and too often it causes mental anxieties and promotes strifes and jealousies from which poverty is free.

Collectively, you constitute the Patapsco Institute; though in order to complete the organization of the body, a head is wanted, and this, the officers of the institution constitute in their combined capacity, while others in a more humble sphere are as hands and feet to the whole. But there is not only the institution considered as unity, its various members all combining to complete this unity, but each of those members are units, each has her own world of thought, her own separate emotions, and her own sphere of action. In addressing all, it is difficult to adapt my remarks to individual cases;—the timid need encouragement, while the presuming, or those too confident of success to make the necessary efforts require to be reminded that talents without labor will bring no fruit to perfection. Some are too eager in the pursuit of knowledge, and require a warning voice to repress their ardor, lest they sacrifice health and ultimately destroy their mental vigor by disregarding the laws of their physical constitution.

But the number of those who injure themselves by hard study is comparatively small; more, through indolence, neglect to take the proper bodily exercise, existing in a dreamy state of reverie, rather than making that exertion which is necessary to a healthy state of mind or body. Some acquire a morbid desire for such stimulus as is afforded by trifling works of fiction, where the imagination is gratified by romantic incidents and scenes, without any good effect upon the heart, or acquisition of any useful knowledge. Even the books which compose our Sunday Libraries are, but too often, highly wrought fictions, which, though intended by the authors to convey important religious truths, are read by many merely for the sake of the story, while the sentiments conveyed take no hold upon the mind;—thus, there are some plants which convert to poison the elements that combine with them; such is their habit—while plants of a different constitution, imbibing the same elements, are healthful, and perform their useful offices in the economy of nature.

Since your tendencies, your habits of mind, your faults and your virtues are so varied, how shall I address you, so that all may be benefited by my remarks? Let us seek for some general principle of action which exists in every individual; we will look into the science of the human mind, and hope we may there find some light to guide us in this search.

You are all here for the purposes of education. Is it not so? Or, have some of you come here because you fancied your acquaintances would esteem you more highly if you should spend some time at a Boarding-school, and, perhaps, obtain a Diploma? Or, because your parents said you *must* go to school, and you were sent away, as if to endure penance for a time, banished from all you love, and that can render you happy?

I will suppose that you all came with the desire of *improvement—education* means improvement, and improvement, in one sense, means education. I would address you then as rational beings, assembled in this place for the purpose of *improvement*, stimulated, as I would fain believe, by the wish to render yourselves acceptable as a living sacrifice to your Maker, and to fulfill the duties incumbent upon you, as rational and intelligent beings. We now stand upon high ground;—we have carried you in imagination to an elevated region of pure and lofty purpose. Would that you all really stood upon this ground, and that you could with full purpose of mind, and with the concentration of all your faculties, devote yourselves to duty, at whatever sacrifice of taste or inclination;—then would your *improvement* in all that is good and praiseworthy be certain and constant; then would you go on from one degree of perfection to another.

The first step in *improvement* is to root out the evil which exists where we wish *good* may be. If an architect desire to erect a useful or beautiful edifice, he clears away all rubbish, and makes a clean place to begin upon. If a gardener would plant a good tree in place of a barren one, he digs out the old roots and makes the ground ready for the reception of the good tree; so must you try to clear away the rubbish of evil inclinations and corrupt tastes, to eradicate bad habits and low tendencies; you must do this work faithfully, and keep a constant watch against the shooting forth of bad roots which may lie concealed within your hearts. Then you can go on with your work of improvement.

We will consider what kind of improvement is meant, when we speak of educational improvement? This leads us into a vast region; let us enter and examine what is here presented to our view. We will suppose many *temples* occupy this space, each dedicated to some particular kind of improvement;—let us pass on. We enter an edifice and read the inscription;—"Dedicated to *religious improvement*." The revealed word of God is engraven on the walls of this temple, illuminated by rays of divine light beaming directly from the great source of light. Here we learn our duty to God and man. We learn that the young are commanded to "Remember their Creator in the days of their youth"—that their Maker demands their heart, with its best affections and desires. The various means of grace or religious improvement are set forth on the walls of this temple ; and the institutions of the Christian religion are here offered for our contemplation and participation.

We will leave this temple in which we behold many devout worshippers—but, only for a while, we leave it ; hither will our footsteps often turn ; hither will we repair when wearied with earthly cares, or suffering under trials and afflictions, we need direction or consolation. Here is deposited the armor which amidst future conflicts and trials, we shall often require. Fortified by the hopes and encouragements we find in the temple dedicated to religion, we may proceed on our way.

Another edifice meets our view—we enter, and scenes of domestic life appear ; the home fireside, where aged grandparents in their arm-chairs watch with satisfaction the happiness of those to whom life is yet fresh and full of promise ; or the child listens with deferential attention to the words of parental instruction. We enter and behold a group of young persons surrounding one who speaks to them of their moral duties, the right cultivation of the heart and its affections ? and we behold the inscription over the doorway of the temple ;—"*Dedicated to moral improvement, and the study of duties to others and to ourselves.*" Here we find books of advice as to the "Proper improvement of time," "The regulation of the temper," "The education of the heart." The genius of this temple is a person of benign, but grave aspect. If a group are seen in angry contention, the genius appears, and holds before them a card on which is engraven the words, "*Be kindly affectionate one to another*;" at the sight of this the flush of anger is seen to subside, and sweet smiles to irradiate countenances but a moment before distorted with rage. A poor woman holding in her arms a sickly looking infant approaches a lady clad in elegant attire and asks charity; in disgust she is turning away, when the genius holds before her a tablet containing these words, "*He that pitieth the poor lendeth to the Lord*," the lady gives liberally to the poor woman, and kindly looks upon the little heir of poverty she holds to her bosom. Two young girls are seen in low and earnest conversation;—shrugs and winks and other significant signs pass between them; the genius frowns and holds before their eyes a tablet on which with confusion of face they read the words, "*Slander and backbiting*."—But we could never recount all the scenes in the temple exhibiting human life, and dedicated to the improvement of the heart and its affections.

We approach an edifice situated on an eminence; and here we find many engaged in deep study. One group are contemplating from an observatory the starry canopy of the heavens, measuring the distances of the stars by means of curious instruments, or explaining the motions of the heavenly bodies. The laboratory of the chemist attracts many—air, earth and water, once considered simple, are brought here for analysis; and elements before unknown and unthought of, are detected in these common substances. Flowers bloom here, and many love to watch their growth, and contemplate the curious symmetry of their formation. Even the smallest and most humble of the vegetable tribe seem to delight these cultivators of botanical science. While natural history thus employs its votaries, with its specimens of animals, plants and minerals, and all created material things receive their due attention, other groups are studying the faculties of mind and investigating the laws of the human understanding. But even to name all the subjects presented, would require almost a lifetime.

We see that with finite, or limited faculties, the scope for investigation is infinite. The greater part of knowledge must be reserved for that future state of existence when time, so short and inadequate for all we have to do, shall be no more, and eternity, in its ceaseless round of progression, opens before us its illimitable expanse. Here, we can but lift up one little corner of the vast curtain which conceals from our view the wonders of creation, the mysteries of science, but in the future world we shall "know as we are known." To those who have no interest in knowledge and no desire for improvement, the eternity which awaits them cannot we believe be blessed; while to such as have, shall more be given, those who have little, and do not desire more, shall be forever excluded from all sources of knowledge and improvement.

In reference to those grand temples dedicated to *religious*, *social*, and *intellectual improvement*, we should say, that as age advances and the strength fails, the first temple becomes the favorite resort. Here the weary repose; here faith sustains the drooping heart, bruised and crushed by affliction, and deprived of the hopes and blessings which make life desirable. The inscriptions on the walls seem to stand out bolder, and the light from above beams more brightly upon the humble worshippers. Here the wayworn traveller rejoices as he reads, "To him that overcometh will I give to eat of the tree of life."

To these temples, you, my beloved pupils, have access —you are constantly incited to your duties, to industry and perseverance, by every bell which reminds you that one portion of time has ended, and another has begun. Can it be possible that amidst all these incentives to effort, and encouragements to virtuous conduct; all the discouragements and mortifications which attend the neglect of the means of improvement, any can recklessly go on, throwing away time in trifling pursuits, and disregarding duties?

But we trust that among us are none who are not, in some degree, desirous to resort to all the temples which may be accessible to them, where truth is to be learned, and wisdom imparted.

——, 1845.

ADDRESS XVI.

PERFECT HAPPINESS NOT TO BE FOUND ON EARTH.

LIFE is not "a succession of pleasant holidays," but to all, and each one, it presents scenes of trials and temptations, and to many, of sorrow and suffering. No situation offers greater temptations than one of prosperity; and earthly prosperity cannot be permanent. Children gather around the family board, and the family hearth, protected and cherished by kind and indulgent parents; day after day, and year after year, passes, and this circle remains unbroken; but it will not always be so. One member after another may be called away to engage in necessary business; the young must soon see that as their parents advance in life, they cannot depend on their care and exertions. In our country there are few fortunes so ample as to secure competency without labor or industry of some kind. If a son receive from his father a fortune sufficient for all his wants, how will it be when this patrimony is divided among several children?

The genius of our government is opposed to family distinctions; and thus the entailment of estates, as in Europe, is not allowed by our laws. In monarchical governments where the crown is hereditary, fortunes and honors are held by the same tenure. The eldest son of a noble family inherits the estate and family honors, younger branches are provided for by the government with places in the public service where they are supported.

Thus is aristocracy sustained and perpetuated; but in our country, there cannot be, under our existing laws, any other aristocracy than that derived from talent and industry.

The family circle may be suddenly broken up by the death of parents; the father taken away, and all is changed in the once happy home. The talents which sustained, or the industry in business which supported the family have passed away; and those who never thought from whence the supply of their wants came, are compelled to think, and to act for themselves; and not only so, but they are bound to take care of those who are yet helpless and incapable of judging, or of doing anything for themselves.

But though the outward circumstances be fair and prosperous, what domestic circle can be a happy one where its members are not governed by right principles, and in their intercourse with each other do not manifest amiable and conciliatory dispositions? It is not always that the virtuous and honest are kind and tender in manner towards their nearest relatives—this is a sad view of human life, and convinces us more than anything else that we are not to be perfectly happy in this world. Too often those who are conscious of rectitude in the weightier matters of the law, omit within the sanctuary of the domestic circle, what they regard as lesser duties, offering sparingly the incense of affectionate looks and words upon the home altar, and recklessly wounding the feelings of those nearest and dearest to them. How little do we know of the sorrows and cares which oppress many who seem placed in enviable circumstances! We heard not the unkind word, the taunting sarcasm, we saw not the cold or scornful glance, which have inflicted deep wounds in that heart, supposed by us to be happy in the midst of prosperity. How many trivial circumstances in the daily intercourse of life, call for forbearance and forgiveness!

A daughter returns from school to take her place in the family circle. If her chief thought is for her own enjoyment, if her imagination continually roves abroad in search of something to interest, excite, or amuse, what happiness does she bring with her? If her parents have sought to give her accomplishments, have they not a right to expect that for them and their happiness those accomplishments are chiefly to be valued, and to be brought forward at their pleasure, and for their gratification? But do we not often see the wishes, and even urgent requests of parents disregarded, while the presence of a stranger will elicit dulcet sounds of music, flashes of wit, or interesting conversation? Is this the fruit of good principles, is this obeying the command of God, to "honor parents?" Good principles alone can secure the young from the temptations of a deceitful and corrupting world; they alone can sustain the heart suffering under sorrows and trials. It should be considered as the first and most important object of your youth, to arm and fortify your minds with such principles as will save you from error, and lead you in the way of truth and virtue. The period of great temptations, of great trials, and sufferings may be more distant in respect to some of you than to others; but come they will to all, unless some stroke of Divine Providence remove you suddenly from this mortal scene. This alone could save you from the dark hours of life; are you prepared for the change? Is your soul, as it now is, fitted to appear before God in judgment? If so, you are prepared to live, to encounter the dangers and difficulties of life; for a preparation for death is a preparation for life—and whoever is prepared to live, is also ready to die.

Before any of you leave this place, whither you have come to prepare yourselves for future life, may you seek and find that wisdom from above which will prove the best and only security for your virtuous and worthy conduct in the scenes which lie before you; which will also be an earnest of your acceptance with God, of your preparation to appear before him in judgment. Think of these things! and inasmuch as the time before you is short, the change to be effected great, and the objects to be gained of infinite importance, may you apply yourselves with all care and diligence to learn those things that belong to your everlasting peace.

—— 1845.

ADDRESS XVII.

A GOOD BEGINNING.

THE past is inexorable, holding with a firm grasp all that is committed to it; no regrets, no wishes, can wrest from its grasp aught which it has once held. The future is at our disposal, should God grant us longer life; but in order to be faithful to our own best interests, we must think beforehand, as to the best method of filling up the time which may be given us, so that it may go down to the past richly laden with good reports. How many live with no plans for the future, acting only from impulse, and as inclination prompts.

The young are naturally averse to restraint; they are not inclined to give up present indulgences for future good. But this must be done by all who would live a virtuous life, who would form such habits as will fit the soul for heaven. Whoever will allow himself to follow his inclinations without considering consequences, acts contrary to his reason and conscience, and must reap the bitter fruit of his own planting. We see the intemperate, not in strong drink merely, but in the various indulgences of the appetite which injure the health; we see a woman fond of admiration, intoxicated with flattery, and giddy with excitement—she cannot deny herself even the doubtful pleasures of society, where she can command attentions for which others sigh in vain. She finds that a certain giddiness, and defiance of restraints and proprieties, attract around her those of the other sex, who seeking pleasure in excitement, avoid the more thoughtful and serious woman, as tiresome and uncongenial. Many a girl who begins by being merely a trifler, goes on her thoughtless course, until she finds herself fast sliding down the smooth declivity, at whose base yawns a frightful gulf. The guilty and abandoned woman might once have been lovely and innocent—her decline was gradual ; from the bowers of pleasure, she passed imperceptibly to the dark purlieus of infamy.

The school-girl is continually solicited by duty on the one hand, and inclination on the other—to rise early, to set about doing what is required of her, to break off from her amusements or her indolence at the call of duty, are all, at first, hard to her. She prefers, perhaps, to follow her own desires, and receives reproof and loses standing. But what a reward follows the doing that which is right, what happiness attends the discharge of duty ! In the one case when we follow pleasure at the sacrifice of duty, we become dissatisfied with ourselves and unhappy ; in the other we have turned away from pleasure, preferring to do what was disagreeable because it was right, and behold the bitter becomes sweet, and the rough places smooth, we find what we had not expected, happiness in the train of duty !

Have each of you formed your plan for the future, or do you intend to leave all to chance, and your own foolish desires? As to those few pupils among us who have scarcely yet passed the years of childhood, we do not expect from them the power of self-control and maturity of judgment, which will enable them to direct themselves, and we therefore place them under the more immediate care and direction of older persons. But I address those who are responsible for their conduct, as capable of judging between right and wrong; who are no longer children, but rapidly advancing to that state of maturity when the full development of the character, as it will be seen in future life, is to appear. The form and tint of the flower, are visible in the expanded blossom; time may imprint deeper and richer hues, and give more symmetry to the outlines, but essentially the flower will remain the same—until decay comes which takes away its beauty, and leaves but the fragrance.

To live by a plan, to make a good beginning, this is what we will now speak of. A good day should be preceded by a good night. That is, when you retire to rest, it should be with the intention of beginning betimes in the morning, to perform its duties, and of spending its hours in the work of improvement; that work for which you were sent to this place. You have, as a Christian, been accustomed to read God's Holy Word before composing yourself to sleep, and to commend your soul to Him, beseeching His blessing upon your good resolutions. After that, you should avoid, as far as possible, all that would disturb your thoughts. You have prepared yourself for sleep, which is the emblem of death, and you should not let your soul again go forth into the world. How calm and sweet is sleep to the young who are pure in heart, and love God, their Father in Heaven! As His all-seeing-eye looks down upon the earth, may we not suppose that our home is regarded by Him with peculiar complacency. Here in the dark watches of the night, He beholds many fair young heads reposing in the sleep of health and innocence; they have the look of angels, yet God who seeth, pitieth their infirmities, and would help them to become perfect.

You are resolved to make a good beginning—therefore when you hear the summons for rising in the morning, do not wait to parley with your conscience, but spring from your beds with the alacrity of a youthful pilgrim, who sees a journey before him which requires all his activity. It is unnecessary to remind the Christian young-pilgrim, that God's eye is upon him, and that a good beginning of the day requires a lifting up of his heart to the source of all virtue and strength; thus, though he may meet with difficulties and trials, he may overcome and endure them, so as not to do wrong himself, or disturb the happiness and tranquillity of others.

Those helpless young persons are greatly to be pitied, in whom habits of indolence are confirmed, and who are accustomed to depend on the services of others for the supply of their wants. Children thus brought up become unable to exert themselves, their bodily powers do not strengthen as they should, and their minds are, in proportion, weak and feeble; yet their tempers often become violent and imperious, and their manners are usually unamiable and repulsive.

How is it with you, my dear younger girls, do you wish to be strong and healthy, industrious, amiable and intelligent? In order to become all this, you must form your plan of living, and try to conform your actions to it. Suppose you should make resolutions like these: "I will go to bed without saying my prayers, or only in a hurried manner, then I will talk and make as much noise to disturb others as I please. In the morning I will not get up till a few minutes before breakfast, when I will hurry on my clothes without properly washing myself, or combing and arranging my hair nicely. I will go down stairs to the dining-room in a noisy manner, running through the halls and pushing rudely by others, especially those to whom I ought, particularly, to be respectful. At table, I will eat fast, sit awkwardly, help myself to what I want, before others have had an opportunity, call on the servants to attend to me when they are helping others, and create as much noise about me as I can, without being so rude as to be sent out of the room. Then in my plays with my companions, I will make all the quarrels I can—if a word is said that will make mischief between others, I will be sure and report it, and advise those who are friendly to have no more to say to each other. I will induce my companions to break rules and be disobedient; we will agree together to do things which we know to be wrong; we will linger away from our duties, go secretly into forbidden places, skulk about as those do who are conscious of doing wrong, and when detected we will pretend to be surprised that we should be blamed, we will say we did not know the rules, we did not hear the bell, or give some other reason, no matter whether true or false, so that we escape punishment." No girl would avow such intentions, but should we see one living day after day in the practice of such conduct, must we not think she has either formed her plan to do these things, or that she is living without a plan? It would be well for you all, younger or older, to write down your plan of life, so that you might have it ever before you. I am sure your parents would like to see your good resolutions *written out*, and still better *carried out*, in practice. "Just as the twig is bent, the tree's inclined." We have seen a tender sapling bowing down before the northern blasts, and we knew that if we would have it grow straight, we must put props to keep it upright, until the fibre of the wood had gained firmness; so do the young who are readily acted upon by passing circumstances, with their flexible feelings and feeble resolutions, need to be sustained by the careful hand of experience until the period when firmly established principles and maturity of judgment shall give consistency and strength of character. If a young tree, no longer a twig or sapling, has grown up bent and crooked, the most skillful culture will scarcely avail to make it upright. Ye are our twigs, saplings and young trees; are you flourishing in a healthful growth, so that you will be upright in character and fair specimens of womankind, with such principles and such firmness of purpose for good as will insure your future well being?

—— 1845.

ADDRESS XVIII.

HUMAN LIFE—ITS BEGINNING, ITS PROGRESS, AND ITS CLOSE.

"You'll tell me man ne'er dies, but changeth life;
And haply for a better. He's happiest
That goes the right way soonest. Nature sent us
All naked hither, and all the goods we had,
We only took on credit with the world;
And that the best of men are but mere borrowers,
Though some take longer day."

HUMAN life is a state of *probation*, or, in other words, of *proof*, to be applied as appointed by the Judge of man, to the soul, as it may, or may not, be fitted for the communion of the spirits of the just made perfect in a future state of purity and blessedness. Such is the great problem of life before us—we cannot shrink from this scrutiny. God's eye is upon us all. He watched over us when we were incapable of thinking of our own existence; He is ever with us. God is our Father in Heaven, we need not fear that He will be cruel or hard with us. "He knoweth our frame, He remembereth that we are dust." As a father pitieth his children, so tenderly doth He regard us.

"Then why," you may ask, "are we taught to fear God, and tremble lest we may offend Him?" This, my daughters, is the solution of such an inquiry. God has given you intelligence, souls which are emanations of His own spirit—He has not made you machines to be acted upon by external force merely; but you have an internal power of resistance; you are endowed with the faculty of choice between good and evil—there are two ways before you, the one straight and narrow, leading to life eternal; the other, the more alluring path whose end is destruction. You may ask, as skeptics have done, "why God, if He love man, should have allowed him to be tempted?" In other words, you might ask, "why is man made a free moral agent?" for to be this, he must be capable of choosing between good and evil. So we perceive that even Almighty Power could not give moral dignity to a being, whose virtue was not that of choice—of free will. But God has provided all needful helps for our infirmities—in His revealed word, He has pointed out the dangers, and the way of escape. Let us, therefore, trust in Him; He will lead us by the hand through dark and slippery places, and at last set our feet upon the rock of ages, never more to slide.

Life is around us, in the vegetable and animal kingdoms, existing under various forms. We will confine our thoughts at this time to *human life*, in which the physical and moral are inseparably blended in this mortal existence.

Infant life, how mysterious does it appear! the little

unconscious lump of mortality, incapable of putting forth its tiny hand to avert danger, insensible alike to looks of tenderness or indifference, lies in its cradle-coffin, dead to all around it, except in its sensual nature, as if its eyes were closed in the last earthly sleep! Can the tiny form of this miniature man or woman, enfold a spirit destined to battle with life; to meet and foil in his assaults the adversary of the human soul, or to join with him in his unhallowed warfare upon the fallen race of man? Who but the Omniscient One can foresee what that infant shall be, when the germ of life having developed itself, the mature being in his physical and moral lineaments shall stand revealed? The mother with tender love watches over her little brood, to her all are alike lovely—for each she "weaves her song," it may "be of melancholy joy."

> "No lingering hour of sorrow shall be thine,
> No sigh that rends thy father's heart and mine
> Thy fame, thy worth, thy filial love, at last
> Shall soothe this aching head for all the past;
> With many a smile, my solitude repay,
> And chase the world's ungenerous scorn away."

But in this one little family, what a diversity of character may hereafter appear! A noble Christian philanthropist has helped to rock the cradle of his baby-brother, who grows up to be dissolute and unprincipled, an open violator of God's laws and a blot upon social life. Of two sisters who shared the same little bed in the nursery, and the same kind mother's care, one may become an exemplary Christian woman, while the other may sink to infamy and shame.

> "'Tis aye a solemn thing to me
> To look upon a babe that sleeps—
> Wearing in its spirit deeps,
> The unrevealed mystery
> Of its Adam's taint and woe,
> Which, when they revealed lie,
> Will not let it slumber so."

Infant life quickly passes away; the beaming of awakened intelligence is seen in the glancing eye, in smiles and frowns. The child begins to exercise its own will, and to seek to subjugate the wills of others. At this point, education should begin; the first lesson is that of obedience; the child must be made to do what is commanded and to abstain from doing what is forbidden. With serious aspect he is taught to say, "I must submit myself to all my governors, teachers, spiritual pastors, and masters," and this early lesson should be followed up by a steady course of discipline, so that the habit of obedience may be early acquired; thus only can the evils be averted, which are sure to fall upon those who have not learned, while young, to submit themselves to authority.

The life of childhood passes rapidly away; dolls and playthings soon cease to be cared for, and to amuse. Girlhood and school-days come. There is a great change in the life at this period, little was expected of the child; she was suffered to amuse herself. Happy childhood had no hard lessons to learn, it was allowed to pass unburdened with care and labor.

But there is no stopping in the journey of life, and the stage of *girlhood* comes with its many restraints and its onerous tasks—in the higher walks of life, these restraints are confinement to a given routine necessary to secure advantages of education, and these tasks are the bending of the mind to study and research, and the wearisome practice necessary to acquire elegant accomplishments.

The young girl emerging from childhood has her trials—she is no longer regarded as a mere plaything ; her actions becoming more constrained as she feels sensible of having grown to be a large girl, she loses the grace of childhood, and perhaps becomes awkward and embarrassed ; this tendency is heightened by her being told of her faults of manner. The young girl from twelve to fifteen often has many mortifications ; she does not know exactly how she ought to behave—if she should appear too womanly she thinks this might seem like *putting herself forward ;* if she is childlike, this may appear ridiculous in one so old. She does not know her place, whether it be with the children, or the older persons. It is at this period of a girl's life, when a boarding-school is often a desirable asylum. The change has come, and the girl in her first teens can no longer be fondled as a child ; even her parents seem to be more distant towards her ; and, sometimes, she feels sad and jealous ; thinks nobody loves her, that she is not lovable, and wishes she were away from home, or could do, or be, something else.

She is sent from home to school, and this school-life is a new state; the school-girl has many responsibilities, and is obliged not only to learn a great deal, but to unlearn. She must arrange her own clothing, take care and keep her things together. She has no mother, aunty, or black mammy to run after her and pick up; what she throws down, or leaves about carelessly, will probably be lost; if she tear a dress she must mend it, or the rent will be made worse; if a string be torn off a night-cap she must sew it on, or it will be lost, and this appendage of her night-dress become useless. She must learn to keep a watchful eye over her books, music and other belongings, so that nothing be lost; thus she may be expected to acquire ideas respecting property; and she is obliged to learn to respect the rights of others, as encroachments upon these are followed by ill-feelings, loss of reputation, and disgrace. She must learn to be active and industrious, is obliged to rise early to perform her morning duties, to assist in arranging her room, and be neatly dressed for breakfast at an hour when at home she would be indulging in her morning slumbers. She finds there is not so much fun and amusement in a school-girl's life as labor and thought; but she must consider the importance of the objects in view—that the thoughtless, careless child is to be formed and moulded into a prudent, judicious, useful woman. To accomplish so great an object, demanded an entire change of life and habits; and the acquirement of knowledge, varied and extended, of the *savoir faire*, or *knowing how to do*, as well as the learning of books. No one should wonder that oft-times the school-girl is discouraged, especially at first, before she has fully emerged from the chrysalis state of childhood into the fuller light and knowledge of the world she inhabits. She longs for home and its indulgences, and to be again the little pet of the family; but that could not be—if she could compare one of her little-girl frocks with the dresses she now wears, she would see that nature has been working a change, and she, too, must work; at home, living idly and indulged, she would be awkward, disagreeable and ignorant; at school, diligently devoting herself to the work of improvement, she is laying the foundation for future honor and respectability, preparing herself to be loved for worth of character, to be the pride of her parents, and ready to act her part in life. But to insure all this there must be self-sacrifice and labor.

School life, with many of you, is fast drawing to a close, your first teens have disappeared, with some, a score of years may be counted; you have persevered in a long and thorough course of school education, and there can no longer be any good reasons for your remaining as pupils—the ripe fruit separates itself from the bough when it has matured; this is nature's law. The immediate stage before you is that of taking your place at home, as young ladies; having had advantages of education, much will be expected of you—that you will appear easy and affable in manners, knowing what to say, and how to act on all occasions. You must require much of yourselves in respect to exercising an influence at home for the welfare and happiness of all within its circle ; you should have a quick eye to discern disorders and irregularities in the household, and energy to remedy them. Carry home with you the habits of early rising and industry which you have here formed. How much might be done by an energetic daughter in a family, where servants sleep away the best hours of the day, and rise to lounge about, doing things in the most careless and slovenly manner, because they will not take the proper way of doing them. How much might be accomplished in the way of reformation by the young lady returned from school, who should be seen to rise early, to walk about and notice what is going on. Servants would be ashamed to lie a bed late, or to indulge in idleness when their young mistress should set them an example of early rising and activity.

A good daughter may do much towards rendering home pleasant—if a father's brow seem shaded by care and anxiety, she may, by her cheerfulness and winning ways, dissipate the dark thoughts which press upon him. Perhaps he thinks of debts which he cannot well pay, and sees around him luxuries which he knows he cannot afford—the good and wise daughter will have tact to discern the associations in his mind, and instead of beginning to talk of what she wants, and *must have*, and to plan new expense, she will show her father that she is careful, and trying to learn and practise economy; that she realizes the fact that he has expended a great deal for her, and is now determined to begin to help save expense. She finds her Arithmetic very useful in reckoning up amounts, in showing her what things cost, and how soon a large sum of money may be dissipated where unrestrained expenses are indulged in.

There is, probably, more domestic unhappiness in the world on account of female extravagance than any other cause. Those who earn money know how hard it is to be obtained, and they usually spend it cautiously, while those who are accustomed to disburse what others acquire, often do it with lavish prodigality. A husband soon becomes disgusted with a wife who thoughtlessly incurs debts which he must pay, or forfeit his reputation—for the extravagant wife escapes the law, while the industrious husband suffers for her faults. Often we see a care-worn man, seldom smiling, or if he does it seems as if it were in mockery of his own gloomy thoughts, toiling day after day in his store or his office, slavishly performing the duties of his calling, whatever these may be ;—seldom he allows himself indulgences, he has no leisure—he must coin himself, yea his life, his heart's blood, for money—"I must have money," cry his wife and daughter. To be able to answer that call, there have been men of high standing in society, who have stifled the voice of conscience, bartered reputation, and ended a life of wretchedness within the walls of a prison.

The extravagance of a wife or daughter has driven many a man to commit forgery, to betray public and professional trusts, to cheat in business, and to incur debts with no probable means of repaying. Should we not, then, as educators of women, seek to give you habits of economy and care in expending money? Begin as daughters to relieve your fathers of their heavy burdens—show that you sympathize in their cares and would gladly assist them if you could. Many good daughters do aid their fathers by writing for them, by keeping accounts, and helping to arrange their business papers; they may steal quietly into a business office where no servant would be permitted to go, and with ready tact manage to remove rubbish and waste papers which had accumulated; put in their places in the library, books which are scattered about, and thus give an encouraging air of taste and neatness to a place which before looked gloomy and confused; and a little vase of flowers by its fragrance would speak to the father's or brother's heart, of a daughter's or sister's care and love, and thus lighten the task of wearisome labor.

A wife who is a help-meet rather than a spend-thrift will confine her wants to her husband's means; there are noble and accomplished women, even in these days of female recklessness and extravagance, who, forsaking the fascinations of society, devote themselves to their domestic duties, and even keep the business accounts of their husbands, while the latter are devoting their energies to the duties of a laborious profession. Such women should be honored, as they surely are, by the good and wise, and their daughters, we may expect, will, in their turn, make good wives, in whom the hearts of their husbands may safely trust.

How long continued may be your life at the home of your parents will depend on God's will and Providence; but changes must come—you will not always be *young* ladies, though all of you may not assume the responsibilities of married life. You will not always have parents to live with; the circle in your childhood's home must one day become a broken one. The pillars of the edifice will fall, your parents must be taken from you, and one after another of your beloved ones be removed from this earthly scene. But you will ever find enough to do to fill up the measure of your days with usefulness. You may find some friend of your early life, perhaps some school-mate whose marriage entailed upon her misery and suffering; you may by your sympathies soothe her afflictions, and if you have means, may minister to her who has been impoverished by a dissolute and improvident husband. As years advance you may not be disposed to count your single life an unblest one; and yet, we do not say you should not marry. The ordinance of God's appointment, we may not condemn; but the subject should not be lightly weighed—not decided in a party of pleasure; or disposed of as an author winds up his romance, by marrying the heroine because the readers expect it.

"Some at the bridal, some at the tomb;"

In a few years what changes appear among the youthful travellers who go forth with joyous feet from our classic shades, to tread the paths "of life's enchanting way." By the past, I see the future reflected as in a mirror. An accumulation of wedding cards—of letters announcing the death of former pupils appear among my sacred relics. Here one writes to tell me of the loss of a beloved parent, brother, or sister; and again, another informs me that she is thrown dependent on her own exertions, and asks to be aided in rendering her education available for her support, and it may be that of a family.

Such is life, its beginning and its progress:

> "To each his sufferings, all are men:
> Condemned alike to groan;
> The tender for another's pain,
> The unfeeling for his own."

The close of a life which was well begun, and continued in the practice of Christian virtues—whether this close come sooner or later—is not to be dreaded. It is but the entrance into a new and better life, for which this has been a preparatory state.

—— 1845.

ADDRESS XIX.

TIMES AND SEASONS.

"To everything there is a season, and a time to every purpose under heaven."—ECCLE. iii. 1.

THESE words of divine inspiration emanate from the same Mind which directs the course of the seasons, the succession of day and night, and the changes in human existence, from infancy to old age.

How beautiful is everything in its season! In the spring of the year the bounding rivulet as if rejoicing in newly recovered freedom, rushes joyously on its way, murmuring to the fresh springing blossoms which deck its verdant banks. The birds, which had been driven from their summer haunts by the ungenial frosts, return to the groves and forests, and hail the return of foliage with their most cheerful notes. The sun comes forth from his chamber, as with a renovated existence, reflecting from flower, and bud, and leaf, from hill and vale, mountain and streamlet, the most cheerful, and the most beautiful coloring; not as in midsummer, with gorgeous brightness, does this ruler of the seasons and the day, gild the face of nature in the delicately tinted spring.

The young lambs frisk about among the flocks, and

their cheerful bleating bespeaks their enjoyment of the life that God has given them—young and happy life is seen, too, among the herds of the stall; and everywhere we perceive new existences springing forth in the vegetable and animal kingdoms.

We walk abroad amidst the beauty and loveliness of this animated scene of nature, coming forth from the shroud and the grave of winter; and our hearts are warm with love and admiration of that benevolent power which has effected this great change. But the season wears on; we lose the exquisite enjoyment which it at first afforded us; and, as it gradually ripens into summer, we are pleased to see the perfecting of nature's works. The flowers of spring are succeeded by others of more gorgeous coloring; and as the beautiful and fragrant blossoms wither and fade, the swelling germs of flowers, scarcely noticed, perhaps, in their blossoming, give promise of the fruits which are to succeed. The young animals have gained in strength and maturity what they have lost in mirthfulness. We see that nature is in a state of progression, and we are satisfied that it should be so; even sober autumn has its peculiar attractions, and stern winter finds us prepared, by a gradual change, to greet its frosts and dreariness, with a kindly feeling. The warmth of affection is heightened by the cold temperature, which draws the members of a family around the fireside. New scenes and new wants elicit in the mind of man new thoughts, presenting a new field to his imagination, and new scope for his emotions.

In our own existence such is the anology to the changing seasons of the year, that nothing is more common-place, than to compare youth to spring, middle age to midsummer, and old age to winter. But though the comparison be common-place, it is nevertheless beautiful and striking. And as one season gradually slides into another, so do the stages of life imperceptibly follow each other, and we go from infancy to adolescence, from youth to middle age, and from thence to old age, without being aware that the change is going on, until we find that it has passed; though others may have perceived this long before we, ourselves, may have been conscious that the particular stage in life's journey has been completed. The mother tells her young child that he must not cry for trifles, for he is no longer a baby; the little boy is still changing, and when he behaves in a childish manner, he is, by-and-by, reminded that he is now a great boy, and must not behave like a child. The awkwardness or ignorance which might have been tolerated at an earlier period, are considered as unpardonable in the young gentleman, and the pardonable impetuosity of youth is found unsuitable to mature manhood. But ardor and firmness, resolution and decision, gradually decay, and the pride of manhood is laid low at the approach of weak and feeble old age, when "the grasshopper becomes a burden," and "man is afraid of that which is high." And yet the strong man so gradually declines into the vale of years, that often he has been classed by others among the elders, long before he, himself, is sensible that he has passed life's meridian.

"To everything there is a season." To the morning

there is sportiveness and activity, to the mid-day labor and care, and to the evening, repose.

But to what do these observations tend? Is there something for you, my dear young friends, to do, which has any relation to the times and seasons, to which we have referred? Should the beautiful order and regularity of nature, merely elicit a transient admiration; or shall we educe from thence lessons of wisdom for the direction of our conduct in life? In the language of the poet, "Order is heaven's first law," and it should be ours also. We should consider times and seasons in relation to our own employments, and should, in our lives, exemplify the beauty of order and regularity.

You who are now before me, may, in respect to age, be considered as children, older girls, and young ladies; yet we must admit this classification is not so distinctive as to render its application clear, in all cases—for here, as in the world of nature around us, the boundaries are not distinct lines, but one state gradually passes into another.

It was the complaint of a precocious young girl, now a grave matron, that in cases where obedience and restraint were required, her mother would insist she was yet but a child; but when she failed in prudence and dignity of conduct, she was reminded that she had now become a young lady. The mother, however inconsistent it might seem, yet acted conformably to the nature of the case, for girls at a certain age may be regarded as children or young ladies, according to circumstances, and the places they are required to fill. Still each of you should consider the character, as to age, you actually sustain, and appear in, to others. A young girl no longer a little child should neither affect the babyish language and actions of infancy, nor the manners of grown persons; while the young lady should avoid extreme timidity on the one hand, or too great confidence on the other; for manners, which at one age, may please and amuse, at another, would excite disapprobation or contempt.

There is a season for improving the mind and the heart;—it is that of youth, especially the period devoted to education. This season is now yours, but it is rapidly passing away; every day a portion of it is vanishing, and bringing you nearer to the time when your pursuit of knowledge will be interrupted. You will find that future years which will see you removed from the restraints of school, will present few favorable opportunities for intellectual improvement. Various are the interruptions to liberal pursuits, and the hindrances in forming moral habits, in that intercourse with the world which follows an entrance upon its active scenes. Now, then, is your season for learning books, for *learning how to learn*, so that you may best improve future opportunities. Now is your season for acquiring a literary taste, without which books and leisure can do little towards enriching the mind with stores of knowledge, or elevating the intellectual character. An expensive library of valuable books selected by a literary friend, or a hired *littérateur*, may by purchase, be the property of one whose mind is incapable of appropriating the rich treasures it contains.

At this season of your lives, you should study to correct the evil passions which you may have suffered "to grow with your growth, and strengthen with your strength." Think what you would wish to be, and strive to render yourselves such; think what you would *not* be, and endeavor to avoid persons, places and circumstances, which would tend to mould your characters into that form from which you now shrink. The minds of the young, like plastic clay, easily take impressions from surrounding objects.

Educators may do much towards directing the efforts of the young in properly moulding their own characters, but the work, after all, must be in a great measure, their own. If they resist what others attempt to do for them, they will certainly destroy all symmetry and proportion; they can and may defeat all. How important then is this season of education to those whom I now address! How rapidly is it fleeing from you! Is there, then, any portion of it to be thrown away, or trifled with? Surely not. So long as any one of you has one bad passion to subdue, or one bad habit to reform, you have work to perform.

Who can know what he may be led to do if he does not learn to govern his own spirit! How often a person begins a wrong course and keeps on doing wrong, in order to justify or conceal the first bad act which might have been but a trifling sin in comparison to what follows. Beware then of seeking to conceal or justify what you may do amiss ; better retrace your steps, and acknowledge you have done wrong. It is always interesting and affecting to see a young person striving against faults of character, willing to think herself to blame, anxious to do right. God, and good angels love such an one ; she will have help to struggle with the infirmities of her nature, and will go on conquering her faults, and improving in goodness. In the season of youth she will perform the duty and labor which belong to it, and will have a reward in a peaceful and virtuous old age, and in a happy eternity.

I would gladly hope that all of you will remember the words you have now heard. Some will do so ; their hearts have received the good seed; and reflection, and meditation will cause it to bear fruit; others have perhaps listened with curiosity, but with little desire to be made better ; they are satisfied with themselves as they are—or they are not willing to trouble themselves about their faults; it is not a pleasant subject ! Some have been too indolent to listen, but have sat listless and indifferent. To them this is a season for dreaming or reverie ; satisfied that they are not to be questioned at the close of the address so that their inattention may be exposed. What have such to do with seasons or purposes ! the seasons they desire are not seasons for doing good, or gaining knowledge ; their purposes—alas ! how many live without any. Though to "everything there is a season, and a time to every purpose," there are many who disregard all seasons for the improvement of their own minds, all seasons for being useful, all seasons for preparing for a future world—to them there is no settled purpose of action.

May the number of those among you who care not for seasons, who live without a purpose, be small. Now is your season for resolving to be, and to do, what you should. Now is the time for you to form your settled, determined, purpose to turn from all evil ways, and seek for righteousness, and holiness of heart. You may possibly live to reform, if you defer this work, but we have no certainty for the future. Youth is the season you now have. May you improve it aright.

—— 1845.

ADDRESS XX.

OUR GARDEN AND GARDENERS.

"Now 'tis the spring, and weeds are shallow rooted;
Suffer them now, and they'll o'ergrow the garden,
And choke the herbs for want of husbandry."

SHAKSPEARE.

To TEACHERS AND PUPILS:

AFTER a short suspension of duty, we have again met to renew our labors; some to impart, others to receive instruction. But though we have been resting from our usual occupations, nature has performed a great work; she has thrown off the icy chains of winter, and comes forward to greet us in her robe of spring. And yet her great work was going on in the dark and silent tomb of earth, unobserved of all save Him who directs nature's laboratory in which the care-perfected seed and bulb are undergoing changes to prepare them to rise to light and life. At His word their resurrection is accomplished, and the new plant, like a new creation, rises from decay and death. The leaf and flower buds which had been carefully folded up in their scaly or downy covering now expand, and the trees and shrubs are again clothed with verdure and beauty.

"Look all around thee! How the spring advances!
New life is playing through the gay, green trees;
See how, in yonder bower, the light leaf dances
To the bird's tread, and to the quivering breeze!
How every blossom in the sunlight glances!
The winter-frost to his dark cavern flees,
And earth, warm—wakened, feels through every vein
The kindling influence of the vernal rain.

"Now silvery streamlets from the mountain stealing,
Dance joyously the verdant vales along;
Cold fear no more the songster's tongue is sealing,
Down in the thick, dark grove is heard his song—
And, all their bright and lovely hues revealing,
A thousand plants the field and forest throng,
Light comes upon the earth in radiant showers,
And mingling rainbows play among the flowers."

The German poet, Tieck, thus beautifully wrote of spring in the last century; for from age to age, the observers of nature are presented with the same phenomena, and the hearts of men are gladdened by the joyful vernal season.

When you now go forth in our "Sylvan walks," you can gather for your botanical studies the Sanguinaria,* the Epigea,† the Viola, the Anemone, and many others of spring's early flowers; and the blossoms on some of the forest trees have come, as is their wont, before the leaf buds are fully expanded. The late ice-bound streams murmur cheerfully as they flow on, and

* Blood root. † Trailing arbutus.

the songsters of our groves and ancient forests, enraptured, sing their loudest, sweetest strains. "Youth, Spring and Flowers," they are all here—shall we too, not rejoice and be glad! Yes, we should do so; and yet we must reflect, for we have something to do in life, as well as much to enjoy. Spring will pass away, its flowers will wither, and its foliage fall into "the sere and yellow leaf" to be blown about by the autumnal winds, and then sink into the bosom of its native earth. After spring, is the season of fruits, the harvest of nature. The analogy between youth and spring suggests that in the former, as in the latter, there must be a preparation for something valuable to follow the season of beauty and gladness. A garden of spring flowers, or showy plants, would be pleasant to look at, but for the support of life, fruits are required. Bread is from the fruit of flowers which have no beauty of form or color. The wise gardener, though he loves and values flowers, is most solicitous for the perfecting of fruits.

Here, then, is a garden of plants, and here are gardeners to tend them. Our pupils are the plants we are to cultivate; sweet roses and proud magnolias, flourish side by side with white lilies and snowdrops; the blushes of the carnation are reflected by the pale japonica; but have we nothing to do but to look at, and admire our flowers; or, as in vegetable physiology, to study their formation and their habits? If it were so, the work of education would be a mere amusement; or rather, it would become needless. But our plants have minds to be cultivated, souls to be fitted for the vicissitudes of life, and prepared to be transplanted into celestial regions. *Their* habits have a moral element, which must be watched and developed. So, my friends and associate gardeners, our work assumes a serious aspect, and though we began with joyful salutations to youth, spring and flowers, we are obliged by a sense of duties resting upon us to turn our course to the grave paths of reflection, and to consider, what, as gardeners, we have to do. That we have, at least, been considered as faithful laborers in our garden, seems to be indicated by the increasing numbers of the objects of our care.

But laying aside all figurative language as we enter into a subject so practical as the duties of teachers, let us pause a few moments to review the qualifications required in their proper performance. The life of a teacher may, by some, be regarded as one of dull and common-place labor, uncheered by bright or beautiful thoughts and aspirations; the butterfly with gilded wings, fluttering in the sunbeams, if she could think in her giddy round, would doubtless fancy herself the queen of insects; so do the butterflies of society look down upon those far nobler than themselves, because they do not glitter and float in idle enjoyment through the atmosphere which constitutes their world. Should one gifted with reason feel humiliated because the inmates of a lunatic asylum fancying themselves, kings and queens, deck their persons with fantastic array, and put on airs of superiority? These self-deceived lunatics are not more blind to the truth, than are those, who living in indolence and self-indulgence claim superiority over such as devote their lives to their own improvement, and the education of the young, for the former should accompany the latter. There are those who go down to their graves "unwept, unhonored, and unsung," because they have lived but for themselves. They who have worshipped the world, and its vanities, can expect in return but what the world has to give—unsatisfying and empty are its pleasures; its rewards are transient and worthless. But teachers must not be expected to be exempt from human imperfections. Doubtless many are urged into this profession by external circumstances, so that with them it is at first rather a necessity than choice. We will grant that this may be, and often is, the fact; but when once the duties are undertaken by the conscientious and reflecting, their importance is felt, and more and more must the sense of high responsibility become active. We are not now referring to those necessitous foreigners who, for bread, engage in teaching languages and accomplishments, with never a thought beyond the emoluments received, or the popularity which will insure their business success. There are noble men and women, enlightened and conscientious foreigners, who merit respect and confidence for their devotedness to the improvement of their pupils, who labor *con amore*, in their duties, and fill their station with fidelity and dignity.

The lady-teachers in this institution, are a band of sisters, gathered together from domestic circles in various parts of our country. I have not chosen my assistants from any one section, but have desired to assemble here the peculiar characteristics of the various portions of our great empire. From New England, the middle and southern States, I have sought to gather in one circle, intelligent and devoted young women, inspired with the noble desire to cultivate their own minds, and to impart to others the fruits of education. I say young women, for in general, educators who are advanced into middle life have become fixed in their own opinion, and cannot readily follow out the system prescribed by another. By aiding in normal education, I have happily been able to train teachers so as to fit them for their places here. So, as a mother and elder daughters, we have wrought together in the care and guidance of the younger ones. The elder daughters observe whether the various professors, and foreign teachers, are faithful in their duties, and are ever ready to give the alarm if aught seems to be going wrong in our large family. This is a beautiful organization—it is one which binds us all in one close and endearing bond—mother, elder sisters, and daughters! Let us bear in mind these sacred associations. There is another picture, such as Dickens and some other modern novel writers delight in portraying—as in "Do-the-Boy's Hall," the "Young lady's school with thirty boarders and six teachers," where exist cruelty and oppression on the one hand, and mean espionage and vulgar attempts at gentility on the other.

When Charles Dickens was recently in our country

and visiting the neighboring cities of Baltimore and Washington, I had a strong desire to invite him here, that he might see an American school, different from the miserable pictures which he had drawn of English schools. But Mr. Charles Dickens was then a great man, courted and followed by Americans who ought to have stood aloof from such servility—so I gave him no opportunity to complain of any annoyance from me in the way of attentions. I had, when Miss Martineau was in this country, and on a visit to a friend of mine in Vermont (where I then resided), gone by invitation to meet her. While arrogantly boasting of the attentions she was receiving, and lamenting her many engagements, she said in relation to a distinguished family of Boston with whom she was expected to pass a few days: "One would not really wish their friends sick, to be rid of an engagement, but I should be glad if something were to happen which would excuse me from going." After this remark I said to Miss Martineau that I had hoped to have had the pleasure of seeing her at my own home, but under the circumstances, could not of course think of adding to the number of those who annoyed her by invitations. It so happened that this lady wished to attend a great celebration, where a distinguished orator was to speak, at a town some thirty miles distant. It had been my intention to ask her to accompany us in our carriage, but as the case was, I let her take a stage-coach, and make her own way. Yet, after all, I was put into Miss Martineau's book on America, as one who took great pains to see her, "a literary lady who boasted of her housekeeping, etc., who talked of Dr. Brown—and Miss M—— did not know what Dr. Brown until she discovered it was Dr. Thomas Brown, the late Professor at Edinburgh ;—and this lady's sister too, had been to see her on another occasion, and it seems she had gone a long journey to tell this lady in Vermont, what she, Miss Martineau, had said to her." Such is the *twaddle*, if I may use the word, that is too often printed about America in Europe. It was true that my sister, Mrs. W., did on her return from Boston to Troy, visit me in my Vermont home, and spake of having seen Miss Martineau. They were both present at some educational meeting, where Mrs. W., as an educator, was distinguished and Miss Martineau had remained in the background. Mrs. W. had expressed to me her disappointment in Miss Martineau ; this of course I did not mention to her, but merely said, my sister who visited me on her return from Boston, spake of meeting her. Yet, though our names do not appear in her book, we are there; and I have only to add, that if there is as little truth in other portions of it, as in that which had relation to what came within my own knowledge, the book is far from reliable authority.

But this is a digression, though the chain of associated ideas may be readily traced, from schools to Mr. Dickens, and from his American travels to those of Miss Martineau. But we owe much to the genius of the former, for his sketches of life in its various phases; and the latter, in her earlier writings, especially those on political economy, manifested a strong and vigorous intellect;

but it is unfortunate when writers of fiction forget that there are such realities as *truth* and *fact*.

We say, then, that notwithstanding all the obloquy which has been heaped upon boarding-schools, and in too many cases but deservedly, we are conscious of aiming at excellence. I believe that you, my associate teachers, labor from a noble sense of duty, and that the services you here render, are not given from mere worldly considerations. Your love for me, and those whom you assist in educating, is deep and sincere. Living together as one large, united family, we can forget the outside world—some of you have left pleasant homes to aid in the great work in which we are engaged; you now say, and think, that you shall never wish any other home, but far be from me the desire that you may never depart hence to preside in your own domestic circles, or to found other educational establishments to prepare for which you are now gaining the rich fruits of experience. No, let us enjoy the present, trusting in each other's affection, and chiefly anxious to make the most of time as it flies, in the cultivation of the moral garden which we are called to "keep and dress" for our Lord and Master. Be content, faithful teacher, with your profession. Even in this world you are doubtless happier than the daughters of pleasure. You are also free from the often harassing cares and the peculiar physical ills to which those are subjected who have entered into the marriage state. We would not use arguments to dissuade from this relation when God's providence seems to lead to it. We believe in Providence, and that man should follow its leadings in humble submission. This Divine Providence has led us all hither, Principal, Teachers and Pupils ; God saw us a few years ago in our various homes, and in His omniscient mind, He then saw us here, as we are now, dwelling together in one of the loveliest spots of earth which He had created; and He has made us love one another, and feel happy in our mutual relations.

This has been a very rambling address ; it was my intention to have dwelt somewhat in detail upon the duties of Teachers and Pupils, but I have indulged in expressing emotions which the subject has naturally excited. We will not now come down from the height to which our imagination has raised us to the enumeration of special duties. It is certain that if we all have love for each other, zeal to do right ourselves and to influence those around us for good, there will be peace and happiness within our circle, and the great work of improvement both in ourselves and wherever our influence may extend, will be steadily carried forward.

——, 1846.

ADDRESS XXI.

RELATIVE DUTIES OF TEACHERS AND PUPILS.

In a late address commenced with the intention of discussing the relative duties of teachers and pupils, we did not proceed directly to our subject, but indulged in some digressions, which might have been more interesting, if not so directly useful as the consideration of practical duties ; this we are now to engage in, and for a short time let us give our serious thoughts to the subject.

"Duty," says an anonymous writer, "is above all consequences. It commands us to look neither to the right, nor to the left, but straight forward. Hence every signal act of duty is an act of Faith. It is performed in the assurance that God will take care of consequences." In education, especially, must we be influenced by this single regard to duty. Thus a teacher, who, in the hope of gaining the love of a pupil, neglects discipline, or any other duty, does not look straight forward, but consults consequences rather than duty—and what consequences will arise from such remissness on the part of the teacher ; what but a want of respect for, and confidence in her who fears to do her duty ? Let no teacher think to gain the love of pupils by failing to perform her own duties ;

but go forward, and do what is right, leaving the consequences to Him who can overrule all, for good. That teacher is to be distrusted who evinces a strong desire for popularity, who is usually seen with her train of attendant satellites; who singles out her own favorites, and leaves others, perhaps, equally or more worthy, to feel themselves neglected and uncared for. It may be very hard to maintain perfect impartiality, but it is a duty which should not be violated by the conscientious teacher. Neither is any parent justified in showing partiality in his family—so that it should never be said, such a child is his or her mother's favorite, as we often hear.

Experience shows the evils incident to particular stations and situations. In a former address we took a poetical view of our associations together here, where principal, teachers and pupils are united in one family, forming one household. But does not discord sometimes rear its snaky head in the sacred family circle, and shall we, where so many and of such various tastes and habits are congregated, escape from all assaults of the serpent? Human nature in its best estate is prone to err. Those who are willing to devote themselves to labor and duty, are sometimes most tenacious of being appreciated by others. Any supposed impeachment of their motives, or depreciation of their merits, may change the calm current of their thoughts and disturb that equanimity of feeling which is required in order to act well the important part they have undertaken, and to render them examples to others. Dr. Johnson says, that "so far is it from being true, that men are naturally equal, that no two people can be half an hour together, but one shall acquire an evident superiority over the other." If this be so, how is it when many persons, whose lives are devoted to improvement, and whose duties call them to govern others, are brought together within one social system—shall they be planets revolving each in her own orbit around a central point, or shall each, striving to be a sun, jostle others, in trying to fix herself into a position where her gravity shall overcome the attraction of all the other bodies in the system?

We cannot deny that habits of solitary study and meditation may be often unfavorable to cheerfulness, and that ready interchange of pleasant conversation which constitutes agreeable social intercourse.

> "Universal plodding prisons up
> The nimble spirits in the arteries."

To this evil, teachers are exposed, and therefore it is important that they should often break off from solitary musing or study, and go forth among the pleasant scenes of nature which in this favored spot so lovingly invite you. Wherever you look, to whatever point you turn your footsteps, you see beauty and grandeur, united. Where can we find on earth, scenery in which these two qualities more harmoniously mingle!—the more we contemplate it, the more deeply do we feel the power of external nature to soothe and elevate the mind. Cowper says:

"Scenes must be beautiful, which daily viewed,
Please daily, and whose novelty survives
Long knowledge and the scrutiny of years."

But then according to Byron:

"To view alone
The fairest scenes of land and deep,
With none to listen, or reply
To thoughts with which our hearts beat high,
Were irksome."

Therefore it is well to have companions in your walks; not such as would encourage any morbid sentimentality, but those who are natural, and, who

"Nature love in all her varied forms."

There is an evil which arises from anxiety for self-improvement and great conscientiousness—it is that of wishing to know what others think of us, that we may be thus assisted in forming an opinion of ourselves; this is generally unprofitable, and therefore it is well in *tête-à-tête* conversations, to avoid discussing our own faults or virtues. Confessions are often a lure for praise; and it is difficult to speak of ourselves to others with perfect sincerity.

To those who love and study natural science there are never-failing subjects for observation and discussion; here, is a beautiful species of moss with its tiny flower, or a lichen with its fairy cup. A fossil shell sets the imagination to work to invent a cause for its being found so far from the river's banks; a stone of volcanic origin gives the mind a new impulse, or a shining lizard seen from his lurking-place suggests another train of thought. So it is better to throw away sickly fancies and the idle complainings of the school of Byron and L. E. L.,* and be happy as those should be, who love God and the world he has made, and believe that, here, they have his work to do, and after he shall have done with them on earth they will be taken by him, to a higher and happier state of being.

Teachers are in danger of becoming dull and moping, or sentimental and romantic, and therefore should they invent for themselves a pleasant variety of recreations; they should not fear sometimes to indulge in reading lighter works of humor, or romance, avoiding in poetry or prose the *too sentimental* class. They should talk and laugh, and love to see others do the same, in proper times and places. It is very desirable too that we should cultivate with those around us a spirit of cordial regard. This requires that we should have confidence in others, especially in their good will towards us. It is one of the great faults of authors, and others devoted to literary pursuits, to brood over fancied neglects, to imagine themselves unappreciated. It would be but natural that teachers, associated together in one household, should sometimes be infected with this jealousy. A woman par-

* Miss Landon, a poet of the present age, whose signature was L. E. L. was the victim of unsanctified and ill-directed imagination; her writings, like those of Byron, have a sickly influence on the young.

tially insane, went to her neighbor's house, and after some commonplace remarks, said to her, "I am going to kill you." "Why would you kill me?" asked the lady. "Because you do not reverence me enough," was the answer. Perhaps we may sometimes feel displeased at others, because we imagine they do not *reverence us enough*; but it would be well if we could care less for the estimate in which we may be held by those around us; indeed it is an unprofitable speculation at the best.

Laying aside then these analyses of our own minds and characters, we will turn to the more profitable inquiry of what *we have to do*. As I look around, I perceive a large assemblage of the young of various ages—a few who may be called children, many between this age and that of the young lady, and a large number of those who have arrived at mature years. They are all sent here to be educated, which according to our great statesman Webster, means, "that the feelings are to be disciplined, the passions are to be restrained: true and worthy motives are to be inspired, a profound religious feeling is to be instilled, and pure morality inculcated under all circumstances." Thus weighty are our responsibilities who have undertaken to perform all this, and chiefly do they rest upon her who is the head of the institution, to whom these young persons have severally and individually been intrusted as a precious charge from fond and anxious parents. To aid me in this great work of education, I have selected the teachers whom I see before me, some of whom have been for years my associates. Each teacher is invested with authority and influence, and acts in her particular station as the representative of the Principal, whom parents properly regard as accountable for the acts of her chosen associates, or neglect of duties intrusted to them, in relation to pupils. It is therefore right that every teacher should understand well what she engages to do, and prepare herself for the performance of her duties by every means in her power. No kind of knowledge of literature or science is useless to a teacher ; if she understand Latin or Greek, she will be the better able to teach the meaning and derivation of the words of her own language. History furnishes interesting anecdotes and illustrations. Rhetoric, if well understood, will aid in teaching composition, and the critical reading of the best writers. Moral Philosophy is not merely for the recitation room, but its rules and principles should be reduced to practice, and the judicious teacher will not want for opportunities of illustrating and enforcing them in the conduct of life. One who is familiar with Botany and other branches of Natural History, has the key to the hearts of her pupils in the power to amuse and interest them in their walks abroad, by being able to unfold the wonders of a little way-side plant, a chance pebble, or insect. A beautiful sunset, or a rainbow is a grand exhibition of the laws of optics ; and the canopy of night, to one versed in Astronomy, is a never-failing subject for conversation.

A person of cultivated mind, may thus not only add greatly to the happiness of others, but thereby acquire an amount of influence which may be turned to great account in education. Pupils soon observe whether their teachers are confined to text-books, or can draw illustrations from their own stores of knowledge. Almost everything you can learn by observation may, at one time or another, aid you in your educational labors. The human mind is a curious instrument intrusted to you to tune, and play upon ; to touch its cords aright requires a skillful hand. A humorous anecdote, a happy touch of well-meant satire, an affectionate smile, often permanently affect a stubborn spirit which appeals to reason might fail to influence.

In addressing these remarks to teachers in presence of pupils, I have thought that good may arise from bringing before the mind of the latter the sacrifices made for them, and the preparation which is required of the former, to fit them for their responsible duties. But as duty and obligation are reciprocal, pupils may consider what should be their conduct towards those who thus devote themselves to their happiness and improvement. "The authority of instructors," says Wayland, "is a delegated authority, hence the analogy between him and the pupil is analogous to that of the parent and child, it is the relation of superiority and inferiority. The right of the instructor is to command ; the obligation of the pupil is to obey. The right of the instructor is however to be exercised for the pupil's benefit. In the exercise of his authority he is responsible to the parent whose *professional* agent he is. He must use his own best skill in governing and teaching his pupil. He must use his *own intellect* in the exercise of his profession, and in the use of it, he is to be interfered with by none. When he and the parents cannot agree, the connection should be dissolved." "Such" says Wayland, "being the nature of the relation between the instructor and pupil, it is the duty of the former to enforce obedience, and of the latter to render it. On the fulfillment of this duty on the part of an instructor, the interests of education and the welfare of the young, vitally depend. Without discipline, there can be formed no valuable habit. Without it, when young persons are congregated together, far away from the restraints of domestic society, exposed to the allurements of ever-present temptation, every vicious habit must be cultivated. The young may applaud a negligent and pusillanimous instructor, but when in after years he shall suffer the result of that neglect, he will not fail to regard with bitter feelings, him who betrayed the trust committed to him."

And will not the pupil bitterly repent in after years, if her conscience reproach her with having by her own misconduct, made sorrowful the hearts of her faithful instructors? While teachers admit the force of their duties, let pupils also realize their obligations, and strive to render those duties pleasant, by self-control and earnest endeavors to perform their own part.

It is comparatively easy to assign to others their duties, and to give them rules of conduct. It is easy, too in respect to ourselves, to see what at the present moment lies within our circle, and to mark out for ourselves a line of conduct. But there is a constant change going on around us, to which we must assimilate ourselves, varying our actions to meet the present exigencies. Thus, quickness of apprehension, the ability to shift our course to suit with the gentle breeze or the boisterous winds that may spring up, are essential to the navigation of the sea of life. We must have our charts, our compass, and general rules, but cases will often arise, where these seem insufficient guides. In this little world of ours, we all, in our several stations and relations, have our peculiar trials and perplexities, and must at times be thrown upon the resources of our own judgment and conscience to direct us through unexpected difficulties arising from the caprices of others, the misapprehension by them of our actions, or from our own unintentional deviations. She to whom in God's providence are intrusted the hopes of so many parents, has a fearful responsibility resting upon her. She has chosen you, the lady-teachers here present, to be her assistants in the work of education. She is accountable for your acts and for your influence. Years have passed since some of us have sustained this relation. But years with their changes have their influence in rendering persons more tenacious of their opinions, less yielding and accommodating. Increasing years, especially if accompanied with physical debility, doubtless tend to increase morbid sensibility. We may be afraid that others do not "reverence us enough," we may be unwilling to yield to others any points we have made—we may become less loveable in character as in person, as years increase. Be it so—God orders all, and the Christian will say, "Though He slay me, yet will I trust in Him." Let the elder children affectionately sustain the steps of the parent whose feet may sometimes slide. Let the younger ones seek by cheerful obedience to make their home gladsome, and so to improve the advantages given them, that when they become actors in the scenes of life, they may do honor to the training of their school-home.

——, 1846.

ADDRESS XXII.

PROGRESSIVE IMPROVEMENT.

The current of time bears us onward, and is ever changing the relations of intelligent beings. Thus, although our granite edifice remains unchanged, though the same walls which echoed the words uttered in former years, now reverberate our accents; though the same lofty trees exhibit their rich foliage in our majestic groves, and the same shrubs offer their annual tribute of spring flowers, there is a great change in the living *tableau* before me—not all are here who have formerly met with us, but we see strangers in their places.

There is sorrow in parting forever with beloved pupils, who must leave us when they have become inured to discipline—as their intellectual powers have become developed, and they have endeared themselves to us by dutiful and affectionate conduct, then we must part with them. What parent would not be sad to see his children depart, and their places filled by strangers! yet though you all came as strangers, you remain not long as such, you are added to the large family, and are hereafter to be considered as its children. But when I look around, there is a sad vacancy—they are not here, many beloved ones whom for years I have been accustomed to meet in this place, and whose bright intelligence often enkindled thought within my own mind. It was remarked by a professor in a European university, that when lecturing to his students, he was in the habit of fixing his eyes upon some particular member of his class, and judging of the merit of his address by the changing expression of his countenance. I can say that not *one* but *many* pupils, who are not now here, have been thus often particularly observed by me; that their respectful attention to my words, the kindling expression of their countenances, beaming with love and intelligence, have given to these occasions an interest never to be forgotten. An impression of moral beauty has been thus made upon my heart, which time cannot erase, and which I have faith to believe will accompany my spirit into the eternal world, where may be my next meeting with many of those dear children of my care and love.

And yet, they might at first have been impatient of control, not perceiving the importance of restraints to which they were subjected. Perhaps at first, as some of you may now be, they were anxiously counting the days and months they should be obliged to *endure* such confinement and self-denial; but, when their school days terminated, and they were called upon to bid a last adieu to a home where they had received kindness and protection, to leave forever the guardianship of those who in all sincerity and faithfulness had watched over their welfare, then how sorrowfully did they look upon the past, how deeply regret that they had ever in aught grieved those friends, or despised the home which had sheltered them from temptation, and afforded them intellectual sustenance; where good habits had gradually been formed, and where they had learned to fear to do wrong, and to shun all "evil ways and works."

May heaven's blessings rest upon the heads of those who have gone from us, and may they long live to prove the benefits of a liberal and thorough course of female education, to do good in the world by an example of correct and elevated conduct, and in the faithful discharge of all the duties of life!

Many others are now treading in their footsteps, their juniors, who have had the benefits of their good examples, and who will, it is hoped, finish their scholastic course with the approbation of their *alma mater*, and the satisfaction of their friends.

But strangers are here, whom we have yet to *study* and to *know*, for be assured that you are forming for yourselves a character and reputation, while perchance you are only occupied in making up your minds respecting the persons and the place, with whom, and where you are to pass a portion of your future life. When a young girl goes from home to reside among strangers, how seldom does she estimate aright the importance of the first impressions she may make, of herself, upon the minds of others. While thinking of the indulgences of home, weighing trifling inconveniencies, and looking upon persons and things in the most unfavorable light, how much better to try to render herself agreeable, and gain a good standing in her new position. She should reflect that others will take the liberty to form opinions respecting herself; and that while she may be free in her censures upon what to her is new and strange, she perhaps is rendering herself an object of severe and unfavorable remarks to those about her.

One great advantage to the young in going abroad, consists in their being taught the value of *character*. A young girl accustomed to servile attentions at home, to consideration on account of the wealth or respectability of her parents, has yet to learn what it is to stand upon her own merits.

All pupils meet here on an equality, except so far as greater moral worth, intelligence, or more agreeable manners, may create distinctions. We do not inquire whose parents are more wealthy, more distinguished, more fashionable, or more ancient and aristocratic. Those pupils who are most worthy of esteem and love, stand highest while here, and are most remembered for good after they have left the institution; such leave behind them the best characters, and it is not difficult to predict that they will hereafter, in life, take precedence of those who may have trusted to their wealth or the respectability of their friends, rather than their own intrinsic merits.

We call on you all, therefore, to look well to yourselves, to consider what are your dispositions and intentions—have you come hither intending to devote the energies of your minds to the attainment of knowledge, to perfecting yourselves in accomplishments which may hereafter fit you for refined society, gratify your friends and enliven the domestic circle ;—above all, have you come hither intending to be *better* than you ever *have been*, and to do better than you ever *have done?* If improvement be your object (as assuredly it was that of your friends in sending you hither), let me assure you, that you shall have every possible assistance in this work. We have no rules that are intended to annoy you, or to place you under any unnecessary restraint—none but what we consider necessary to the good order, welfare, and happiness of the pupils.

We ask you to form no habits here, which will not be for your future happiness, usefulness, and respectability—we ask no servile obedience to tyrannical laws ; no constrained deference to those who have no love or care for you ; but we ask your love and confidence. We ask you to be sincere and open, to be what you ought to be, rather than dissemblers concealing as under a mask jealous and corroding thoughts, and willing to do wrong if you can do so without detection. God's eye is ever upon you ; He sees what are your motives of conduct, how you spend the time He has allotted you, and what improvement you make of advantages which His providence has afforded you. In our excellent morning service you will find petitions for all needed grace. First, after asking God to pardon your sins and give your true repentance you pray that He will put from you "*all evil ways and works.*" Think upon this prayer when you are tempted to fall into evil ways, and do evil works, and in sincerity of heart call upon God in the language of our daily evening service: "Deliver us, O merciful Lord, from the *dangers* that beset us; from all *evil* and *mischief*, from all *vanity* and *lies;* from *pride*, *impatience*, and *impertinence;* from *envy*, *hatred*, and *malice*, and all *uncharitableness:* from *inattention*, *carelessness* and *sloth;* from *selfishness* and *self-indulgence;* from *lying deceits* and *corrupt examples.*

Would you become the children of God, resist the suggestions of the adversary of your souls, who would seduce you to evil; resist him and he will flee from you; you must be in earnest in the work of your own improvement, for "the hour cometh when no man can work." Piety must be at the foundation of all your good resolutions, or they will be fleeting as the morning dew. "The fear of the Lord is truly the *beginning* of wisdom;" with their hearts imbued with this, the young may walk safely through the fiery trials of the world, and pass unharmed through its dens of lions; all is included under this one word—*piety*.

Some may conduct well for the sake of reputation, and others for the approbation of friends, but the pious would do right, because they love and fear God; they would avoid sin, not to please others, but because their own soul abhors "*evil ways* and *works.*"

We who are charged with the instruction and care of so many young persons, have much to do. What can sustain us under our duties and privations, but the desire to do our Master's will, and faith in his divine assistance? "Feed my lambs," said the blessed Jesus to his disciples; —though educators are not set apart for the sacred work of the ministry, they have a high and holy calling—they are appointed to aid the young in their preparations for life; and the principles formed while under such influence may fix their condition in the world to come. Shall teachers be as bright examples to the young, or stumbling-blocks in their way to eternal life? Serious and weighty are the considerations which should press upon our minds in view of this responsibility. Let us bear with patience the imperfections and errors of the young, considering our own deficiencies in the sight of God;—let us strive by kindness and affection to win them over to the cause of truth and virtue, and to the work of their own improvement. But let us never, through the desire of popularity, or fear of offending our pupils, indulge them in what is wrong, or pass over their offences through fear of their resentment.

We are all accountable to God for the manner in which we discharge our duty, and we should be fearless where principle is concerned. It would be very easy to do right if this were always to act in a way to please those who are about us, and whose love we desire to secure. The most difficult part of our duty to our pupils, is to say and do that which will cause them, for the time, to dislike us, or which may lead them, for the time being, to doubt our wish to make them happy; but we must not by such considerations be deterred from acting according to our understanding of duty and right; and we may be sure, that hereafter, if not now, we shall be rewarded by the love and gratitude of such as are capable of noble sentiments;—yet we must look to a higher source than earthly affection or approbation, for our reward. We have all, Instructors and Pupils, met under this roof as a family, united by many common ties and interests; let us therefore *love one another*, and strive to render each other's burdens light, by mutual sympathy and kindness.

For myself, I would ask indulgence from all; all of you have cares and duties common to some others, I have those peculiar to my own position as Principal, and in which none can wholly sympathize because they cannot feel their weight and pressure. In years past, my thoughts have often reverted to my pleasant home among the green hills of Vermont, and I have said, "there will I rest when the labors in which I am engaged may be laid aside, and an evening of calm old age may follow a life of toil." It was natural I should sigh for that quiet home, and for the literary leisure I there enjoyed while preparing many of my educational books. I seem now to see it, as it stands overlooking a beautiful New England village embowered by forest trees, presenting with its appropriate architecture a picture of beauty such as the eye seldom rests upon. What a crowd of associations are connected with that home! Every shrub and flower has its history; in a small village * at a little dis-

* Guilford, three miles from Brattleborough, Vermont.

tance stands the old church where is now our family pew, with its books, carpets, and cushions, as we left them nearly seven years since—and there is the cemetery, seen on yonder eminence, beneath whose solemn shades I had thought, at last, to rest !

A few months since, when the Green-mountain region was decked in the rich tints of a New England autumn, I visited that spot, more lovely in reality than even my recollection had painted it. A strong desire to remain there, and to escape from the cares and labors which Patapsco required, seized upon my spirit, and it was not without tears, that resisting such temptation, I tore myself away, leaving as my tenants a refined and intellectual family, who were capable of enjoying the natural beauties of the spot, appropriately called "Boscobel." * May it not be in vain that I have returned to toil for a few more years, should my life be spared, in the duties of education, and may we all during our future life on earth, and in Heavenly Mansions, be enabled to review with satisfaction the period of time which we shall here spend together in the great work of progressive improvement.

May, 1846.

* Meaning *Beautiful Grove.*

ADDRESS XXIII.

STUDY.

"If you devote your time to Study, you will avoid all the irksomeness of this life; nor will you long for the approach of night, being tired of the day; nor will you be a burden to yourself, nor your society unsupportable to others."

When we commenced the school session which is in a few days to close, spring with tardy steps was following in the train of winter. A few early flowers greeted us with their cheerful smiles, giving the assurance that an ever-watchful Providence during the apparent vegetable death of winter, had been busy within the dark, cold earth, perfecting the germs of beauty and loveliness which were to adorn the face of nature in her more genial season. And so, day by day, we were greeted by new flowers, which seemed to hold up their heads to us in friendly salutation, as if to say, "you see I have come back again, God has taken care of me as well as you, and though I have been buried in the damp, cold ground, I have been raised again to life, and all the happiness of which my vegetable nature is capable." Have we read aright this lesson taught us by every plant which springs up from the dark clods of earth? If we have, our hopes of a resurrection from the cold sleep of death have been confirmed;—the analogy is too striking to be overlooked.

As new flowers diversified the scenery abroad, sc a succession of new faces presented themselves to add a new interest to scenes within. Many who a few months since were strangers to each other, have formed intimacies which, however widely you may be scattered in your future life, will never be forgotten, though new friends, new scenes and new relations may in some degree lessen the vividness of your present feelings. The current of life, animal, vegetable, intellectual and moral, has been moving onward, and now, we number by days, the close of the present school-year. We have all had much to do—first, improvement of the mind in the studies assigned to you has occupied much of your attention—or if not, it should have done. But what a difference between a thorough and a superficial scholar! To the former, the most difficult sciences are made to yield up their truths. The thorough scholar will not be satisfied with a partial, indefinite knowledge of subjects, but possess herself of their nature and bearings. She may have to study hard, but she knows of no other way; she has not learned to skim over a lesson, and consider it as learned, when in reality she knows nothing about it; that is, of its true meaning. When attempting to learn a language, the thorough scholar makes sure progress—she does not go by mere sound in conjugating or defining words; she does not require that her teacher shall give her the key-note to begin with. For instance, if called upon to conjugate the French verb *aimer, to love,* in the indicative mood, present tense, the good scholar can begin *j'aime,* and go on, *tu aimes, il aime*—but the superficial scholar will need to be set a-going or wound up like a watch, by being told the first person, and then as a stone will move for a little distance when it is pushed, our superficial scholar will go on, perhaps through the different persons; though when she comes to the third person plural, she will be likely enough to say, *ils ai-ment,* although she has been daily told for a year, that *ent* at the end of words in the third person plural is silent. If it be the Latin verb *ămārĕ,* the thorough pupil is asked to conjugate, she remembers that it is a regular verb of the first conjugation, that its indicative mood, first person is *ămō,* and then she can go on to *ămās, ămăt,* etc.—but the superficial scholar is in a mist; she has not learned understandingly, but as a parrot, to repeat after others, and she looks vacantly, or with a beseeching glance, waiting for the teacher to commence, and then after *ămō* has been said, our stone begins to roll on, and we have *amas, amat,* and the tune naturally brings out *amamus, amatis, amant,* though the change of accent by the addition of a syllable may daily have been explained and pointed out by the teacher, especially in that very case of *ăm-ā-mus* and *ăm-ātĭs.* The superficial scholar can never be made to understand why *y* is used in French in such cases as *il-y-a;* nor how in *il aimerais, he might or could love,* the words *might or could* are expressed; though she may have been repeatedly told that the words *might or could* are denoted by the ending in *ais*. If the superficial scholar can remember long enough to recite something which some one else has found out for her, she thinks she knows her lesson, when, in reality, she has no understanding of it whatever.

In mathematics, the superficial scholar is satisfied with the mere ability to say something, no matter whether to the point or not. She will run on with *plus* and *minus*, confounding these distinctions until she proves herself to be *minus* of all thorough knowledge of the science of algebra. In geometry, she will say that A is equal to B, and D is greater than B, because B is equal to A; thereby proving that she, in intelligence, is equal to a superficial thinker.

But our time would fail in attempting to show the difference between the thorough and the superficial scholar in the various branches of education. The disposition which can rest satisfied with superficial attainments, is found to diffuse itself through the whole round of accomplishments, as well as literary and scientific departments.

In music, this is seen in the false manner in which notes are played or sung; many a young lady conscious of her want of thoroughness, solaces herself with the idea, that if she make a noise upon the instrument, put on an air of *nonchalance*, and seem self-satisfied, others will suppose she performs well; but very superficial must she be, who does not know that at this day, when music is so generally understood, her incorrectness as to time and tune will be readily discovered.

In composition, of all branches, the superficial mind perhaps most discovers itself—attempts to steal the thoughts and language of others will be here apparent; ignorance of the rules of correct reasoning, of the power and value of words, and even of grammatical construction, is exhibited; or perhaps there may be fluency of language with very little sense; for shallow minds may have words at command, though they can hardly be said to stand for ideas, as words are nothing except as they represent thoughts.

Besides the cultivation of the mind in the attainment of knowledge, which some falsely imagine to be the chief and almost the only branch of education, is the improvement of the heart, or the cultivation of the moral and religious feelings. You have all found as you went on from day to day, that you had constant need of watchfulness, to keep within the path of duty amidst the trials and temptations which befell you in your way. Trials of temper from the thoughtlessness or unkindness of others, and trials in overcoming your love of ease and self-indulgence; indeed no day perhaps passed without some trial; temptations, too, from various sources have been in your pathway.

In reviewing your conduct during the school-year which is now expiring, you may be conscious of having injured the feelings of others by unkind treatment, or passing them by with haughty indifference not less wounding to the sensitive heart than open contempt. You may have made uncharitable remarks, or circulated slanderous reports, calculated to injure another; you may have sown the seeds of suspicion and jealousy among friends; you may have ministered to folly by flattering the vain, and depressed the meek by pride and arrogance. You may have fostered in yourself a spirit of discontent, refusing to enjoy the blessings bestowed upon you; or, through indolence, you may have neglected your advantages. Above all, you may have trifled with religious privileges; you may have profaned the Lord's day, neglected his holy word, and done despite to the spirit of grace which has striven in your hearts.

In a few days our circle will be broken up, and never again shall we all dwell together as we have done in the same home, and sustain to each other the same relations. Many of you may never meet again in this world—you may not again behold the face of her who, however imperfectly her duties have been discharged, has yet desired to be faithful, knowing her own great accountability to the Father above. You may not again behold the faces of those kind teachers who have labored for you, often under discouragements; you will think of their efforts, hereafter, differently from what you perhaps have done. When you reflect how much easier it might be for a teacher to pass by deficiencies than to remedy them, and that it is those who are strictly conscientious who are willing to take upon themselves unpleasant duties, you will feel the higher respect for those who have had the moral courage to do what is right.

In the education of the young it requires firmness and

resolution to pursue what is right, fearless of giving offence, and a high, unswerving moral purpose. The young talk a great deal of teachers being kind. Well, what is kindness in a teacher? Is it best displayed in trying to do all possible good to the pupil, or in allowing that which is hurtful, through fear of not being called sweet and amiable? Suppose we are sick, and send for a doctor, and the doctor, though finding our heads badly affected, our hearts diseased, and our stomachs in a disordered condition, instead of prescribing suitable remedies, though unpleasant, for the bad heart and the swelled stomach—suppose this doctor, finding out what we like best to eat and drink, and what amusements please us most, tells us to indulge ourselves in all desirable gratifications, though he knows they will make us worse; he knows they made us sick—that what ails us, is the effect of self-gratification; but he wishes to please us, to be popular, to have us say, "What a sweet doctor! How I love him!" No, you would not long love such a doctor; and as soon as you thought about his conduct rationally, you would say, "I would never have that doctor again; I would never put any friend of mine under his care."

The educator finds patients in his pupils—many heads badly affected, many hearts diseased, many stomachs filled with indigestible pride, and swollen with vanity. We must be faithful to our duty; we must use proper remedies, even at the risk of being called cold-hearted and severe. But when our patients recover, then we have our reward in their gratitude and love; and the first sign of their being convalescent, or of not requiring *treatment*, is when they show the proper feeling towards those whose lives are devoted to their improvement.

But doubtless, too, there may be something to be regretted on the part of the teacher as well as the taught, on future retrospection. It would be better for the teacher to err on the side of indulgence rather than that of severity, as it would be better for the doctor to let nature alone than to give too much medicine. The present happiness of the young should not be lightly regarded, nor should heavy burdens be laid on youthful shoulders. Those who have passed their bright days of youth, may be refreshed by mingling with the young and light-hearted, while the latter should seek to learn wisdom from the more experienced.

> "Something of youth, I in old age approve,
> But more the marks of age in youth I love.
> Who this observes may in his body find
> Decrepit age, but never in his mind."

——1849.

ADDRESS XXIV.

FOR A CLOSING SESSION.

THERE is something in the word *last*, when applied to any period of time, which falls mournfully upon the ear; all closing scenes appear in a degree sad; even joyful occasions, which yet mark the termination of any course of time, are mingled with sorrowful associations. The last hour of the day, the last day of the week or of the month, and the last day of the year, suggest each their peculiar reflections. The closing of a school-year is now the subject of our contemplation.

There are some who pass through the varied scenes of life with little apparent thought of the past, or care for the future. To them, the gathering of a family group, after a period of separation, suggests no thankfulness to God for His preserving care; sickness and death in this circle of family or friends cause a transient, profitless sadness, which passes away with the occasion, leaving in the heart no germs of suggestive meditation to develop the fruits of wisdom. A marriage scene, to such, is merely one of gaiety, feasting, and bridal attire; they think not of dark shadows which may lie in the pathway of those whom they see setting out together in the journey of life. The solemn vows pronounced at the altar are, to them, mere words of ceremony; an unmeaning simper or giddy laugh often attest their want of thought or sensibility.

We pity those who strive to banish from their minds all reflections which, by presenting life in its true aspect, might render them less gay, and less inclined to follow after the vain and unsatisfying pleasures of the world.

But why should any child of earth wish to deceive himself as to his true condition? We commiserate the deluded maniac who, sitting down amidst want and wretchedness, exults in fancied riches and power;—or one upon whom some impending calamity is ready to fall, who is yet wholly unconscious of his situation; should we not, then, pity those who act the part of the imbecile in their self-delusion and blindness to realities, amused with toys and trifles, when they should be seriously applying their hearts to learn wisdom?

It has been the great object of my appeals to you, to awaken the powers of reflection and conscience with which you are endowed, but which too often seem to remain dormant and inactive. The earnest desires which some of you have recently expressed to be instructed, and the attention with which you listen to my words, give me courage to proceed in my course of moral teachings; would that my ability were more commensurate with the great work to be accomplished—that the experience of years might be accompanied by the energy of youth!

In all human organizations, where a number of individuals are combined to form one body, each has his own particular office; the head plans, the limbs execute—the former must depend on the latter to carry out and perfect its designs ; and it is important for the good of the whole body that the directing mind should be at liberty to consider general results. The bearing of a heavy weight requires strength and endurance, and one thus situated might seem quiescent, even while making great efforts to sustain the burden. Thus, though your progress in literature and science, or your class-teaching, may be chiefly intrusted to others, my own most important duty is that of helping to form your characters—to frame the different parts of education into one symmetrical and perfect edifice, founded on truth and virtue, and perfected according to the best models of Christian excellence.

Time has flown on rapid wings since a pilgrim band came hither with faith and hope to cheer their lonely steps. And have we not been rewarded by the smiles of heaven upon our labors ? That you are all here, representing the fairest portions of our great country, from East and West, and from North and South, is the living answer. Devout faith has been more than realized, and the most sanguine hope exceeded. What shooting forth of the tendrils of affection has not this "garden of immortal plants" witnessed ? Many of our beautiful flowers have been removed to their native homes, and some have been taken to celestial regions. But love is not lost, it exists on earth, however distant may be the hearts in which it has taken root; and in Heaven it is strengthened and purified.

The atmosphere of a home-school is favorable for the development of tender emotions. The young girl who leaves her home to come among strangers, meets with others under like circumstances, and sympathy soon becomes a strong bond of union; new ties are gradually formed—the warm love of newly-found sisters, and the kind regards of those who have assumed the parental office, fill the void in the heart, and give the conscious happiness of a new home, enriched by many new and delightful associations—not taking away any of the love for the old home, but suggesting much that is hereafter to make that home more perfect and happy.

Those who were affectionate, amiable and obedient in the domestic circle at home, brought hither the same good qualities, and in their new relations exhibited the same dispositions which heretofore made them lovely or otherwise. Change of place does not alter the heart; one does not part with bad habits and feelings on leaving one place and going into a new scene; though from the restlessness and desire of changes we often see manifested, it would seem as if many deemed that in new scenes they should be different persons; that in another place the "Ethiopian would change his skin and the leopard his spots."

Neither when we leave this state of existence, and our souls wing their way to the world of spirits, shall we be essentially different from what we now are; we shall be placed in a new situation, with new associates, and with new and enlarged faculties, but our minds will retain their identity. It is supposed by some who have dared to speculate upon the condition of the disembodied spirit, that it will resemble in its lineaments and appearance the body to which it has been united, but freed from its grossness and materiality; and that, purified from all earthly stains, it will exist a glorious and spiritual body, but yet bearing the stamp and semblance of the terrestrial body.

The disposition of the mind is now apparent, in a greater or less degree, in each individual; and character is, in some measure, read in the countenance; hereafter, when the spirit shall no longer be concealed by an earthly covering, we shall doubtless appear without any disguise; here we see, and are seen "through a glass darkly," then shall we "know even as we are known."

How fearful are such reflections to those who pretend to be what they are not; who endeavor to conceal their real characters and motives! We must believe such will hereafter appear in their true characters; that their thoughts and emotions will shape their spiritual forms; and that their proper place and associates in the world of spirits will need no other designation than will be given by their own external appearance.

The virtuous are often misunderstood in this world; their good, perhaps, evil spoken of; and bad motives attributed to those whose intentions are too pure and noble to be understood by the sordid and selfish—the path of the good may be overshadowed by suspicion and jealousy; they may meet with ill-will and unkindness where they had most reason to expect love and gratitude. When such are oppressed with a sense of injustice, and anxious that their motives may be known, and themselves vindicated from the charge of what they detest and abhor, how consoling the thought that the time will come when all these misunderstandings will be rectified! In such reflections upon a future state, we have the strongest inducements to seek to be truly just and upright in heart, so that our souls may be fitted to appear before the just made perfect, before angels, and before the Great Father of our spirits.

1849.

ADDRESS XXV.

To the Graduating Class:

My dear Pupils: It becomes both my painful duty to address you for the last time as members of this institution, and my pleasant office to announce to you your honorable discharge from school-duties and the restraints of scholastic life. The object you have so long had in view is attained; and you will now leave this place of your education, having passed through its course of studies, and with its highest testimonials. You may sometimes have been tempted to pause in your course—indulgent parents, fearful of your tiring in the race, have perhaps left you to choose between the enjoyments of home and the privations of school. The temptation was great, but you overcame it, and have purchased the gratification which ever follows the sacrifice of inclination to the dictates of reason and duty.

Your minds have become more matured and better disciplined by habits of research, your characters more formed, and strengthened, by the practice of self-denial, and you are in consequence better prepared to enter upon the duties and trials of life.

In the seclusion of these classic shades, no less healthful to the moral than to the physical constitution, you have been carefully guarded from evil influences ; and now, with unclouded brows and firm steps, looking to heaven for its blessings and guidance, you go forth to assume the responsibilities of woman's mission.

You are about to enter upon new scenes, while those who have so carefully watched over, guided and guarded you, will not be near to encourage you in goodness, or to avert from your pathway temptation and danger. Dearer friends in their caresses and indulgences may not weigh consequences, as those have done whose calmer reason discerned in the minute germ, the poisonous flower or bitter fruit. Does the father, when delighting to indulge his daughter in all her fancies—perhaps smiling even at her caprices, and regarding her as lovely in whatever mood she may chance to fall—does this fond father consider the relation that these caprices may bear to the future woman? Does he think by what a different standard than his own the character of his daughter *may be* estimated by a husband? The latter may dislike extravagance; *he* may regard caprice and childishness as studied methods to obtain power over him—as attempts to govern him by affected weaknesses. Children, too, are severe in their judgments upon parents. They are quick to detect the slightest weakness or defect in a mother, whom they will not revere if she be not self-denying, exemplary, and free from all reproach.

Inasmuch then as pupils and daughters become wives and mothers, those who have the forming of their minds and characters cannot be too assiduous to train them for future dignity and usefulness in those relations. But should Providence decree to the young lady a single life, so that it shall be her lot to walk alone through its vicissitudes, surely she will require all the strength of mind, firmness of purpose, and dignity of character, that the most judicious training can bestow.

More than half your number, my daughters,* will enter upon life with no mother to watch over you. God has seen fit early to deprive you of that tender, sympathizing friend; and though a father's affection be richly bestowed upon each one of you, yet there will be many occasions in life, when that father will look to you for prudence and mature judgment, perhaps to fill the place in the family circle of your lost mother; and there will be seasons when your hearts will yearn for sympathy, such as only a mother can feel—in such moments may you be led to seek for communion with the Father of your spirits! We trust you go hence, in some measure prepared to be the friends and comforters of those who have so long looked forward to your return to them as an event which would unite a broken family circle, and diffuse over it some of the cheerfulness of former happier years.

What time can any of you, my daughters, have for the worthless frivolities of fashionable dissipation? What peace of mind would you be willing to barter for a short-lived admiration, even were it to gain the *éclat* of being called the belle of the season.

It has been too common for writers, especially in the

* The graduating class consisted of nine pupils.

department of romance, to describe woman either as too sublimated or etherial for any earthly toil or duty, or as divested of all that is attractive and fit only for the labors and materialities of common life. The manners and language of polite society are flattering to the young and attractive woman; they tend to mislead her as to her true position and real value, and after a short dream of power, she too often wakes to find herself—a slave.

Alas, for woman's lot! A being often gifted with lofty powers of intellect, and capable of high moral purpose, but possessing strong impulses, an excitable imagination, and capable of emotions which, left to act without restraint, carry her into the wildest excesses of passion—what shall check those impulses—what shall curb the vagaries of fancy, and keep this wandering star within a fixed orbit—what shall speak peace to the turbulent passions of her nature, and convert the dangerous tendencies of her soul to the best and noblest ends? One power alone is able to produce such effects—the power of religion acting upon the heart and conscience. That power which led the pious Marys to follow the footsteps of their Redeemer, the last at his burial, and the first witnesses of his resurrection.

Would we see what woman may become without religion? Let us look at France—misguided, bleeding France! We see in the streets a procession of women, clamoring for their rights, threatening to destroy property and lives, and not merely threatening, but performing horrid deeds of cruelty, with blasphemy upon their tongues and murder in their hearts. The picture is too sickening, we would pass it by; but let us dwell a moment upon the causes which have led the women of a country boasting its refinement, to such degradation and wickedness. Fourteen years ago, Madame Louise Belloc, a great and good woman of France, in communications addressed to my sister, Mrs. Willard, and myself, deplored the progress in her beloved country of the doctrine of the St. Simonians, or Socialists; and especially that her own sex were among the first to be fascinated by them. With prophetic vision she foresaw the gloomy destruction of social ties which lay concealed in embryo, beneath specious principles of liberty, and a pretended desire for the amelioration of human society.

French literature, since that period, has assumed a new phase. We will not even name one among the many works of genius which have helped to sap the foundations of all moral distinctions, and subvert the institutions on which all that is valuable in human existence depends. When you hear of what the French women have dared to do, casting off the delicacy of their sex, and becoming ruffians and murderers, and all that is wicked and despicable, remember that these are the results of the principles to be found in the modern French novels, which fashionable American ladies allow to ornament their boudoirs, and with which young American girls do not hesitate to acknowledge themselves familiar.

Any attempt to lay aside the restraints imposed upon

our sex by time-honored custom and by the holy word of God, should be frowned upon by every virtuous woman. Our mission upon earth is to do good. As woman was first in transgression, she should be first in penitence and holiness of character. In the private scenes of life, its daily round of cares, duties and trials, woman's virtues should be preëminent. As the perfume of flowers and the rich juice of the grape are *crushed* out by pressure, so the sweetest qualities of woman's heart, the rarest excellences of her character, are brought out by the heavy pressure of affliction! But why, it may be asked, speak to the young and light-hearted of sorrow? Ask the faithful guide why he tells the traveller, in a perilous journey, of the difficulties he must encounter before reaching its termination.

Even this hour, so joyous to you in anticipation, so triumphant in its fulfillment of long-cherished hopes, is saddened by the sundering of ties closely entwined around the heart. But soon will the consciousness of time passed in this place be to you among the recollections of by-gone years, as "a dream when one awaketh." Thus will all earthly scenes successively fade into the dim twilight of the past, until that last scene shall come when each of us shall bid adieu to earth itself, and our disembodied spirits pass into the unseen and spiritual world—there, in a new school, to learn the mysteries of our own being and of God's providence.

PARTING HYMN.

SUNG BY THE PUPILS AT THE COMMENCEMENT, AUGUST 1ST, 1842.

God of the young! Creator, Friend,
To Thee in lowliness we bend;
Oh, hear us in this parting hour,
Support us by Thy mighty power.

God of the young! In humble prayer
Oh, let us seek Thy guardian care;
Our trust in Thee securely place,
And rest devoutly on Thy grace.

God of the young! Our footsteps guide,
Where flowery paths are open wide;
Keep us, Thy daughters, free from guile;
Teach us to fear each tempting wile.

God of the young! To Thee alone,
Our course in life is fully known;
Dark waters rise upon the sight,
Thy presence only giveth light.

God of the young! Thou once on earth,
A feeble child of human birth,
Didst feel the ills of mortal life
And meet temptation's awful strife.

God of the young! Who for us died,
Oh, keep us ever near thy side;
In sorrow's hour be thou our stay,
And bring us to thy perfect day.

END OF THE FIRST SERIES.

WE have passed over a period of eight years, from the founding of the Patapsco Institute in 1841, to the close of the school-year in 1849, having selected from written addresses such as seemed least local in character, and most generally applicable to the young in school, at home, and in the various other circumstances of life. We have kept in view the wants of teachers, who may not have the leisure to prepare addresses on moral subjects, but conscientiously consider that the literary instructions of their pupils, do not constitute their highest duty. We have remembered our debt of gratitude to those, who in years long passed, wrote books of instruction for the young ;—a debt incurred in youth, by the appropriation of the counsels in self-education, and in after years doubled by the aid received from them in the training of others committed to our charge. To discharge this debt to the rising generation, and to those by whom they are educated, is the great object which induces me to bring from their dusty repositories the time-worn manuscripts in which are embodied my instructions to my pupils, and my system of education.

NOTE.—During the years 1847–8, instead of the weekly addresses, were occasionally read, in serial numbers, stories written for the pupils, among which was "Ida Norman," with some others, as yet unpublished.

THE following extract is from a report of the Board of Visitors of 1849, among whom were the late Chancellor Johnson of Maryland, Rev. Dr. Atkinson (now Bishop of North Carolina), Hon. J. P. Kennedy, late Secretary of the Navy, with other distinguished gentlemen:

The scheme of education which has come within the view of the Board of Examination, matured as it has been by the discriminating and accomplished mind, and by the rare experience of the lady, MRS. LINCOLN PHELPS, who presides over the Institute, and not less effectively sustained by her talented coadjutors in every branch of instruction, would seem to leave nothing to be supplied for the increase of its value to the community. The studies of the Institute embrace within their scope an unusually large range of scholastic acquirement. They are drawn from the best sources, and are illustrated by authors of the most approved excellence. The course marked out for each class, seems to be singularly well adapted to the age aad progress of the pupil, and calculated to ensure the largest amount of instruction compatible with the condition of those to whom it is imparted.

The moral discipline of the school not less favorably attracts the regard of the undersigned than the scholastic. The invaluable impressions of good precept and good example in forming the characters of the young, in teaching the decorum of life, its virtues, its charities and its courtesies, are duly and prominently brought within the social government of the Institute, and are inculcated with a success and effect that are everywhere visible throughout the establishment.

In closing their report, the committee are not willing to pretermit the agreeable duty of renewing the expression of their testimony to the signal merits of the distinguished lady, whose reputation no less than her judicious control, has given character to the Institute; and the eminent deserts of that assiduous, skillful, and accomplished company of teachers and aids, who have so effectively seconded her efforts. Throughout a wide range of useful science and graceful art, everything appears to be well taught by those competent to the task.

SECOND SERIES,

Commencing with the School-year of 1849–50, and closing July, 1856.

ADDRESS I.

WHAT SCHOOLS OUGHT TO BE—AND WHAT SCHOLARS OUGHT TO BE.

When we say there are in our country few *literary* institutions for girls, you may be surprised at this assertion : almost every pupil, here, remembers that her parents were perplexed, among the multitude of schools, to decide where to send her to complete her academical education. There are, indeed, many fashionable, and popular schools for young ladies, but few, comparatively, that are so conducted as to secure the pupils the advantages of a thorough, practical, education, combined with good moral and religious influence.

In some schools, much valuable time is spent in crochet-work, embroidery, the manufacture of toys and trifles; and, in some, claiming to be of a higher order, the principals do not even profess to understand the literary or scientific branches taught, but are satisfied with employing teachers in these departments, of whose qualifications they are incapable of judging.

What would be thought of the president of a college, or principal of a boys' school, who should be found ignorant of the different literary and scientific branches taught in the same?

There are schools for girls conducted by gentlemen of learning—these cannot be called superficial; true, they are not liable to that objection, and they may present advantages for a thorough literary education; but a gentleman may be very learned, and yet very ignorant of the associations which are most powerful in the female mind; he may not, nay, he cannot know how to advise young girls on many points of importance connected with prudence or propriety of conduct; and there are subjects of interest connected with physical education on which he could not speak to his pupils.

The female mind possesses its specific characteristic traits, which women, themselves, best understand and appreciate; they know the peculiar weaknesses of their sex, their course of thinking, their moral dangers, and the temptations which life presents. Women should, therefore, be prepared to act as educators of their own sex. For this purpose, they should, themselves, be educated; their reasoning and reflective faculties should be exercised, and their minds cultivated by study and systematic training. They may thus become fitted to guide and educate the young, either as mothers or sisters at the home fire-side, as governesses in families, assistants in schools, or as principals of educational establishments for their own sex. We would not that women should be presidents of male colleges, but is it more absurd to suppose a lady presiding over an institution for young men than to imagine a gentleman as sole principal of a young ladies' school? Associated with a lady of education and dignity of manners, who is vested with authority to act as principal in such cases as more especially belong to the care and direction of girls, a gentleman may, with propriety, preside over their literary education. As regards the cares of business, and financial direction of a large establishment, we must admit that, in general, women are less competent managers than men.

In the organization of this institution, it was designed as a place for literary education, in connection with such domestic and religious training as might fit the pupils for the peculiar duties of their sex in this life, and prepare them to act with reference to the world which lies beyond these earthly scenes. Yet we approve and encourage feminine pursuits—thus, we expect you, once a week, to assemble with your work-boxes and materials for work, that you may be busy with your fingers while listening to the reading of select pieces or original compositions; but we also aim at a certain degree of thoroughness in the higher departments of learning. We do not think that girls must, of necessity, be superficial; and though they cannot become so learned in the classics and mathematics as college students, who devote most of their time to these studies, they can learn well as far as they go; and they can go as far as they have time consistently with the varied accomplishments which they are expected to acquire, as music, and perhaps drawing, with some knowledge of domestic affairs, of arranging their rooms neatly, a knowledge of plain sewing with the ability to execute some fancy-work—the latter has been found of much use in the fairs gotten up to build, or furnish churches, and even to found literary institutions for the education of young men. To sustain the reputation our Institute has acquired will demand the continued efforts of teachers and pupils. We profess to have a good and thorough system of education; let us consider what this requires of us, that we may not fall below our own standard.

Our standard of *manners* should be high. This forbids all that is low in speech or action, all that would be inconsistent with refinement and delicacy, all tricks and meannesses, which some foolish girls consider as proofs of cleverness. What great errors do the young commit who make themselves buffoons for the amusement of others, or who seek to gain notoriety by daring to set aside proper restraints!

It is not necessary to go to modern teachers of politeness and good manners to learn rules for behavior—the Holy Scriptures, on this subject, as in more important matters, contain ample directions, and if your minds could be thoroughly imbued with its teachings, so that they would enter your hearts and influence your lives, you would be perfect patterns of gentleness, simplicity, truthfulness, politeness, and true Christian loveliness of character. The Bible teaches that we should in honor prefer others to ourselves, and that we should be kind and courteous, doing to others as we would they should do unto us. If such were the motives by which society was influenced, how different would be its aspect from what we now see, where politeness is often a cloak for the most selfish and unworthy designs.

We profess to have a high *literary* standard, and whatever is taught, is expected to be thoroughly understood. In learning a language, you should enter into, and master difficulties—you should study independently, not looking to others to help you out of difficulties. You should think, reflect, compare, and examine, using your own judgment; memory will then have something committed to her worth the keeping. If you try to learn by rote, without first understanding, poor memory will be sadly troubled to keep together a mere mass of words—but give her thoughts and ideas to take care of, that is, your own thoughts which you have carefully dug out of the mine of knowledge, and how will she brighten up, how tenaciously will she guard the treasure committed to her! Without this hard study, this finding out for yourselves, your deficiencies will be apparent to all, and you cannot even deceive yourselves. When you study the conjugation of a verb, or the declension of a noun or pronoun, you should so learn, that let any part be taken by itself, you can at once translate or recite it. The superficial scholar requires to be told how to begin, and then poor memory is dragged in to help out with the rest, and, like a parrot, goes on, "*eram, eras, erat,*" etc.; or "*je porte, tu portes, il porte,*" etc. Now, this is not knowing, nor would a thousand years of such study make a scholar. We often observe when younger pupils are called on to answer, simultaneously, questions upon their lessons, there will be some who watch others to catch their accents, and then, with an air of confidence, repeat what they have said, or are saying. Whatever you study, try to know, not merely for the day of your present lesson but for your whole life.

After hearing a botanical lecture, you should pursue, in your own mind, a train of investigation ; think of the peculiarities of the plants examined, the principles to be applied to new cases, and make deductions for yourselves from facts stated. One pupil may merely remember that the teacher analyzed a blue or a red flower, that it had a long or short stem, large or small leaves; while another pupil has comprehended the laws of construction illustrated by particular plants ; she has exercised her powers of comparison and generalization, has passed from the individual to the species, from them she has made deductions as to natural affinities between this and other known plants, she has learned to perceive specific and generic characters, and having become acquainted with individual plants, to group them into their appropriate natural orders and classes, according to the laws of her own mind. Thus, by its generic characters she can recognize a Veronica, Viola or Orchis, though of a species before unknown to her. This recognition, indeed, requires practical acquaintance with plants. The attentive student, in the first stages of the study, learns the methods of analysis, and acquires a facility in finding out the names of plants, by examining their structure, and referring to her guide-books. These books will teach that this analysis is but the first step in the study of plants, and that the student should not rest at the threshold of this science.

The subject of learning things thoroughly, in its application to different branches of education is too extensive to be followed out, at this time, but I would urge upon each of you its due consideration. If you have more studies than you can learn well, your burden should be lightened ; but first consider whether you do improve all your time allotted for study to the very best advantage, whether you are not indolent and listless, and do not let the hours slip by with little exertion ; whether you do not spend much time in getting ready to begin to do something, looking up books carelessly thrown down, or finding some one to help you to get your lessons—or, perhaps you have not yet learned the best way of pursuing your studies. Whatever you do, do it *earnestly.*

Our standard of *morals* should be high—even above intellectual eminence, should morality be placed. What is to become of our country, if schools for its future women are not pure fountains of morality ? What will be the character of future generations, if the mothers who are now being educated are not intelligent, virtuous women, who will be ready to sacrifice pleasure to duty, and set an example of strict and undeviating integrity to those whose characters will be committed to their forming hands ?

Our standard of *religious duty* should be high. We profess to be a *Christian school.* The character and teachings of the blessed Saviour, whose name we bear, should be our example and guide. We should study his character and teachings. In the History of His life, we observe first, His humility—His early years were spent in lowly circumstances, laboring with his hands for his daily subsistence. After he had become distinguished as a great teacher and benefactor, he was still simple in his habits, and chose for his associates and friends the poor and humble.

The outward observances of religion are of little importance, unless connected with the inward sentiment. Suppose a monarch possessed of the power of reading the hearts of his subjects, beholding among the crowd of courtiers, one in whom he sees indifference or enmity; he is scrupulous as to all the ceremonies of the court, bowing exactly as etiquette demands, gracefully presenting himself before his sovereign in the most humble posture, repeating with great correctness whatever the forms of court etiquette prescribe.—How would such a subject appear in the eyes of his master—would not his professions be despised, and his real character odious? God is this monarch; he requires the homage of the heart, he desires of his creatures no "vain oblations"—outward observances are the mere circumstances in religious life, and should be so regarded. The "Sermon on the Mount," which contains the first public teachings of our blessed Saviour, may be considered as embodying the principles of his religion; meekness of spirit, humility, desire for holiness, a merciful and forgiving temper, purity of heart and life, and willingness to suffer in a good cause—these are enumerated as Christian graces. While the peace-makers, those who are kind to the poor, and who are ready to forgive injuries, are pronounced blessed; such as make hypocritical professions of great piety, or who think they "shall be heard for their much speaking," are condemned.

We might enlarge upon the topic of what a school ought to be, and what pupils should be. But our subject spreads out in extent before us, and like everything in life, must be broken off. A broken shaft may well represent the termination of human researches and human plans, which can never be completed, never finished—something must be omitted, something wanting—and so our subject, so full and inexhaustible, must now be broken off.

1850.

ADDRESS II.

LETTERS.

Some persons excuse themselves from writing letters to their absent friends, because they have no *news.* What a frivolous reason ! as if those who love others, and are interested in their welfare, would not prefer to know their *thoughts* and *feelings*, rather than to be informed of *events* in which they have little or no interest, or what is commonly called *news.*

What child can find it difficult to fill a letter to a parent, with warm, affectionate, and grateful sentiments ! What child, on reviewing the past, cannot see in memory's tablet, some records of disobedience, of conduct which has grieved a parent's heart ? and when sitting solitary, and looking into the chambers of thought, such sad images arise, how sweet the privilege to address that injured parent in the language of penitence, even to magnify the past error, that the humiliation may be the greater.

In writing a letter to your parents, my dear pupils, endeavor to prepare your mind for the duty, by some previous reflection; think whom you are to address, think of all the benefits they have bestowed upon you ;—before you could know them they watched over you ; when you were helpless and feeble, they guarded you from harm, suffering for your sakes many privations and anxieties such as none but parents can know.

Think of the trouble you have since caused them by your wayward temper, your neglect of their advice, and disregard of their admonitions ;—and can you have nothing to say to them about all this, when you are separated from them, and your consciences are awakened to feel that, in respect to them, you "have done the things you ought not to have done, and have left undone the things that you ought to have done?" You can little realize how precious to the heart of a parent are letters from a child which express grateful sentiments, sorrow for past undutifulness or neglect, and the warm gushing of filial love.

Your parents send you from home for your improvement. Their solicitude for you is great ; it may be that they were not well able to afford the expenses they are incurring ; but they have said, "the education of my child shall be my first object; I may soon be taken away from her, and she left alone to meet the troubles of life ; she will need a cultivated mind, under all circumstances ; to endow her with this gift every effort must be made." The days seem long to them which separate you ; but your letters are looked for, as messengers of happiness to cheer the family circle.

Think then, what kind of letters you should write to your parents, and to others in the home circle. Will it be pleasing to them that you should dwell on every disagreeable circumstance, that you should murmur at privations, or express your envy of those who are permitted to remain at home? In short, would you follow them when absent, with those bad traits of character which troubled them when you were at home? For who are, usually, the discontented at school? Surely not the most affectionate daughters when at home; but those who are restless in their dispositions, who love to find fault; who, when with their parents, rendered them unhappy through their perverseness of temper.

The good and affectionate daughter leaves home for school determined to spend her time to the best advantage; in proportion as she loves and respects her parents, she honors and confides in those whom they have chosen to direct her education. When she writes letters she tries to do it in such a manner as will gratify her parents in respect to her improvement. She has no need of news, to exaggerate inconveniences nor to manufacture falsehoods, for her heart is full of kind and loving thoughts, and words cannot be wanting where such exist. She is capable of gratitude, and appreciates the kindness of strangers; all is seen by her in the reflective light of her own good nature.

We will give you two specimens of letters written by school-girls to parents. Perhaps some of you knew Miss Snarl, who writes as follows: the sheet of paper is soiled and rumpled, the date appears scribbled half-way down the page, so as to leave less space to be filled up.

"UNFEELING PARENTS: I would of written before if I had any news, but shut up in this prison, we don't of course have any, so you can read the newspapers for that (I should not write now only I want you should send me some money). When we arrived at this mean village of Ellicotts Mills, we were directed to get upon some rocks, and climb up a narrow passage; in this way we proceeded for *some miles,* I should think (though this may be exaggerated), but any how, it was the worst climbing I ever *done,* and we were nearly ten minutes in coming from the depot to this place. But one would be willing to make some exertion to get to that which is agreeable; but all this fuss was to find a school, to be confined in like a prisoner. After we had groped our way along, ever so far, we came to a road that led up to the *Institute. The Institute!* Yes, it is no doubt *instituted* for the torment of poor girls banished from everything that is pleasant. I really do not see what pleasure folks can take in such a life as they lead here. If they had any kindness of heart they would let us do as we choose, and not as *they* think best. But no, I do believe they love to torment us; we must get up when a bell rings, we must be silent in study hours, we must descend to the mean employment of putting away, and even mending our own clothes; and if we talk and laugh in our classes we get a *mark.* As to *these marks* which some dread so much, I don't care for them. I mean to do what I please; but if you will only let me go home, I won't quarrel *no* more with Ned and Molly, and keep the house in disorder. I have eat up all my *goodies.* I am really hungry, and would like to live in our pantry for one week, and do nothing but eat. The *fair* here *isn't but tolerable!* I am tired of eating candy so much. I have carried it about in my pocket till I am sick of it. The piano keys where I practise are always stuck up with the candy which my fingers leave on them, and I expect every day to hear a mark read for it; but I say again, I don't care for marks. I have had my will at home, and I mean to have it here. We have been expecting to have some awful sickness, the scarlet fever, measles, small pox, or yellow fever; but I do believe the poor girls are afraid to have anything which is not according to rule.

"No more at present from your distressed and miserable child,

"GROWLINDA SNARL."

It is a relief to turn from this snarling epistle to one of a different character. You all know Miss Goodchild, and she writes as you would have expected.

"MY DEAR PARENTS: Though somewhat fatigued with my journey, I will not let a day pass without informing you of my welfare. On reaching the romantic village of Ellicotts-Mills, we were directed to the Institute by a winding path which leads up a steep ascent; but were amply rewarded for our labor, by the delightful prospect presented on every side.

"In my own mind I compared this with the pursuit of

knowledge before me. The way may be rough, I may have to pursue it alone, or unaccompanied by those whom I most love, but yet, great rewards will attend perseverance in my journey. Yet, thought I, as panting for breath I ascended the lofty eminence leading to the Institute,

"'How hard it is to climb the steep,
Where Fame's proud temple shines afar!'

"Determined as I am to be happy, and to accomplish the objects for which you have, at so much expense and such sacrifice of your own feelings, sent me to school, I shall find no difficulty in controlling my thoughts and fixing them upon my studies.

"If I am ever tempted to murmur at any duty, the thoughts of my dear parents, their anxiety that I may be found among the best pupils, and the idea that my disgrace would be reflected upon them, shall stimulate me to renewed efforts;—but indeed, our tasks, so far as I understand what is required, are not hard, and I think there is, around us, everywhere, a disposition to render us happy, as well as every facility for improvement; I shall write more fully soon.

"Your affectionate daughter,

"Agatha Goodchild."

It is said that "while there is life there is hope;"—Miss Growlinda has spirit—even her willfulness *may* be turned to good account; and we should not wonder if she becomes a favorite among us. We will be kind to her, and endeavor to teach her that there is something sweeter than candy—even the consciousness of becoming better and wiser. And we must be careful not to spoil little Agatha by praising her for being good,—"Let him that thinketh he standeth take heed lest he fall."

—— 1850.

ADDRESS III.

ON THE CHARACTER OF MISS MERCER, THE TEACHER, PHILANTHROPIST, AND CHRISTIAN.

Few among you are unacquainted with the character of the late Miss Margaret Mercer, who for many years was the honored Principal of a female school in Virginia. It is well that those young persons who do not properly appreciate the claims to honor and respect of faithful and gifted instructors, should contemplate some one particular instance of devotedness and merit, that thus they may learn to place a different value upon those engaged in the noble work of education.

Miss Mercer was nurtured in ease and affluence, but she declared in the midst of trials, and too often the ingratitude of those for whose benefit she labored, that she found more true enjoyment in the occupation of teaching, than she had ever done in all the pleasures and indulgences of gay and fashionable life. The father of Miss Mercer was the intimate friend of Jefferson and Madison, and himself distinguished by the confidence of his fellow-citizens. He devoted much time to the education of his daughter ; to his instruction she ascribed her fondness for literature ; and to him she was, in a degree, indebted for a high tone of intellect and morals. Her biographer says of her, "beautiful and accomplished, and occupying a high social position, she entered upon life with the brightest prospects before her, and for a time participated in the usual amusements of the circle in which she moved. But she very early learned the 'luxury of doing good,' and gave indications of that benevolent and self-sacrificing spirit which in after life shone so conspicuously in her life and character." In one of her lectures to her pupils, "On Patience," she relates an affecting story of the sufferings and resignation of a poor woman, on whom she personally attended ; thus incidentally disclosing her own benevolence and sympathy, even at an early, and too often thoughtless age.

The religious character of Miss Mercer gradually unfolded itself in beautiful and attractive features. She, herself, spake in after life of a change of heart, which in her case had been the gradual development of a religious principle, the first unfoldings of which were scarcely perceptible. At the age of twenty-three, she writes to a cousin in Essex Co., Virginia, in answer to a letter referring to the supposed amusements in which she was considered as indulging. She informed her cousin that so far from being engaged in worldly pleasures, she had been for the last month waiting by the sick-bed of a beloved aunt, expecting that disease would forever remove her dearest and best friend.

"Thank Heaven," she says, "I have hopes that the Almighty has heard my earnest prayer, and that a merciful Father will not withdraw this model of our imitation. Last night I had such a golden dream about going to Essex! I do think if you had a church it would be a heavenly place. I could cry when I think there is no church for such dear good people to collect in, and offer their thanks to Heaven for being so blest. I was confirmed, and had the pious blessing of our venerable old bishop (Bishop Moore) the day before I came from home. You cannot think how humble, how penitent, and yet how happy I feel. It seems as though I still feel the pressure of his hand upon my head."

"Such," says the biographer of Miss Mercer, "were the first dawnings of that spiritual life which was more and more developed until it shone bright and clear, to the glory of Him who had thus begun a good work in her, to be perfected only when after forty years' trial she was taken to the rest prepared for His people."

There was a beauty in the mind of Miss Mercer which was singularly reflected in her person, at an early age; but, in after life, when sickness had made its ravages upon her physical frame, she appeared decrepit, and her countenance bore traces of suffering. But the mind triumphed over bodily infirmities, and waxed more and more lovely, as the external investments became less attractive.

She had in early youth a just and refined taste in literature, and though delighted with the beautiful in style, she was not forgetful to scan the sentiment as the ultimate criterion of literary merit. With such a standard in her mind, she condemned Byron; while admiring his genius, she was disgusted with his infidelity and heartlessness, and abhorred the malice which induced him to desire to infect others with the sentiments which rendered him so wretched and hopeless.

Yet at this time Byron had not written his later works, which no female of delicacy would even wish to read, or have in her possession. And since we are upon this subject, it may not be amiss to caution you respecting the indulgence of imagination in the perusal of improper books. Indelicate ideas may be expressed in smooth and poetical numbers, and the most corrupting sentiments may be conveyed through the medium of beautiful language. Some, indeed much, of the poetry of Thomas Moore is of this character; and when all his poems are brought together, it would be better never to read those which are unexceptionable in sentiment, than to attempt to pick out amidst the corrupting mass, the gems which may be imbedded therein.

The letters of Miss Mercer to her cousin and young friend, even at an early period of her life, are beautiful specimens of pure and elevated composition. Her letters contain no vulgar phrases, no low conceits, or malicious slanders, no frivolous gossip or unmeaning tattle; but they bespeak a mind elevated, earnestly seeking wisdom and knowledge, and desiring to make others wiser and better.

We have not time to proceed with the circumstances which led the gifted and accomplished Margaret Mercer to devote her talents and life to the education of the young, which she did in the spirit of the most devoted self-sacrifice ; and yet, here, she found the element her soul sought after ; here she found that happiness which the world had never imparted. In the midst of her pupils she found the opportunity she so much desired of doing good. She loved to direct their thoughts to the great and good God through the medium of his works. She regarded the study of nature in its various forms, as tending to refinement of taste, and especially as conducive to pious feelings. She loved flowers—to paint them from nature, and to study their botanical relations. She observed with wonder and awe the laws of attraction, magnetism and affinity, and made every lesson in science conducive to higher attainments in piety.

Miss Mercer's great desire was the moral and religious improvement of her pupils; she watched over them with a mother's solicitude, and grieved over the thoughtless and erring, even as a tender parent sorroweth over a wayward and unpromising child. She possessed in an eminent degree the love and confidence of her pupils ; those who sought improvement, knew how to value the advantages which, under her care, they enjoyed. But all her pupils did not appreciate her labors, her talents and high moral worth. Thoughtless and impatient if restrained, or possessing bad traits of character which they wished to hide, some did not like the government which would control irregularities ; others feared a penetration into character which would reveal their secret faults ; to such young persons Miss Mercer was doubtless repulsive.

To them she was only a diminutive woman of singular plainness of dress, and destitute of any attraction; they did not like her. But to those who could appreciate her talents and worth, who could understand the beauties of her mind and heart, there was a perception in her presence (as I have heard her pupils describe) of something angelic—a charm almost supernatural, which attracted to her. Some of her former pupils have been members of this institution; I have delighted to listen to their descriptions of her. She was truly one of those noble educators who adorned their profession and made it honorable. The principal teacher * at Miss Mercer's school graduated (under my instruction) at Troy, N. Y., Seminary. She was privileged to be at the dying-bed of this interesting woman, and reports that her last words were, "It is sweet to depart and be with Jesus."

May we live the life of the righteous, that our last end may be as theirs!

* Miss Ingersoll of Massachusetts.

ADDRESS IV.

GOOD WORDS AND WORKS.

Again we have arrived upon the confines of Christmas and New-Year, and many of you are eager for expected meetings with friends, and the pleasure of being released from school rules.

Some of you, having been absent a few short months from home, are about to return thither again. It may be that those whose homes are too far distant to be reached in a few hours, feel sad that they must be deprived of the enjoyments connected with such visits. But in general it may be remarked, that pupils entirely separated from home influences and associations while at school, accomplish more than those who, by frequent visiting at home, return to old habits and associations, so that each time of coming again to school they are obliged to begin anew the work of improvement.

It may be considered but a poor compliment to the home of a pupil to suppose that she will not, there, be trained up better than elsewhere ; yet, without any disrespect to parents or home influences, it must be acknowledged that children do, at home, often acquire habits of idleness and self-indulgence which must be overcome to fit them for the duties of life ; and that when they return to the accustomed scenes of former indulgence they naturally fall into the same routine of life and behavior.

At home you like to indulge in sitting up late, and wasting your morning hours in bed; you prefer to be waited on, rather than take useful exercise in doing things for yourself. You like to complain to your parents, because they pity you, and seem to care more for you when you appeal to their sympathies. You like to eat irregularly of such things as suit your appetite, whether good for health or not. With servants you may be capricious; with brothers and sisters, perhaps fretful and exacting, unwilling to make the exertions and sacrifices, yourself, which you demand of them.

Now, the great advantage in going from home to school, is in breaking off all bad habits formed through the indulgence of parents too often blind to the faults of their children, or if seeing them, destitute of the resolution to carry out effective plans for their reformation.

Doctors are often unwilling to prescribe for their own families in sickness: they prefer trusting to the judgment of other physicians. Parents are, indeed, often the poorest physicians for the moral ailments of their children; and so, it is well they should intrust them to others for a certain time at that period of life when bad habits must either be conquered, or become masters.

Now, what are your moral complaints, the bad habits, the disagreeable ways, and unpleasant tempers which you should be cured of; which have hitherto stood in the way of your own happiness, and that of your home fireside?

It is not likely there is one of you who has not something to regret as to the past, some amendment to desire for the future.

Those who are going home, will do well to consider how they ought to deport themselves. When one is going to any place, it is natural to form some plan beforehand as to how she intends to act, and to form some idea of the impression she will be likely to make upon others. Because you are to meet parents, brothers and sisters, should you be less careful about your conduct than if you were going among strangers?

You might say, "Our feelings will prompt us to act rightly. We love and honor our parents, and, of course, we shall be affectionate and obedient;" but it is not *of course* that this will be so; there are in the world a great many selfish, undutiful, hard-hearted children; and often when the indulgence is greatest on the side of the parent, there is most ingratitude on the part of the child.

It is not by showing excess of feeling when you meet your parents, that you will manifest any essential improvement in your characters. You must think in what duties you have hitherto most failed, to what faults you have been most liable, and begin by doing those things that you know you should do, but have formerly neglected. Rise in good season in the morning, and dress yourselves neatly; look about and see what you can do to make home more cheerful. Shut doors carefully after you, in rooms which should be closed; ask servants kindly for what you want. When they do things awkwardly, and you can think of a better mode of doing the same, suggest this to them in a pleasant way. After servants have cleaned rooms, there is usually required the hand of taste and neatness to arrange things so as to give a pleasant, sociable and refined look or *coup d'œil.*

Be attentive to little things: take your father's hat, cane or umbrella, if you meet him as he comes into the house: it is so pleasant to parents to see their children observant and thoughtful. Think what you can say or do to make home pleasant;—exercise there, your accomplishments if you have any; if you can play or sing but tolerably well, do the best you can. You can all read; try to find something in books or newspapers to suggest subjects for conversation, or read in the family circle such passages as you think might please. Do not be too anxious to go somewhere or have company: it is sad when families can find no happiness in each other. Above all, cultivate no intimacies, nor make any acquaintances, except as your parents approve; nor invite company to your homes but with their knowledge and consent.

Children may see faults in their parents. What shall they do in such cases? It is hard to say—but a virtuous daughter of mature age, loving a parent above all earthly friends, might wisely suggest, with caution and tenderness, thoughts tending to good.

Suppose a father, worldly-minded, bent on gaining wealth at whatever cost of health and principle; a pious daughter might speak of the vanity and uncertainty of riches, and allude to enduring treasures in another world.

A mother, careful and troubled, like Martha of old, might, by a daughter's pious reflections, or a word spoken in season, be led to see her fault in being too careful about "much serving."

There are tendencies to evil, even when pursuing what is proper and right in the conduct of life. It is not in human nature to stop just at the right point, but there is a tendency either to go beyond, or to stop short of the proper limit; either of which is faulty. We can often see better what is right, in the case of others, than in our own. When moving onward, there is sometimes a difficulty in discovering the right stopping-place.

A wise and pious young person may be a blessing and honor to her parents and her family. Striving to do right, herself, she diffuses around her peace and happiness, so far as may be in her power. Brothers are made better by the influence and example of a good and judicious sister—not one who sets herself up for a pattern, who would exalt herself and put down others; but one who quietly moves on in her proper sphere, cheerful, attentive and obliging, refined and active in doing for the happiness of others. But how seldom we see in young girls good sense and sound judgment united with piety and conscientiousness. Such things do exist, but where are they to to be found? Not usually among the children of luxury who have never felt a necessity for exertion of any kind. Such may wish to act nobly, may have good aspirations, but how seldom can they conquer their fixed habits of indolence: putting off duties till a more convenient season, they satisfy their consciences by feeling that they love goodness; that they would like to be good, if it were not so much trouble. They have, what Lord Kaimes calls "the sympathetic emotion of virtue," which he proves, hardens the heart when felt without leading to action; the mind becomes satisfied with itself, and regards the sympathy felt, as an equivalent for actions performed; the wish to do right, as a substitute for having done so. At length, the sympathetic emotion of virtue may cease even to prompt to action. Look at the novel-reader pursuing with absorbing interest her tale of virtue and distress. She may let fall some tears of commiseration, and indignant at the oppressor, wish she could step forward to the relief of the heroine;—yet she lies at ease stretched out upon her luxurious couch, or lounging in her cushioned rocking-chair, fancying herself good, because she has sympathized with virtue in distress. Perhaps she calls a servant to hand her a glass of water, or perform some service, which she might better have done for herself, and the servant, it may be, is sick, and with evident feebleness performs what is required of her; how does our sympathizing novel-reader act? She probably takes little or no notice of the languid air, or feeble step of her attendant; but fretfully complains that she had has to wait, and wishes she might be better served. Perhaps she hears of a case of sickness or distress in her neighborhood or among her friends, but she thinks not of offering to assist by her exertions; she feels far less sympathy with actual suffering near her, than with the imaginary actors of romance. Such is sentimental virtue! How poor and inoperative, how little to be admired or esteemed!

Behold the young woman who dreads not labor, whose step is quick and elastic, whose activity shows a desire to promote the happiness of those around her; she lives not in a dreamy state of reverie, admiring the virtue she has not the strength to imitate; not only on her tongue is the law of kindness, but her deeds are worthy effects of principles of benevolence and love.

Happy is that young person; her course in life must be one of usefulness; in her breast morbid and gloomy feelings find no place; her time is employed in doing good to herself or others—or improving her mind by useful study, or in works of love and kindness.

In the last chapter of Proverbs, the mother of king Lemuel describes a good woman: this chapter is worthy of much study, for it is rich with instruction as to the good qualities of woman. First, it is said that "her husband hath not need of spoil," by which is to be understood that she is not wasteful or extravagant, but knows how to make the best of a little, by her prudence and good management. "She will do her husband good, and, not evil, all the days of her life." It is of a woman of good sense, industry and economy, only that this can be said.

The good woman is said "to work willingly with her hands," not in fancy needle-work merely, but in providing clothing for her family, so that her husband appears with fine linen, when he sitteth in high places, or "with the elders at the gates." "Her household are not afraid of the snow," for they are warmly clad through the care and activity of this good mistress. She herself appears clad in beautiful garments by the labor of her own hands. Her conversation is seasoned with wisdom and discretion, and she studies to govern her conduct with judgment and prudence.

Think, my dear pupils, of such a character; strive to resemble it. When you see levity, indolence, extravagance and folly, pity but do not imitate.

Those of you who are going from the Institute for a short time, should improve this pause in your scholastic life. Carry home with you activity, and hearts full of love and kindness to all. Pain not your friends by seeming reluctant to return to your school duties when the holidays are past; but rather surprise them by your zeal to press onward in your pursuit of knowledge: express your gratitude for advantages of education afforded you, and your determination to make the best use of them. Govern your tongues in respect to your school and school companions; circulate no idle tales, which will tend more to your own disadvantage than to that of others; but by excelling in mind, manners and morals, may you prove that you are not of those on whom instruction is thrown away.

—1850.

ADDRESS V.

TO THE GRADUATES.

Commencement, July 31, 1859.

Young Ladies of the Graduating Class: You have, in successive years, beheld your seniors receive their last testimonials of approbation, and have wept to see them depart, sorrowing that they were no longer to dwell among us. Time has brought the hour when you, too, are to go, not for a short vacation, a season of recreation, to return again and resume your relations as pupils;—but you go, to come back no more. You go, to take your places in the world, to act your parts in its busy scenes. But though there may be before you bright anticipations of a dawning future, you cannot, unmoved, sever the ties which bind you to this place, to those you leave behind, and to each other, as sisters and companions. Though sadly experienced in such scenes as this, when cherished daughters depart as they blossomed into loveliness, and their hold upon our affections had become strongest, it is not for us to regard this present scene unmoved.

Your class is the largest which has graduated at this institution—many of you came here children, in person and character; you are now thoughtful, and serious-minded women—and though these traits of character may apply more fully to some of you, than to others, yet that you now stand in your places on this occasion, is an evidence that each one of you has *thought*, and *resolved*, and *performed;* and we trust that the habit of *thinking*, *resolving*, and *performing*, being in some degree formed, none of you will enter upon life unconscious of, and indifferent to its duties and obligations.

At this time, especially, when the world is agitated by revolutions, and our own beloved country threatened with disunion and the horrors of domestic strife, woman has a high and holy mission to perform. May you, my beloved pupils, daughters of the North and of the South, seek in your respective homes to assuage the angry passions which would lead brother to contend with brother. *Woman should be conservative;* on her depend, in a great measure, the destinies of nations, as well as of families.

Go then, my daughters ;—with a parent's love, receive a parent's blessing ;—my prayer for you all shall be, that on earth you may accomplish your mission, as Christian women, so that, in Heaven, you may receive the Christian's reward.

ADDRESS VI.

BAD ADVISERS.

"How blest is he who ne'er consents
By ill advice to walk."

When a fond parent parts with a beloved daughter, committing her to the care and influence of strangers, many fears suggest themselves as to the nature and effects of this influence. With the utmost prudence on the part of parents in selecting a school for their children, evils of a formidable character may arise where least expected. Thus, those who have the care of the young may be faithful, watchful and judicious; their assistants may be in all respects competent to the discharge of their duties; but, by chance, there may be among the flock gathered together from various climes and homes, a few whose habits are evil, whose minds are contaminated by vicious thoughts and feelings, and whose example and advice would be injurious. The stranger, in a moment of sad repinings for home and the dear friends she has left, meets in some private recess a pupil of this class, whose influence may counteract the good advice she received from her parents before leaving home, and the efforts and care of those who now stand to her in the relation of parents.

We will call the stranger, Lois (a name honored in Scripture), and the dangerous companion, Calypso, who was represented as the tempter of the young Telemachus.

Our young friend Lois, having just parted from her parents, is very sad; she thinks no one cares for her, everything is new and strange, new places and new faces, new duties, new employments, and new privations! She perceives movements which she cannot account for; bells are rung, and all change their places; if it were not that they seem serious and busy, she might suppose they were playing at the old game of "*Puss in a corner*," and running from place to place for the mere sake of change. The manner of pursuing studies, of reciting lessons, and of doing many other things is different from what she has been accustomed to;—and she longs for the old familiar objects which are associated with her affections, and seem to be a part of her existence. Sad at heart, Lois sits down in a corner of her little room, perhaps on her trunk, the only familiar object near her, the only possession in the wide world which she can claim as her own. In her despondency Calypso enters the room: she sits down by Lois and begins to talk with her.

"And so you are left here alone, my dear; it is really too bad that strangers should be so treated. I have been wanting to call and see you ever since you came, but Miss Crabapple kept me in her room after school to study over a lesson just because I did not know it; for the truth is, I hate study, and am determined not to become as stupid as those who are called the good girls here; such a dull set, you have no idea! But how long since you came—where do you live—have you been classed yet—what are you going to learn—how long are you obliged to stay—do you expect to have to be here in vacation?" But we cannot repeat all the questions which, in rapid succession, are asked of the new scholar by Calypso.

Lois, with tears, answers that her parents came with her, a few hours since—that they have left her, and she is very unhappy, for she has never before been abroad to school, and she is afraid she shall find it difficult to do her duty now she is left to herself.

"Left to yourself!" says Calypso, "you will find quite enough to attend to you. You'll be watched closely enough, I can tell you; but come, let us walk out, the walls have ears here, so that I cannot talk confidentially, and I wish to be your friend. It is a great thing to find a good friend when you come to a place like this, and I am sure I shall love you devotedly, you are so like one of my dearest friends, she has just such beautiful eyes as you have, and just such a sweet mouth."

Lois, cheered by the voice of kindness and sympathy, and gratified by the soothing accents of flattery, wipes away her tears, and taking the arm of Calypso, is conducted by her to an arbor, overlooking a beautiful prospect of hills, valleys, and rivers, where, amidst the picturesque wildness of nature, the art and industry of man are conspicuous and add variety to the scene.

And here, where all should prompt to pure and elevated thoughts, does Calypso seek to poison the mind of the stranger, by infusing distrust, suspicion, and apprehension of all around her, magnifying the privations she will suffer, and maligning the character and motives of those with whom she is to associate.

A young girl approaches them, Calypso looks uneasy, she wishes not that she shall make acquaintance with the stranger, lest her own influence should be lessened. Eudosia is one whom Calypso particularly dislikes; often has she been heard to say, "*I hate her.*" When asked why she hated one so good and gentle, the answer was "she sets herself up to be a pattern, she is trying to court favor by seeming to be better than the rest of us girls, but it is all hypocrisy."

"Then let me be a hypocrite," was the rejoinder of the well disposed, "if Eudosia is one ; if I could but imitate her virtues, I should be but too happy."

Eudosia, with kindly interest in the stranger, addresses her in gentle tones. "We do not," says she, "wait for an introduction when a new sister comes among us ; we know, by our own past feelings, what it is to be a stranger in a strange place, and how sad are the first moments after a separation from our dear parents, and when we feel that we are left alone. But you will not, I am sure, be sad, long, here, for we are all so happy."

Lois looked at Calypso, who had just said the pupils were all very unhappy, and wished themselves at home.

Eudosia was a plain-looking girl, with little of the

fascination of manners which Calypso possessed, and Lois thought she would prefer the latter for her friend, but she could not avoid thinking that Eudosia's remarks indicated a better heart than did the slanderous aspersions of Calypso ; and she thought, too, that there was not in the manner of Eudosia any of that coldness and contempt with which Calypso had said the pupils treated strangers.

Calypso, rising and taking the arm of the stranger pupil, said, in a low tone, "You had better not say anything to that girl, she is a spy and a tell-tale."

Lois was astonished at such a charge ; the fine, open countenance and dignified though gentle demeanor of Eudosia certainly indicated no such traits of character. She began to fear that Calypso was not a safe friend ; she thought of the lines which she had learned in her Sunday-school lessons,

> "How blest is he who ne'er consents
> By ill advice to walk ;"

and summoning more resolution than she had before exhibited, Lois said to Calypso, "I like the countenance of that young lady. I do not wish to entertain distrustful thoughts of those with whom I have come to live. I like her because she speaks well of others ;" and Lois, turning to Eudosia, said, to the astonishment of Calypso,

"Is it customary for the young ladies of this school to ridicule strangers ?"

"Certainly it is not a common custom," replied Eudosia ; "I have never seen it done except by a few, who are either ill-bred or unamiable. I assure you that when a new pupil comes, we are generally very desirous to make her happy, and to cause her to forget, as soon as possible, that she is among strangers."

"But," said Lois, "is not a pupil here despised and neglected by teachers and pupils, unless she is of a rich, or distinguished family."

"All the distinctions we recognize here," replied Eudosia, "are such as arise from superior talents or merit."

"But you are kept under very strict rules, I suppose," remarked Lois.

"We have no rules but such as are for our own good," was Eudosia's reply.

Calypso could contain herself no longer:

"This is very fine, Miss Eudosia, to try and get the new scholar to join your set, the '*doing good party.*' I suppose you consider yourselves as patterns, upholding, as you do, the teachers in their treatment of us. A mean-spirited set you are, with your servile obedience and hypocritical pretensions; but if Miss What-do-you-call-her prefers your friendship to mine she is welcome to enjoy it; but she will find herself laughed at, and ridiculed, for there are some of us, here, who are determined not to be governed by tyrannical rules, nor influenced by those whom we consider our inferiors.

As Lois, astonished, looked towards Calypso, her face flushed, her features distorted, and her frame trembling with anger, a perfect transfiguration appeared to have taken place; all the charms she had at first seen in her countenance had vanished, and ugliness had taken the place of beauty.

Eudosia attempted to take the hand of Calypso, begging her not to be angry, as she had no idea of offending her.

"Why," she said, "should my answers to the questions of the new scholar so displease you?"

"Because," replied Calypso, "they were contrary to what I had told her, and you would make me out a liar."

"I am sorry," rejoined Eudosia, "that you, Calypso, should act so unworthily as to attempt to injure this stranger who has come among us. You would destroy her happiness, render her suspicious of those in whom she should confide, so that the objects for which she has been sent here would be defeated. I did not suppose you capable of such acts, but I should have said the same, even had I known what you had previously told her, for we should never be afraid to speak the truth."

Lois had left Calypso's side, and taken the arm of Eudosia. She felt how narrow had been her escape from an intimacy with a false-hearted, unprincipled girl, and regarded Eudosia as providentially sent to be her deliverer from an ill-adviser.

Calypso, with a sarcastic glance and sinister smile, walked away, and finding a pupil of congenial character, gave an exaggerated account of Eudosia's meanness in interfering between her and the stranger; which account was whispered about among those who would listen to scandal. The rudeness of the stranger in repelling Calypso's attentions, was noised about, but no fuel being added to the fire, in the way of defence or complaint, it soon went out; the good principles which had been carefully instilled into the mind of Lois by a pious mother, had saved her from the seductive influence of an ill-adviser. And often did she reflect on her narrow escape from a dangerous intimacy, treasuring up in mind the precious lines, which, like a friendly monitor, had whispered in her season of temptation—

> "How blessed is he who ne'er consents
> By ill advice to walk."

——, 1851.

ADDRESS VII.

"MEDITATE UPON THESE THINGS."

1 Timothy, iv. 15.

To man alone, of all the beings who inhabit this earth, is given the power of contemplation. The flowers of the field are beautiful to the eye, they are lovely and fragrant; but they do not meditate. We love flowers because they are attractive ; God has created them for us, and adapted them to give pleasure to our senses and imagination ; some fulfill the objects of their being, when they look beautifully, and give out sweet odors ; others are made for useful purposes—they are the gifts of a kind Providence; we should love and cherish them, and be very thankful to Him who so profusely scatters them in our pathway; but they cannot think, and therefore they are not accountable to their Creator, or to us who cultivate them.

"Ye are of more value than many sparrows." Animals are higher in the scale of existence than plants ; the birds can sing ; how sweetly sound their notes at the early dawn—in the morning twilight, when Nature is awaking from nightly repose, the spirit of harmony seems to pervade the groves and forests, the air itself is full of melody. Poets have loved to think that birds sing hymns to God, that "insects murmur his praise, and quadrupeds salute Him at the dawn of day," when they walk forth in His beautiful world—but this is poetry merely, it is not fact; —the feathered songsters, by their music, may help to excite devout aspirations in hearts which can meditate; but these musicians, themselves, know not God, they enjoy a mere animal existence.

We can bless God for His great goodness in creating so much beauty, and harmony, and perfection—we can meditate upon Him, and His works—we can go forth in the freshness of morning, or in the pensive evening twilight, and rejoice in all that we see around us, of the beautiful, the picturesque, and the sublime. How noble our faculties! How delightful should be the task of cultivating them, and of continually seeking to raise ourselves to the dignity of which our nature is capable.

Education is designed to lead the young to habits of reflection. The study of arithmetic is not valuable merely because this science is necessary in the business of life, but for its effect on the mind, in leading it to reflect, to think, to reason; so it is with the higher branches of mathematics, with grammar, languages, natural sciences, etc.—all conduce to that one great result, the cultivation of the reasoning and reflective powers. But there are meditations of a higher and holier nature than those connected with the intellect; the thoughts and feelings of the soul directed to moral and religious subjects; the study how we may best perform our duties in that station of life where God has placed us. The thought of moral obligation or duty is not, naturally, pleasing to human nature in its present imperfect state.

The child loves sensual gratifications; in him the animal nature is predominant. The young girl begins to love admiration, and for a time this may be a ruling passion. Alas! that with many, this passion is allowed in maturer years to engross the mind, leaving no room for nobler and better feelings. When such persons think, it is not in meditation upon subjects of an elevating nature. One whose mind is devoted to the world and its vain pursuits, may meditate upon the flattery offered to her personal charms, or may study how to set forth these attractions to the best advantage. For the sake of appearance she may pay a decent respect to virtue and piety, but her own tastes and inclinations are opposed to the pursuits and meditations connected with an elevated course of moral conduct.

The pupils collected here, come not merely to learn various branches of education, and accomplishments for this world alone, but to be disciplined in mind and character with reference to the two worlds which lie before them.

Meditate on what you are, on your relations to those around you, to your Creator, and to a future life. Such meditations will give seriousness and earnestness to your characters; they will moderate your love of admiration, and teach you to value above all else, the approbation of God and your own conscience; they will impart to your minds serenity and peace; they will raise you above the trifles of earth to that heaven of purity and love to which the good aspire. "Every saint in Heaven," says the great Dr. Edwards, "is as a flower in the garden of God, and holy love is the fragrance and sweet odor that they all send forth, and with which they fill the bowers of that paradise above. Every soul there is as a note in some concert of delightful music, that sweetly harmonizes with every other note, and all together blend in the most rapturous strains of praise to God."

"Favor is deceitful and beauty is vain, but a woman that feareth the Lord, she shall be praised." Such are the words of inspiration—meditate upon them. Do you care too much for favor, for praise, for human love—remember that they are incapable of making you truly happy, for it is the approbation of conscience only which can give your soul peace. The persecuted good man feels

"A peace above all earthly dignities;
A still and quiet conscience;"

while his oppressor cannot forget the All-Seeing Eye which beholds his actions. Milton, in his "Comus," beautifully expresses this thought:

"He that has light within his own clear breast,
May sit in the centre, and enjoy bright day;
But he that bears a dark soul, and bad thoughts,
Benighted walks, under the mid-day sun,
Himself is his own dungeon."

"I had a thousand times rather," said a young man, in writing to a parent, "be supposed in fault when innocent, than to suffer the bitter shame of receiving undeserved praise." Much more we might say on the topic before us, but we forbear, at this time, for nature invites you forth to enjoy her loveliness, and it is not fitting that the young should be required to think too much, or too seriously. Go, then, and gather wild flowers, inhale the fresh breezes from our hundred hills, and watch the sylvan brooks in their meandering course. Forget lessons for a time—be thankful for all the blessings of your lot, and for the future leave all to your Father in Heaven. But yet should the serious tones of the address to which you have now listened, linger around your thoughts, softening youthful gladness into sober contemplation, we may hope your happiness will not be the less now, and that greater good may await you hereafter. So you see I cannot even advise you to go and amuse yourselves, without adding a word of *meditation.*

——, 1851.

ADDRESS VIII.

TO THE GRADUATING CLASS.

YOUNG LADIES OF THE GRADUATING CLASS:

THE circling year again brings us to an anniversary of peculiar interest—a period to which you have looked forward with anxious solicitude. You stand here to receive the meed of intellectual labor, and exemplary deportment. This should be to you a proud and happy hour;—nor should you fail to recognize the kindness of your Heavenly Father who has crowned His many gifts by bestowing on you the means and advantages of education.

Human life, my dear pupils, is but a tissue of events,—scene follows scene in quick succession, until, at last, the drama closes, and the curtain falls. There was a day when each one of you came a stranger to this place, whither by Providence you were sent to receive instruction, that you might be fitted for the future scenes of life. This present moment then seemed far distant, as you regarded the vista of the future, in your prospective "Temple of Time." But it is even now here, and the moment arrives for you to depart—not strangers, as you came, but loving children, affectionate pupils, and fond sisters, to those whom you met as strangers.

Desiring that this scene may not be without its influence on your future lives, permit me, ere you go, my beloved daughters, to address to you a few parting words. You are now to take your places in society as women; may you walk carefully along the straight and narrow road of virtue and piety, consulting in matters of worldly prudence those who have had experience in life, avoiding all peculiarity of conduct and manners, and refusing to sanction, by your presence or example, whatever is offensive to propriety or principle. Seek rather to be useful than brilliant, to be loved and respected rather than to be envied or admired. Take no important steps involving your future happiness without the sanction of your parents or guardians; trifle with no solemn obligations. While you are careful not to be yourselves deceived, beware of being found selfish deceivers of those who may intrust to you their happiness. May you be able to fill with propriety whatever station may be yours, neither despising nor neglecting the humblest duty, nor found deficient in the proper discharge of the highest. Whatever may be your allotments in life, receive your portions with cheerful submission to the will of the Great Dispenser of all, remembering that even in this world virtue and piety have their reward, and that misery is the natural consequence of ill-doing.

The great faults of the female character, and those which education often fails to check, are vanity, love of admiration, and of pleasure, faults which too often destroy domestic happiness, turning the energies of the mind to frivolous pursuits of dress and fashion, or the dangerous chase after exciting amusements, or associations that are often fatal to virtue and reputation. Let educated Christian women frown on all writers, however gifted with genius, who, perverting their gifts of intellect seek to veil the deformity of vice, and who dare attempt to introduce into American society the dissolute manners of Europe—all who return from foreign travels to ridicule what they call our strict notions of propriety, and who would seek to familiarize us with scenes where vice, under the slightest and most transparent disguise, appears in fascinating colors. Home! this sacred word is even unknown in some of our modern, fashionable languages, which American girls are sometimes taught while allowed to remain ignorant of the rudiments of their own. May you, my dear pupils, ever love your homes;—bear thither all the treasures of knowledge and the accomplishments you have acquired; seek to gladden those homes by cheerfulness, industry, and intelligence; and let piety consecrate those sacred precincts where your affections may freely expand, and your energies be safely employed.

Two short years since, there stood one before me, as you now stand, beloved and esteemed by all: to her was unanimously assigned the honor of the farewell address to her class. We listened to the thrilling tones of her voice, saw her kindling eye and deeply glowing cheek, as she read her beautiful and touching allegory of "The Voyage of Life;" and we could almost fancy her slight form that of an angelic spirit, even then, rising to its native skies.

She has gone—Mary Johnson* has passed from this earthly scene to those heavenly mansions to which her thoughts were often turned, and an entrance into which, as a humble disciple of her Saviour, she sought to secure.

Listen to her last words, for they were the last she uttered in this place, which for years had been her home. "We are happy," said she, "my class-mates; for go we not to gladden the household hearth, to minister to the happiness and comfort of beloved parents, and to hold communion sweet with those unto whom we are bound by the dearest ties of kindred? The sorrow which we feel at parting with the loved guardians and companions of our scholastic life, is but the one bitter drop which must be mingled in every cup of earthly joy; and this is all of which I would remind you. I would only say, remember the fleeting nature of earth's best gifts, and beg that ere we have left the calm and peaceful precincts of Patapsco's shades, and become surrounded by the perils of the uncertain and dangerous sea of life, we shall each resolve to steer our course in that direction which, we know, would be pointed out, could the *guiding star* be still allowed to hover over us. Let us go forth with the determination that the siren fashion shall never entangle us in pleasure's bewildering maze, that we will not waste in her courts our heart's best affections, but that home and domestic peace shall be our watchword, and chief delight."

Short was the time allowed our beloved young friend to

* A daughter of the late Chancellor Johnson, of Maryland.

dwell in her pleasant home on earth. The summons came for her to go to her heavenly home; and in the spirit of the closing words of her Valedictory Address, she expressed her willingness to depart;—and we can readily imagine her, in her last earthly moments, saying to weeping friends, "Time has brought us to the very moment of our departure, I can only say a single word, farewell!—our chain of union has, link by link, been severing, 'tis now forever broken."

Other memories of dear, departed ones crowd upon us—they will often come to you in hours of silence and solitude, and possibly in scenes of gaiety and pleasure, admonishing you of the uncertainty of human life.

For a time after you leave this place, its associations will seem to fade in the excitement of new scenes, or amidst the attention and applause which may greet your entrance upon the stage of life;—but, should you, too, not be called away in the flower of your days, Time will soon bear you to a period when trials or cares may come upon you; then, in solitary and anxious hours, will the guides of your youth appear before you, with their serious counsels drawn from experience, and you will gladly receive from faithful memory what, unconscious to yourselves in pleasure's hour, she had carefully treasured up.

Education will not only be required for guidance in domestic and social life, but as American women, it should imbue you with an enlightened patriotism, such as may be of service to your country. The pages of history teach us the dangers of disunion in republics; that nations, like individuals, may destroy each other by blindly yielding to the influence of passion, which refuses all *compromise*, which rushes onward regardless of consequences, and would bring destruction upon all that is most dear and sacred, rather than yield to the monitions of prudence, or the counsels of moderation. Misguided, indeed, is that individual, and terrible is the fate of that nation, thus blinded. We may seem to be wandering out of our sphere on this occasion, yet the circumstances of our country cannot be regarded with indifference by its women. It would be absurd to say to the passengers of a vessel in danger of shipwreck, that none but the commander and pilots need give themselves any concern ;—such as are too weak to labor, might be of service, by encouraging others to assist in extricating the ship from peril. So may you, my daughters, do something for your country by using the influence within your sphere, to allay the strife and contention which endanger its prosperity, honor, and the stability of its government. If every American woman were at heart a patriot, and would frown indignantly upon all attempts to sunder the chain of Union which connects in one vast nation our States and Territories, soon would the voice of disunion cease to resound, hoarsely, through the land. Let patriotic women of the Northern and Southern States seek to allay angry passion and bitter prejudice, and to soothe the agitated spirit of fathers, husbands, and brothers ; this done, our country is safe, and intermeddling fanatics seeing their hopes disappointed will cease from their incendiary efforts. On this subject you may think little now, yet the time may come, when you will appreciate the vast importance of the duty I suggest.

But I can no longer detain you from expectant friends ; with my parting blessing I would say, may you in youth remember, that "favor is deceitful, and beauty is vain : but the woman that feareth the Lord she shall be praised;" thus in age may it be said of each of you, "many daughters have done virtuously, but thou excellest them all."

——, 1851.

ADDRESS IX.

BOOKS.

We have found it necessary to establish a censorship in respect to books. The influence of these silent companions is too great to be permitted without some advice or restraint. The young may not perceive the reason of this caution, and think themselves justified in evading rules, by smuggling in such books as are not among our authorized volumes. Yes, such things may be done—there is no situation in which a person cannot, if he choose, do himself an injury. The young can find improper books to read, and may manage to conceal them. They can talk with others on subjects which are unprofitable and corrupting. Is it wise to do so?

There may be cases when reasoning would be out of place; as, for instance, in the case of a good old servant, whom his mistress was about to employ in something a little out of his usual routine of duty, and sought to convince him by the use of cogent arguments that she was not unreasonable in her request—old "Uncle Tom," began rubbing his forehead as if to quicken his reasoning faculties, and finally said, "Please, mistress, tell me just what you want me to do, and I'se satisfied to do it."

The lady saw that her servant was right, but making the best of the case, replied, "Yes, I know you always do as you are told, but I wish you should think that I do right as well as you." But it is proper that your reason should be appealed to ; it is not enough in education to require implicit obedience to rules, the young should be made to understand that such are designed for their own well-being.

You have time for recreation and amusement—is it not your own to be spent as you choose? You have books which have been given you, or purchased by yourselves—should you not be allowed to spend your own time in reading your own books, or those borrowed of a friend? Would it not seem tyrannical to interpose any power to prevent the exercise of free-will in this case? You have perhaps heard of the child who said that his jack-knife was his own, and so were his fingers, and he had a right to cut them with his own knife if he chose to do so.

But so obvious are the evils to the youug of reading improper books, that little argument may be needed to convince you all that, as your appointed guardians, we are in duty bound to examine your private libraries.

An inundation of unprofitable reading has swept over us, and it has become necessary to clear away the literary rubbish found within our premises. So much trash is now published which is worse than useless, that the young, left to themselves, are in great danger from the evil influence of the literature of the day. Booksellers must live by their business ; they cannot afford to publish that which will not sell; therefore the question with them is not so much what will do most good, as what will be popular, and bring the greatest profit by rapid sales. Not that a good man would publish a book which he considered as decidedly immoral, but a bookseller might be tempted by the prospect of gain, to publish books of a doubtful tendency.

Then there are books so sparkling and lively, that they become favorites, before they are discovered to be worthless in themselves as to sentiment or information. Their whole value consists in their style. A young person being asked how she liked the style of a book she was reading, answered, "I have not yet come to the *style*"—but the books we refer to are all *style*. Exclamations, dashes, interrogations and mysterious breaks, keep alive the attention, and are, it may be, suggestive of something unexpressed. A book is amusing, and it sells well; the writer becomes popular, and a new work by the same author is eagerly sought for by the mass of readers, who would be saved the trouble of thinking.

Books are silent, and may be, dangerous companions, conveying through the medium of the eye a moral poison to the mind. As an illustration of this, I will tell you a true story. An unprincipled young man (and there are, alas, such in our world), artfully threw in the way of an innocent girl, a book of an immoral tendency. Attracted at first by curiosity, she began reading it. Day after day, did the seducer watch his victim; he knew that the poison was doing its work in her mind, and so at length he triumphed by the help of that insidious ally, the bad book lying concealed in its secret hiding-place, unseen by all but her to whose once pure mind it proved as the destroying angel.

We may better point out the books we do approve, than the trash we would condemn ; and this I have often done in private conversations with many of you who have asked my advice as to the furnishing of your libraries. There are writers whose names are a guaranty for good moral and religious influence ; no book of theirs is to be feared or suspected. There are unexceptionable books which it would not be well for you to have in your school libraries, because they would tend to draw away your thoughts from the pursuits which here demand your attention. One who possesses in a high degree the susceptibility of ideal presence, cannot well break off in the midst of one of Scott's interesting novels, at a bell-call, and, with the reasoning powers in full exercise, enter upon the study of a dry lesson. Therefore we do not generally advise that novels should have place in your school libraries—yet there are some works of fiction written expressly for the improvement of the young which we would not exclude.

Some time since, an interesting pupil from a distance, was introduced ; with her travelling bag she held in her hand a book which attracted my attention—it was one of the forbidden class. You know me too well to think I would have spoken to the stranger unkindly ; but to a suggestion respecting the book, she said with perfect simplicity, "it was given me by an acquaintance in the car, as I was passing through B——, but I have not yet looked into it." Of course she was innocent of any offence.

A young lady enters a steamer or railway car, and the vender of cheap literature comes round with his books—"Love at first sight," "The Mysterious Rag-Picker," "The Interesting Shoe-black," "The Robber's Bride," "The Neglected Wife's Lover," "The Happy Elopement," "Parental Tyranny," etc. Our young lady having in her purse some gold dollars or silver quarters, thinks it would be a charity to buy something of the poor fellow who seems so anxious to sell; and she wants something to read, as papa or brother may be too much engrossed in his newspaper to notice her, so she possesses herself of one of these choice volumes. On the table before me lies a pile of these contraband wares which have found their way up the "Hill of Science." Suppose we should call upon the owners, or readers, and inquire what good they have gained from their perusal—would not a blushing cheek and downcast eye be the eloquent reply? You were disgusted with the "Mysterious Rag-Picker," and the low company to which she introduced you. The "Robber's Bride" you found was no fit associate for a refined young lady—and the "Neglected Wife's Lover," though very handsome and interesting, proved himself a villain, and the wife a weak-minded woman, not deserving the respect and attention of her husband. As for "Parental Tyranny," you were ashamed of reading such stuff, and acknowledged to yourself that the love of parents is shown in care and needful restraint. "The Happy Elopement," did not, on the whole, seem so happy when you reflected on the long train of consequences which might follow such a misstep on the threshold of life.

None of you have a word to say in favor of these worthless books—but we might name works that have found an entrance into good society, and whose authors have attained an ephemeral celebrity, which help to corrupt good taste and good morals. Genius, though it may give brilliancy to bad metal, cannot turn it to pure gold. There must be a high moral purpose in the heart accompanying the products of the brain, to give the latter sterling value.

But here are Byron's and Moore's works ; are they not found in all libraries ? Can the most fastidious find any fault with these standard works ? True, the genius of these poets has immortalized their names ; while the English language shall continue to be read or sung, will Childe Harold, Lalla Rookh, and the songs of Byron and Moore touch the finest chords of the soul. But we will not even name the licentious and corrupting writings of these poets, which render their complete works unfit for the library. Moore was ashamed of his earlier poems, and sought to destroy them, but they were too luscious a morsel for the depraved to give up, aud his repentance could not recall the poisoned arrows which his genius had winged.

Byron, with fiendish malignity, seems to have excelled in his power of voluptuous imagery, and his unblushing effrontery in violating decency under the guise of refined language. Far better read the cheap novels whose coarseness of style is often an antidote to their bad morals, than sigh over the exceptionable writings of Moore and Byron. The latter hated human nature, he loved to represent it as bad, and to make it worse. He could soar high as an angel of light, but he chose rather to descend into regions of darkness, with fiends for his companions. So in social life; he left its higher walks, its pure domestic enjoyments, to grovel in sensuality with the abandoned. So bad was his life, that his diary given by him to his friend Moore, to publish for the benefit of the latter, was by him condemned to the flames, as unfit for the public eye. There may be many men who would be ashamed to publish the daily record of their lives, but Byron was willing the world should know of his infamy, and that his friend Moore might for pecuniary profit have the benefit of it.

Setting aside the immoral portions of Byron's writings, there is in all his works a tone of feeling, which has been found to act unhappily on the minds of others. An indifference to life, a recklessness of social obligations, and a want of all faith in a Superintending Providence; therefore is the best of Byron's poetry to be perused with fear and caution.

But here comes the immortal Shakspeare. Can there be any objection to his works? Yes, the young should not read them unless selected, freed from the low and vulgar allusions which pervade many of his plays.

It was said by one who well understood human nature,

that curiosity had caused more women to swerve from virtue and innocence, than evil passions. There is a deep meaning in the history of the temptation and fall of the mother of the human race; curiosity and disobedience, then "brought death into the world, and all our woe."

In examining the books before me which have been the companions of your private hours, I find many marked passages, indicating emotions of various kinds—sometimes sadness and melancholy, such as would not be expected from such bright and blooming young girls. Disappointed love, bitter experience of life and blighted hopes—impassioned sentiments seeking a safety-valve in "words that breathe, and thoughts that burn." Surely those who have yet scarcely passed life's threshold, should not require the relief of such out-pourings; if the buds are thus blighted, what will be the ripened fruits?

But we are consoled by the thought that it is only while you are reading, that you have these fancies; the first walk you take abroad, or the first romp with your companions, dissipates them, and your merry laughter does not sound like the wail of the disconsolate.

Throw from you, my daughters, all books which affect your minds unfavorably, or which crowd out good sentiments and desirable knowledge. Select your reading no less carefully than you would your friends. And until your judgment is more mature, avail yourselves of the experience of those who are able and willing to advise you in the choice of books.

1852.

ADDRESS X.

TO THE GRADUATING CLASS.

MY DEAR PUPILS:

THOUGH according to custom I address you as Pupils, I must not forget that the interesting relation we have so long borne to each other is dissolving with the passing hour. Some of you have been members of this institution for more than the usual Collegiate term of four years ;—the time which seemed so long in the perspective of the distant future is, is even now, here—the last scene of your scholastic life is closing, and as a Class you will assemble in this place no more. As there are hope and joy in the various opening scenes of Life's drama, there are regret and sadness in their termination.

As a Class, I see you together in this place for the last time ;—there were others who thought to be with you on this occasion ;—five of them in God's Providence are now in distant States, engaged in transmitting to others the instructions here received. And there was *one* * who now belongs not to earth ;—ere the roses of spring had shed their perfume to the vernal breeze, she

* Jane Singleton Garner.

had faded away ;—dust had returned to dust ; but "the germ of immortality," which in the sight of her Creator constituted her identity, will be "safe with Him," until at the final resurrection that "which was sown in weaknes shall be raised in power," and the "corruptible shall put on incorruption."

As the Class of 1852, your names will stand associated in the annals of the Institute. In reviewing those annals we find that Death, who "loves a shining mark," has taken from different Classes of Graduates some of their brightest ornaments—the beautiful, the meek and gentle, the lovely in heart and life, and the trusting devoted Christian, have passed away from the things of earth. Clad in sable garments of widowhood, are others who, a few short years ago, went out from us full of joyous anticipations of the life on which they were entering ; they can now but too well understand why they were taught by the warnings of experience to look for trials in this state of probation.

The Class of 1852—what will be their future life,—their future history? The oracle responds, "even as it hath happened to others, so will it be to them." Carry with you then to your distant homes in the valleys of the Connecticut and Mississippi, the Schuylkill and James Rivers, the shores of the Potomac and the banks of the Chesapeake, subdued thoughts and expectations as to future earthly good,—receive with thankfulness whatever happiness or prosperity may be yours, seek to be useful in your lives, whether they be long or short, and in the days of trial and sorrow, for such must come, meekly bow yourselves in humble submission to the Providence of God.

Thus feeling and thus acting, we shall all at last find ourselves united in the "land of the blest," where partings with beloved ones shall be no more:

> "Joys on high can never die,
> Though all below must fade."

1852.

ADDRESS XI.

BEHAVIOR AT HOME AND ABROAD.

The approach of Christmas and the New Year renders it proper for me to direct your attention to some practical considerations connected with this season of holidays. A large number of you are to return to your homes to spend a few days in the enjoyment of family reunions, and of the social affections, in that domestic circle, where your hearts most freely expand

The affectionate, loving daughter thinks of the pleasure she can afford to those who have watched over her infancy and childhood, and she revolves in her mind what she can do to promote their happiness. The self-loving daughter is thinking what new gratification her parents are to afford her, what advantage in respect to pleasure or presents she shall gain from the holidays. Look steadily into your hearts, my dear pupils, and decide impartially, to which of these classes you belong; to that of the affectionate, disinterested daughters, or are you of those who care mostly for themselves, who love their parents chiefly as the dispensers of good things, and who repay their past kindness by exacting new favors. How disgusting is selfishness! When witnessed in the domestic circle, how hideous! I once knew of a case where two sisters in a family of respectable condition, carried their selfish spirit to such a point, that at the death of their mother, as she breathed her last, one sister locked the door against the other, that she might get possession of the gold-beads upon her mother's neck! You start with terror at such an act, but the unconscious dead was not afflicted by it;—a living parent grieves to witness selfishness in a child. Go, then, to your homes with loving hearts, not loving yourselves chiefly, but those who have done so much for you, to whom you owe obligations never to be cancelled. Think what you can do while there to make your homes happier—regard everything in its best light; do not say "why do we not have things, so and so," or "as such and such persons do;" do not begin to suggest your own wants, but make the best of everything. Should you find any one of the household feeble in health, or less happy in mind than you would wish, study how you may minister to the comfort, or promote the cheerfulness of that one. Even the placing of a footstool, or arranging a cushion or pillow by an affectionate daughter or sister, is as a sunbeam going warm to the heart. Your parents have many cares and anxieties which you cannot know; they are often disquieted by causes not apparent to you, and with which they may not deem it expedient to trouble you. All that you can do to help them bear the evils of life is but little, and yet that little is powerful for encouragement; parents are willing to toil and suffer for their children, and they are surely excusable if sensitive with respect to the love and gratitude of those for whom their own lives are devoted. Suppose those of you who are going to spend a few days with your parents should write down some resolutions by which you determine to regulate your conduct while at home; they would be good, too, for other seasons. I will suggest to you an outline which you can vary according to circumstances.

"1st. To appear in the family circle, amiable and cheerful, and to be obliging and conciliating in manners.

2d. To be active, and show that I have improved in habits of industry;—seek occasions for being useful.

3d. To be careful of all that concerns myself, not to burden any one with the care of what belongs to me, as clothing, books, music, etc.; or to require to be reminded of my duties.

4th. Observe all the family regulations; not to be late, or irregular, at meals, family prayers, church, etc.

5th. Be moderate in the indulgence of my appetite at table, and in abstaining from eating between meals, so that I may not injure my health by any excess or imprudence. Never eat or drink anything which I believe to be injurious to my health. Let my friends see that I have improved in self-control.

6th. To assume no superiority over others, because I may esteem myself wiser, more temperate, or more pious.

7th. To keep myself perfectly neat in person and dress.

8th. Not to annoy my parents by any demands for

dress, money, etc., but be grateful for whatever they may give me.

9th. To think more of pleasing my parents, and of making the home-circle happy, than of going abroad or seeing company.

10th. To avoid all impropriety of manners, to respect myself too much to encourage in young gentlemen the slightest familiarity, or to be guilty of any approach to indiscretion—considering that a young girl who seeks to attract gentlemen around her, places herself in a dangerous, and often, doubtful position. Towards those who are relations, or particular friends of my family, to be polite and friendly, but in no case to induce contempt by appearing too forward or too fond of their society.

11th. To attend to my religious duties while at home, with the same regularity as at school;—to value time, and to seek to spend it in the most profitable manner, by improving myself, or in doing good to others.

12th. To comply cheerfully, as far as possible, with the wishes of my parents and friends—to sing or play when requested, without appearing obstinate, affected, or disobliging, by refusing; to perform what I do with simplicity, without airs or affectation—to keep such control over myself that I may always act with dignity and self-possession.

13th. To avoid idle gossip respecting my school, my teachers or companions, remembering that my school is my *alma mater*, that I owe towards it that filial respect, which should cause me to feel indignant at those who would do aught to injure its good name; and that I should do all in my power to maintain its reputation and honor, considering that my own intelligence and good behavior will be my best recommendation of those who conduct my education.

14th. And lastly—to consider myself at all times and places, accountable to God, for my thoughts, words and actions, and to seek to live in accordance with His commands."

Some of you are going to visit, as invited, at the homes of your school companions. Many of the resolutions we have suggested might be properly adopted by such ; but there are others, which occur to me as peculiar to your relations, as guests. In accepting an invitation to visit, you incur certain obligations—one is to render yourselves agreeable to your entertainers ; to appear polite, affable and cheerful, that you may not become burdensome to them. Study how you may please and commend yourselves to the elder members of the family in which you visit ; listen with attention to their conversation, evincing modesty and respect; endeavor to learn all you can from those who are wiser and more experienced than yourselves—ask of them to treat you with candor, and to tell you of any faults which they may perceive in you—acknowledge that you need to be advised (there will be little danger of any of you saying what is not true, by such confession). Try to make yourselves beloved by those with whom you are sojourning. When family affairs are brought forward in which you can have no concern, show no idle curiosity to listen, or to pry into such matters, but withdraw from domestic consultations, when you perceive your presence might be dispensed with. Never boast of what you have at home, or what you have been accustomed to, as if to make a contrast with the house, furniture or modes of living of your hosts. Families of high position often live plainly, and without ostentation, while the *nouveau riche* are often profuse and extravagant ;—and yet if you were visiting where there was elegance of style, and sumptuous living, it would be in very bad taste for you to make such a remark, or *vice versâ*. But you should be no servile flatterers, nor seek to please by giving up your independence of thought or character. Artifice is easily seen through—it defeats itself. If your manners are affectionate and amiable because your feelings are kind and friendly, this will be apparent to those who know anything of human nature; but if you merely put on sweet manners, the dissimulation will be apparent.

When visiting a young lady friend, never do or say anything to tempt her to act contrary to the wishes of her parents. If you hear them express disapprobation of anything, as of a particular book, associating with certain individuals, of peculiar modes of dress, etc., be careful not to countenance your friend in opposing her parents, or disregarding their opinions. You should rather seek to influence her to be dutiful and respectful ; and should you see her, selfish, exacting, or indifferent, it would be right for you to take an opportunity, when alone with her, to express your surprise at her conduct, and your disapprobation of the same. Her parents, noticing that your influence is good with their daughter, would then feel happy to have you an inmate of the household—they would recommend you to her as a safe and worthy friend, and ever remember you with affection and esteem. You would be sorry to have any parent say of you to a daughter, "I do not like your intimacy with that girl; she is wanting in good principles, she is a dangerous friend;" or, "she is weak and silly, she has no judgment, and her heart is as corrupt as her head is weak;" or, "your friend is a poor fanciful girl, with her head full of romance, and deficient in good sense—I would have you regard her rather for a warning than as an example, and discontinue your intimacy as soon as possible."

Speaking of behavior abroad, let me give you some cautions;—a mother, when her children are to go from home, advises them against such bad practices as she knows are sometimes seen in the young. In travelling, remember that you are observed by many—do not disgrace yourselves, your family or your school, by rude, boisterous, or improper manners. Loud talking, laughing, and calling each other's names, so as to attract attention, should be avoided. Talking about your school to each other, while strangers are listeners, is not to be recommended on such occasions, even though you speak kindly.

The conduct of young ladies, particularly school-girls,

in railroad cars, steamboats and stage-coaches, is often imprudent, sometimes ridiculous. Last summer, in travelling, I sat near a young girl, pretty and well dressed, but disgusting by her vanity and frivolous conversation.

She ran on talking to a young man (who seemed not to be more than a slight acquaintance) of the balls and parties she had been to at such a place, of the partners she had danced with, of such and such beaux whom she admired, of young ladies whom she did not think "at all pretty," and of her plans of amusement for the winter. As her companion seemed a *weak* young man (his strength like that of Sampson of old, appearing to consist chiefly in his hair), he seemed to listen attentively to this silly conversation, and perhaps thought it well enough; he might not himself have learned that life has any higher objects than visiting "the springs" or other places of recreation and amusement, or that a young lady has any more noble field of ambition than engaging the attention of brainless fops.

At public tables in hotels, boarding-houses, etc., young ladies should conduct with dignity and reserve. It is improper to talk and laugh loudly, to make remarks upon others; a quiet, self-possessed manner always commands respect. A noisy party at a public place is always freely censured by the observers.

A few words in respect to young gentlemen whom any of you may meet in your approaching absence from the Institute; and the observation may apply to all young girls, at any other times, seasons, or places.

Do not seek to be followed by admirers—severe remarks will ever be made upon young ladies who throwing out their lures indiscriminately in quest of admiration, induce young men to follow in their train. A coquette will throw away true friendship and hazard reputation; to gratify her vanity. Or if a young girl be really so susceptible that she bestows her affection without due caution, she may become a dupe to the arts of the designing. The greatest weakness in the female character is, in general, that which appears in her relations with the other sex. It is right, at a suitable age, and under proper sanctions, to form an attachment which may result in the most intimate and holy relation. But young girls should beware of entertaining thoughts on this subject at too early a period of life, as false steps may be taken before the judgment is mature, and the character formed, which would lead to a life of disgrace or misery. Be cautious, dignified, and reserved in your manners towards young gentlemen—keep near to those whose care and duty it is to protect you, and fear being left too much to your own judgment. At church, remember that your professed object is to worship God, and permit not your eyes to wander about in quest of admiration from idle gazers; when you leave the sanctuary do not encourage young men to accompany you home, as is too common a practice in cities. On the streets, at all times, behave with decorum. While you treat gentlemen of your acquaintance with civility, let it be with that dignified politeness which will repel familiarity, and prevent their joining you when not desirable. A volume might be written on this topic, but I will conclude by one remark,—that if the principles be good, and the heart pure, you will scarcely fail to conduct with propriety.

—— 1853.

ADDRESS XII.

TO THE GRADUATING CLASS OF 1853.

YOUNG LADIES OF THE GRADUATING CLASS:

FOR the last time I address you as pupils—The interesting relation which for a long course of years has existed between us, must now cease forever. There remains but for me to say a few parting words, and you will go hence, bidding a last adieu to your adopted home. and to those who have stood to you in the place of parent and sisters.

I would not move your minds to sadness, nor that tears should be called forth by unnecessary appeals to your tender emotions. This is no *tableau vivant*, nor scenic representation, gotten up for effect. No, it is a living reality, a real and final separation between those who have long held in respect to each other, intimate and sacred relations.

The most unreflecting girl, she who may have complained of the wearisomeness of her school years, and often, and often, wished they were over, approaches not this period without at least a touch of sadness, a mournful sentiment at the thought that her school life has drawn to its close ; that the time allotted for exclusive attention to the improvement of her mind has run out, and that her accustomed places will know her no more. Those of deeper feelings experience emotions which words cannot express—they look back upon the tranquil past, with its hallowed friendships, and associations, and forward, to the uncertain future ;—they shudder at the mysteries of life before them, and vainly wish they might ever remain in happy, irresponsible, childhood. Children, were some of you brought to this place—one, an only child, by her only parent who has not lived to behold this hour so fondly anticipated, and which would have restored to him a cultivated woman in the place of the little girl he left among us.

Children, some of you came here to be watched over in sickness and in health, to be borne with in your waywardness, to be instructed in learning, to be trained in the ways of virtue and piety, fitted to act your part in life as woman, and for a higher and nobler state of existence. Often our task may have seemed but imperfectly performed ; an overwhelming sense of its magnitude, compared with our ability, may have weighed down our spirits; but time waited not for us, nor for you ;—quickly, oh, quickly has it flown, and the children have become women ;—such as they are, they must go forth to act their part for the short period of human existence.

Have you thought, and decided, upon the parts you are to perform in the drama of life before you ? Your particular stations, whether high or low—the accompaniments which may surround you, God alone knoweth ; but if your education have been successfully conducted, if we have done our part, and you have done yours—you will be the same, essentially, in all conditions of life—in prosperity and honor, you will not be proud and high-minded ; in adversity, you will not be, abjectly, cast down. Respecting yourselves under all circumstances, you will command the respect of others for what you are intrinsically, not for those adventitious advantages which do not ennoble the soul, nor, when wanting, affect its true dignity. If you have well profited by education, you will be wise, intelligent, and good women, seeking to apply your talents and acquirements to the promotion of the happiness and well-being of those with whom you may be connected. You will have no sympathy with women who would cast off female delicacy, by invading the peculiar province of the other sex. May the *duties* of woman be your study ; the liberality of man, designed by God as her protector and defender, is taking care of her *rights ;* true it is that woman is dependent—fanaticism may call her the slave of man ; but what the Almighty has created her, that she is, with all her physical weakness, her nervous excitability, and her desire of loving, and of being loved. The lot of woman she may not escape from, without doing violence to her better nature, and the immutable laws of her Creator. There is, in the lives of most women, a period in which they seem called upon to exercise only the feminine virtues, to love, to be loved, and to confide in a chosen protector ;—too happy such a lot to be long continued ; but soon sterner qualities must be developed ; and the trying scenes of woman's life do not usually fail to test her forbearance, prudence, and her power of enduring, not only physical suffering, but a wounded spirit, conscious, perhaps, of injustice. So opposite are the situations of woman at various periods of her life ! Education should provide for all ;—when gentle breezes of affection and kindness waft her onwards, she should be grateful and happy ; but she should possess the ability to encounter the storms of life, and strength, and firmness of character to sustain her amidst rough waters, and stormy tempests.

If you have in the progress of your education, acquired strength of mind and firmness of purpose, we trust you will never abuse these gifts by attempts to go beyond the proper sphere of women, but the rather in judiciously fulfilling the duties of life in that sphere in which it may please God to place you.

But if some among you, endowed by nature with genius, and improved by a cultivated taste, shall be able to wield "the pen of a ready writer," so that you may hereafter be known in the literature of your country, may you be more conscientious as to moral effects, than ambitious of popularity. If celebrity and distinction, as the result of well directed talents, should be yours ; may you enjoy them as the just reward of labor, and consecrate your influence to high and noble purposes.

Society is in an agitated state, and never was there such need as now, of wise and good women to exert their influence in calming the agitations which exist, and in bringing order out of confusion. Beware of listening to the popular delusions of the day, in any form whatever; walk carefully, on, guarded by science, and guided by religion. When the time shall come for God to give us a new revelation, we shall all know it—the evidence will be clear and full. Till then listen to no insane ravings of pretended or supposed spiritual influences. Even should appearances confound you, believe not that the established laws of nature will be changed, except for some great and good object; and what you cannot understand, and revealed religion does not call on you to believe, cast aside as vain and unprofitable speculation. The Almighty can never want man's help in the manifestations of His will, or if He do require it, this, He will, clearly, and fully reveal.

You stand before me no longer children, time has matured your persons and minds;—your regular scholastic life is now to end;—yet the work of improvement should cease but with your life, and then in worlds of bliss, improvement will rapidly advance—the capacity of the human mind is infinite—it is unlimited! We must now part, you go to your parents, all but one * of your number, who remains with her widowed mother. May you, all, long live to bless the hearts of those who love you, and when the time shall come for us to leave these earthly scenes, may we go to dwell in celestial mansions with a Father in Heaven.

* The youngest daughter of the author Myra Lincoln Phelps.

ADDRESS XIII.

REFLECTION.

COLERIDGE, says, "*Reflect* on your own *thoughts, actions* and *circumstances*, and especially the *words* you use, and hear used."

How often do young persons say, in a self satisfied manner, as if this were a complete vindication of bad conduct, "I did not intend any harm, I did not think it was wrong;"—but this not thinking is a great sin. Are you, all, in the habit of reflecting upon your *thoughts*—what kind of thoughts do you have? The most thoughtless must sometimes think, and the character of their own minds must come up in review before them. You are sometimes alone; at night you may lie awake, and then comes to you a solemn sense of your being God's creature, accountable to Him for the improvement of the time and advantages he gives you. What kind of a soul appears before you, do you like its companionship, is it a good soul? If so, a sweet perfume of virtue and innocence will linger around it, a consciousness of good thoughts and good actions will give it a pleasant and tranquil aspect; though you may be in bodily pain or in affliction, such a reflected image of your own soul will make you comparatively happy. But if you see a bad spirit, and know it is your own bad soul, come to show you its deformity, how will you try to turn away from its contemplation ;—but it will not leave you, it will virtually say, " am I not your own soul, which you have neglected, suffered to grow deformed and disgusting? for what I am, you are accountable, you cannot rid yourself of me ; conscience will ever be holding up the mirror in which you now see me, you cannot turn from this spectre—it is yourself.

There are times when all must think ; conscience speaks when all else is silent. Silence and solitude are solemn monitors. But there are, we fear, some whose thoughts are so habitually evil, whose minds are so filled with vain and foolish, not to say impure imaginations, in whom the mirror of conscience is so clouded, that they cannot even feel remorse, cannot see by reflection, their own bad souls.

You who are before me are all young, and it would be hard to believe that you have yet lost the power of reflection ; but if you have not, why is it that some among you continue to do evil after being often and often reminded of your faults, and shown the path of duty?

Reflect on your *thoughts, words, actions,* and *circumstances.*

Thoughts! what are thoughts? You see your external forms, but thoughts are invisible to the bodily eye, to God they have shape and substance. He looks into your minds, and sees what is there allowed and cherished.

What are bad thoughts, what are good thoughts? Bad thoughts are malicious feelings towards others, as envy and hatred—contempt and indifference towards their happiness, the desire of injuring others by wounding their feelings, either by assuming airs of superiority towards them, or in any other way. *Bad thoughts* are evil imaginations of scenes and objects which virtue and purity would avoid. *Discontented* and *murmuring thoughts* are bad; everything is bad in thought which leads to bad words and actions.

Bad words—what are bad words? Evil speaking, and foolish talking, as also trifling remarks on serious subjects; speaking unkindly or disrespectfully of those who labor for your good, and are entitled to your love and gratitude, and saying what will tend to lead others wrong, either in thought, word or act.

Dr. Paley says, one may *act a lie*;—so, one may act pride, vanity and selfishness; contempt, ingratitude and irreverence, they have all their appropriate looks and gestures, and can be represented to the eye without words. This word *acting* is very significant, as applied to many of the thoughts of the heart of which it is the effect. Bad actions are not confined to looks and gestures, or an irreverent manner in religious worship; these may pass away with the occasion, though they make impressions on the minds of the spectators not easily to be erased, and they are noted by God. There may be a course of bad conduct carried on through a series of acts, all tending to a bad end, all injuring the actor more or less, though often intended only for the injury of others.

As in Geometry you often learn truth by studying an erroneous hypothesis, so may you learn to follow good, by considering the evil to be avoided. You well know, what are good *thoughts, words* and *actions,* and you can *have,* and *speak,* and *do,* such if you choose—you may be good or bad, as you prefer. Sometimes we may be at a loss as to what is our duty, but who ever heard of a conscientious, reflecting person desiring to do right, who was really bad? or, if for a season, through the malice of others, such an one should be suspected of doing wrong, the truth will eventually appear; to God it is ever known, and even if we suffer in this world, for righteousness' sake, we shall be abundantly rewarded in the world to come.

Reflect on the *circumstances* by which you are surrounded. You are at school; sent here for your improvement. Some of you are being educated here by means provided for you by parents no longer living; they thought of your good, they left you property that you might enjoy the advantages of education. Whether you have living parents watching for your improvement, or whether your parents are anxiously regarding you from the world of spirits, do as they would wish you to do—reflect.

Reflect on your thoughts, words and actions, and the *circumstances* in which you are placed. Extend your views to future situations in which you may be placed, resolve to fulfill your duties to living parents, or to the memory of departed ones. Reflect that life is not given mortals to be trifled away in levity or amusement, that it is short, and important as a preparatory state to that eternity which lies beyond.

Thus by reflecting, will you avoid evil and secure good. Life is a school, for which this place is to prepare you to enter—from that school you will pass as you may be prepared by the manner in which you live, to an immortal existence.

——1854.

ADDRESS XIV.

TO THE GRADUATING CLASS OF 1854.

IMPORTANT eras in life are significantly marked by appropriate ceremonies. Among the ancient Romans there was a custom of publicly taking from boys, at a certain age, the baubles and playthings of childhood, and investing them with the toga worn by men, as a sign that they were, henceforth, to be admitted to the privileges, and charged with the duties, of manhood. The ceremonies of this day are significant of an important era to you who stand before me. You have now received an honorable discharge from the duties of school, and are henceforth to be considered as women. The roll of parchment presented to you is of itself nothing, but as emblematical of labor, self-denial and victory, it becomes to each of you a valued trophy.

How long a course of training has been required to prepare you for this day! From your first rude attempts to form letters with a pen, from your first imperfect efforts to express thoughts in writing, and from your earliest lessons in thinking, has gradually proceeded that development of mind which has enabled you to become the authors of the literary compositions you have to-day read before this audience. And how long and laborious has been your application to the science of music, to prepare you to perform with skill and execution the most difficult pieces of the greatest masters of the science of harmony. Your late examinations in the various branches of scholastic education has proved that you have all labored, though, it may be, with different degrees of application, to prepare yourselves for an honorable discharge from school, and to merit the honor of graduation.

But in being freed from certain restraints, and invested with privileges belonging to the new stage of life on which you are to enter, you assume new duties and responsibilities ; these, rather than the idea of enjoyment, should chiefly engage your attention ; the flowery gardens of pleasure may attract your youthful tastes, but there you may not long linger—or rather, there you *cannot* long remain. The journey of life is to be performed, and many obstacles in the way are to be surmounted. No kind indulgence of tender parents and friends can exempt you from the condition of humanity, the common lot of mortals. In the Book of inspiration it is said that man is born to trouble as the sparks fly upward—that is, the physical law in respect to the flying upward of sparks of fire is no less certain, than is the moral truth that every human being is born to trouble.

When we look at a collection of blooming flowers, we know they will not long remain in this state ; the blossoms must fade and wither. In beholding a group of young girls, in the freshness of early youth, thoughts of coming change will take possession of the reflecting mind.

You who are now before me occupy the place where for thirteen years successive classes of graduates have stood—like you, their hearts beat with bounding pulse at the thought of the delightful scenes which imagination promised them in the world they were about to enter. Suppose these graduates of past years could now, at our call, be brought forward, and stand, side by side, with you who are looking forward to the future with joyous anticipations. Here would we see a mother bowed down with grief for the loss of her lovely children; and there a feeble woman, with little physical strength to perform the arduous duties which, in her domestic relations, devolve upon her—and here is a daughter bereft of her last parent, and left to feel an orphan's loneliness and sorrow;—each one, however prosperous may have been thus far her career in life, has learned that there is no unalloyed happiness in this world. Mark the change which a few years have made in the appearance of all—the bloom of youth, how evanescent! Like the morning dew upon the blossom, it passes away long before the noon of life. Not a few have exchanged their bridal attire for the garments of widowhood. We start back—for there appears a spectral train with shadowy robes of white—they are your elder sisters of Patapsco, who have passed away from the scenes of earth to the world of spirits—their last school examination, and the scenes of this day, were soon followed by the falling of the curtain upon their short drama of life. Among those who have been added to the land of spirits is Agnes Buck,* a graduate of last year, known and loved by many of you. On the very week allotted for revisiting her school-home, the last summons came, and she departed.

We would not sadden too much this parting hour, but it is right to remind you of the uncertain tenure of earthly enjoyments, and your obligation to live as those who are seeking a better inheritance than earth can give. We trust that none of you will go from this place to be mere triflers, seeking only for pleasure amid scenes of gaiety. More than half your number are professed followers of Christ. You will not surely forget your solemn obligations as Christians "to live soberly and righteously" in the world.

As graduates of Patapsco, may you maintain the honor and dignity of your Alma Mater, exhibiting at all times and in all places a character earnest and sincere, amiable and conscientious, despising the arts by which too many of your age and sex seek to attract a short-lived admiration; frowning upon the flatteries which lead to vice, and jealous of any influences which might cause the slightest divergence from the path of rectitude. Representatives from more than half the States of our Republic, may you ever love our common country, and cherish with a conservative spirit that sacred Union which binds it together as one great consolidated nation.

* Grand-daughter of A. Kirkland, Esq., of Baltimore.

In your own homes will be your proper sphere of effort; make their inmates happy and virtuous, and you confer a blessing on society. The future citizens and statesmen of our Republic may owe to you, as wives and mothers, a loftier patriotism and a purer morality.

But the hour of parting is at hand, and I must bid you, as a class, farewell. Having accomplished the objects for which you came hither, you must now go to fulfill your duties to those kind parents who have so liberally bestowed on you the advantages of education. We shall miss your pleasant voices and affectionate smiles; there will be a void in the places you have filled; and though strangers may come to occupy your seats, the absent daughters will not be forgotten. Though we may see each other's faces no more in this world, we will hope to be reunited in those heavenly mansions which are prepared by our blessed Saviour for those who love and serve Him on earth. You may have much to do before the close of your mortal pilgrimage. God will lead you where He will have you to be, and in His own good time will take you to Himself, if you will be guided by His Spirit.

PARTING HYMN.

FOR COMMENCEMENT.

FATHER above! a sister band
Go forth upon life's troubled wave,
And only Thine Almighty hand,
In sorrow's coming hour can save.
To them, unknown, the dangers lie
Which intercept their onward way,
They dream not of the secret sigh
Which oft invades the scene most gay.

Fair maidens! though with willing heart
Ye go, familiar friends to greet;—
Yet, *Alma Mater* claims her part,
A sigh, a tear, as offering meet;—
And memory, often to your souls
Will speak of early, by-gone days,
As time its rapid current rolls,
And pleasure sings her farewell lays.

Yes, such is life! a mingled scene
Of joy and grief,—of sun and shade—
But yonder Heaven is all serene,
And flowers immortal never fade.
God's blessing rest on those who now
Launch forth upon life's troubled wave,
Give grace to keep their Christian vow,
And from the world's temptations save.

——1854.

ADDRESS XV.

THE VIRTUOUS WOMAN.

"While they behold your chaste conversation coupled with fear. Whose adorning let it not be that outward adorning of plaiting the hair and of the wearing of gold, or of putting on of apparel; but let it be the ornament of a meek and quiet spirit, which is in the sight of God of great price."—1 PETER, iii. 23.

ON this occasion of addressing you, I can think of no more important subject on which to direct your attention, than what is suggested by these words of Holy Scripture. When I consider the great and prevailing faults of the female character, and connect with this the idea that the interests of a never-ending eternity depend on the attainment of purity and holiness in this short state of probation, an overwhelming sense of awe comes upon me, and I am constrained to say to you, "what thou doest, do quickly."

"Chaste conversation coupled with fear," is mentioned by the apostle as a means by which a wife may influence her husband who refuses to hear and obey the word;—and here we may pause a moment, though in anticipation of future events, but which will doubtless arrive to many of you. A wife has a deep interest in the character of her husband ; to retain his affection and esteem after marriage, how important ! the salvation of his soul should also be to her an object of deep solicitude. How little does the young and thoughtless girl, about to connect her future happiness and respectability, and perhaps her own eternal interests, to the keeping of one whom she has met in parties of pleasure, and of whose real character she knows nothing—how little does she think of the coming scenes and events of a life of trial and change —of a life of duties and responsibilities ! She is to be married—her mind is taken up with thoughts of bridesmaids, beautiful dresses, wreaths and bouquets, a pleasure tour, and brilliant parties where she will be the reigning queen, as the bride.

When the ancients were about to sacrifice a victim, they first adorned it with chaplets of flowers and led it about triumphantly—alas, how many victims of imprudent and ill-advised marriages are left to mourn their want of reflection, during a life of sorrow and unhappiness. But the husband may be deserving of love and confidence ; if so, he has certainly a high standard of excellence in his own mind, and he looks to find in his wife, the realization of his dreams of female purity and loveliness. Most miserable she, the wretched wife, who is conscious that her husband is deceived in her, that familiar acquaintance with her faults and deficiencies will deprive her of his esteem, and chill his devoted affection.

"Chaste conversation coupled with fear."—In married life, especially, should a woman be chaste in her actions, and in her words—even a man of little refinement or delicacy, himself, is disgusted with the want of these qualities in a woman ; and a husband is not slow to observe the faults of his wife. Disgust and hatred soon follow love, when disappointment succeeds to hope and anticipation. *Chaste conversation* does not, in the meaning of the Scripture, here refer to words merely, but to conduct in general : to modest demeanor, to actions free from all lasciviousness or shadow of sensuality, and to wise and sensible discourse. This is to be coupled with *fear*. Fear of what, fear of whom ? Fear of acting or speaking wrong, fear of violating any rule of propriety; and, above all, fear of God, who searcheth the heart and before whom all are to be judged for deeds done in the body, for evil thoughts and idle words. Such should be the woman who will have a good influence over her husband, who will lead him, though unbelieving, to respect religion, who will secure the esteem and confidence of a pious and worthy husband—for he shall praise her, his heart shall safely trust in her.

"*Whose adorning let it not be that outward adorning of plaiting the hair, and of wearing of gold or of putting on of apparel; but let it be the ornament of a meek and quiet spirit which is in the sight of God of great price.*" We do not suppose that it is wrong to dress becomingly, that braiding or plaiting the hair, or of wearing ornaments of gold, pearls or diamonds, are in themselves offensive in the sight of God. He has created a world of beauty for our enjoyment ; He decks the flowers of the field in robes of brilliant coloring and silken texture; He has given lustre to the diamond, bright hues to the ruby and emerald, and its inherent richness to the gold—let these things be used by His intelligent creatures as His gifts, but not worshipped as idols. Let the body which he has created in His own image, which is destined to be the temple of the Holy Spirit receive its due care and attention—keep it pure outwardly by attention to cleanliness, and cover it with garments adapted to its comfort, and if circumstances permit, suggestive of taste and elegance.

But when the chief care is expended upon the person, when the great concern is what one shall wear, how shall she dress her head, how have her garments made, what ornaments she shall put on—then it is that sin is committed, and the rights of the soul are set aside for the adornment of the perishing body.

There are some among you who are too much engrossed with the subject of dress. You attach to it an importance that it does not deserve; would you, in order to distinguish yourselves for fashion and elegance, do that which is wrong, and venture on the very verge of disobedience to the known rules of the Institute, in relation to dress on public occasions? Our pupils have often been commended for simplicity and modesty in this respect.

Let not "*the putting on of apparel*," appear to you as a matter of supreme importance. Think of that hour when your body will be shrouded in its last garment. Regard the passing scenes of this mortal life as steps which are carrying you forward to the verge of an eternity you must soon enter. In the Romish church, the novice about to give up the world, puts on the habits of her order. You, who are about to enter into the busy scenes of life, may, hereafter, adopt the vanities of fashion ; you may, perchance, become its votaries, and its leaders, but pay to the institution which has sought to render you something more noble, at least the compliment to be willing to leave her halls dressed with maiden simplicity.

But God forbid that any of you are to become the heartless devotees of fashion ; may you now, henceforth and forever, possess *"the ornament of a meek and quiet spirit, which is in the sight of God of great price."*

—— 1855.

ADDRESS XVI.

TO THE GRADUATES OF 1855.

Time, in its ever-moving current, has brought an hour of deep interest to the members of this institution, more especially to you who stand before me—the class of graduates of 1855. In past years, you looked upon this scene in the dim perspective of futurity ;—it has gradually appeared in more distinct outlines ;—it is now here, the present—to-morrow, it will be of the past,—anticipation will have transferred it to the keeping of memory, where it will ever live amidst your most hallowed recollections.

Some of you have passed here many years of your life; some have been with us a fewer number of anniversaries, but all have been here long enough to have formed strong ties in the place where your closing period of school education has been passed. Amidst the beautiful scenery of nature, your hearts have not been insensible ; and while the outer world has made its ineffaceable daguerreotypes upon your memory, affections, deep and strong, have stamped their impress upon the soul.

The present scene is, of itself, sufficient to excite strong emotions without the aid of words. Why then speak thus of its import! Why remind you that you are forever to leave the home where you have been cared for; your physical, intellectual and moral natures nurtured and trained, that you who have lived together as sisters, in one common family, are now to be separated far and wide from each other, never more *all* to meet together again in this world! Yet you expect from me some parting words, and therefore I speak; not to excite your sympathy to useless tears, but to strengthen the principles of virtue, and the good resolutions which we hope have taken deep root in your minds. The parent sees not his child go out into the world, without giving, with his blessing, counsel to guide his steps amid the dangers which may await him.

This hour should be to you, my daughters, a happy one. You have honorably passed through your school probation, and are going to your several homes, with the approving smile of conscience, and testimonials of approbation. But human happiness is never unalloyed—the expectant voyager about to embark for foreign countries, amidst exciting anticipations of new scenes, turns sadly to those he leaves behind, and to the home which he may see no more—the happy bride leaves not without regret, her girlhood's home, and its dear inmates. Gladly you depart for your native home—sorrowfully you leave this place, and the friends you have here found.

But it is not well at this moment to occupy ourselves too much with mere *feelings; duties* await you, and you go to prove, in the battle of life, the armor with which you have been furnished. In the varying scenes which may await you, your principles will be tested ; your habits of industry and of self-command will be constantly put in requisition. To live an idle, useless existence, would be to forfeit self-respect, and the esteem of those around you. It is *well-directed action*, only, that is truly commendable. The labor to be fashionable, or to gain *éclat* for beauty, accomplishments or learning, is unworthy your immortal destiny. May the daughters of Patapsco ever aspire to be *good women* rather than *fine ladies.* The reputation for talents, or great learning, is not to be anxiously desired. Education should produce *good fruits*, rather than manifest itself in ostentatious show or pretension. Our country needs all the virtue of its enlightened daughters in this period of political excitement and dangerous tendencies, when patriots tremble for the fate of our common republic : and foreign nations, jealous of our prosperity, regard with complacency and encourage our sectional prejudices, confidently expecting them to work out our national destruction. I speak not to you of *woman's rights*, but of *woman's duties.* May the descendants of the noble women of the American Revolution, prove themselves (with far superior advantages for mental culture), not inferior to them in wisdom, virtue, and true patriotism.

Go, then, my daughters, fulfill your mission as wise and good women, faithful followers of the blessed Redeemer of mankind, seeking to benefit others rather than please yourselves. Go, now, to be the light and joy of your respective households, and reward the care of the parents who have made so many sacrifices for you.

Finally, wherever the guiding hand of Providence may lead you in future years, and whatever relations you may be called to sustain, may you be found among the faithful and the true, and at last may we all find a home, together, in heaven.

—1855.

NOTE.

The following paraphrase was prepared at the suggestion of the beloved daughter of the author, to be sung at the Commencement which took place but a few weeks before she was called to join in heavenly music.

PARTING HYMN.

EVENING HYMN TO THE VIRGIN, PARAPHRASED.

Jesu sanctissime, list to our parting strain!
Ora pro nobis! we may not meet again;
Guard us while shadows lie,
Far o'er life's journey spread;
Hear our hearts' parting sigh,
Thine, too, hath bled.
Thou, that hast look'd on death,
Aid us when death is near,
Whisper of Heaven to faith,
Oh! Saviour, blest Saviour, hear!
Ora pro nobis! we lift our hearts to thee,
In life, and death, our Saviour be.

Jesu sanctissime, list to our parting strain!
Ora pro nobis! we may not meet again;
Oh! thou who know'st our frame,
And dangers of the way,
Our erring thoughts reclaim,
And be our stay.
Oh! save our souls from ill,
Guard thou our lives from fear;
Our days with virtue fill,
Oh! Saviour, blest Saviour, hear!
Ora pro nobis! we lift our souls to thee!
In life, and death, our Saviour be.

Commencement, 1855.

ADDRESS XVII.

CHRISTIAN PROFESSION.

The time is now near at hand in which some of your number are to make a public profession of their Christian faith. It is proper that this address should have reference to the coming event, and to topics connected with the early dedication of the young to the service of God, their Creator, Redeemer and Sanctifier

In pursuing this subject, I shall consider those of you here present as consisting of three classes : 1st. Those who manifest no desire to become the children of God, or who may have felt religious convictions, but have said to the Holy Spirit striving in their hearts, " Go thy way for this time, when I have a convenient season I will call for thee." 2d. Those who have professed their faith in Christ ; who are communicants in His church, and who are bound by this relation to Him, to live as becometh children of light. 3d. Those who are about to ratify their baptismal vows, made for them by others when they were in infancy, or who have as adults voluntarily taken upon themselves these vows.

First, to those who choose to remain without taking

upon themselves the obligations to live as becometh the children of God ; who prefer to enjoy the pleasures and gaieties of life, rather than to check the tendencies of their hearts towards those vanities ;—to you I would address a *last* warning admonition—for so short is the period now before us, ere our final separation as "Teacher and Taught," that we may regard this as our last opportunity for the serious consideration of truths which concerns your immortal destiny. Bear with me then, once more, while I would seek to make you better acquainted with yourselves, and the condition in which you now stand, as respects your title to a heavenly inheritance. There are many of you who have chosen to remain free from all self-imposed Christian obligations. You have preferred to cast off reflection ; you have not wished to place yourselves in a situation where you might be reminded that you are acting unworthily of a Christian profession ; you thought that by making no profession, none could reproach you for not fulfilling its conditions. Alas ! for the hardened heart, for the conscience which can slumber on, unheeding the loud tones of the Gospel, "Awake thou that sleepest !"

God speaks to you in His providences. Within the last year, His voice has come to us all, in an event which though touching me most painfully, has been deeply felt by every inmate of Patapsco, even to the humblest servant, for all felt that they had lost a friend.

One in the bloom of health and the prime of life, who

read to you on one Sabbath day * on the uncertainty of this life, and the importance of being prepared for a future state—as if a practical illustration were required by the Almighty, is, on the third day after, suddenly taken from these earthly scenes, when with filial love and devotion she is travelling with her mother debilitated by sickness and seeking health in change of air and scene—you know the beauty and piety of her life : you hear, on all sides, the testimony that she was "*ready to go*;" you perceive how this belief softens the grief of survivors, nay, turns their mourning into joy, and their weeping into songs of praise ; for they look forward to a blessed reunion in the world of spirits, and to a never-ending companionship with her in mansions prepared by the Saviour for his faithful servants and followers.

God speaks again in the early death of school companions ; The good and exemplary Eliza Van Meters † is cut

* On Sunday, August 26, Miss Lincoln in the absence of the chaplain (it was a season of vacation) and her mother being indisposed, gathered for religious worship the large number of pupils remaining, with other members of the Institute family. If she had known what God designed should take place on the third day after (the 29th of August, at that same hour), she might have selected the Hymns and other portions of the worship, as appropriate. She read a Sermon on God's providence, the uncertainty of life, dangers seen and unseen ;—how, in a moment from an accident in travelling, the soul might be summoned to eternity. Again, as the sun was calmly sinking below the western horizon, did she lead in the hymn of praise to God in that circle of pious worshippers ; and with a glowing cheek and brightened eye, after the prayers with which she had closed the Sabbath evening, she came to her mother's sick room, to ask if she should read to her. And thus passed her last Lord's day on earth—a fitting prelude to an eternal Sabbath.

† Daughter of Hon. John Van Meter of Ohio.

down by "sickness in a day;"—while the piously resigned Sarah Young * is seen slowly lingering under the touch of consumption, and after her removal to her own Virginia home, we learn that she has passed away. A momentary sadness has come over you—perhaps a sigh breathed, or a tear shed, or at the least a shade of seriousness for an hour, or a few minutes, and then you turned away, glad to amuse yourselves, glad to cast from you all gloomy thoughts—the dark, cold grave was too horrible for you to think of, you would not turn to the beaming light from Calvary, which can irradiate the tomb with heavenly brightness. Religion seemed to you gloomy and austere;—because you would not become familiar with her, you feared her looking into your trifling and vain hearts; so you failed to secure that friend, who taking you by the hand would have led you safely through dangers and temptations, and finally enabled you to triumph over the last enemy in this our mortal life, even death. Religion would have taught you that Christ having conquered death, His followers have no more cause to tremble before the "King of terrors."

Of what avail to you, who refuse to attend to God's call in his solemn warnings, have been the many addresses you have heard from this place; when the voice which now speaks to you, and which soon will be forever silent to you, has called on you to repent of your past thoughtlessness, and to turn your feet from following after vanities.

* Daughter of Dr. Young of Virginia.

I speak to you as a class—and yet, had I time, I might particularize the different individuals of this class who refuse to interest themselves in religion, who disobey God's calls, and remain as they are ; I might say of one, she is too indifferent, about everything, to mind religion ; she neglects her own improvement in her school education, she only desires to live without doing anything—all effort, physic al or intellectual, is a weariness to her ; how then can we expect her soul to wake up to its immortal interests ! Shall we say, sleep on, take thine ease—alas, how soon thy soul may be required of thee !

I might say of another, she is too eager for present pleasures to regard spiritual interests which are not manifest to the senses—like Esau of old, she would sell her immortal birthright for one savory morsel.

Of one, we might say, she is skeptical as to religion ; she sees the faults of professed Christians, and she doubts the efficiency of that religion which fails to make them what they should be. Of all the devices of the enemy of the souls of men, this is one of the most dangerous, the most successful in keeping back those who are willing to reflect, from entering the fold of Christ. But consider that Christ came to save sinners, consider that as sinners His professed followers came to Him, and though they may often err, and do things unworthy of their high calling, yet they may repent in bitterness of spirit ;—you see the transgression, but the penitence may be in secret between the sorrowing soul and its God. "Lay not the flattering unction to your souls," that the faults of professing Christians will excuse your neglect of "bounden duty and service." Watch not for the failings of others in respect to their duties, but look well to yourselves that ye be not among the foolish virgins, who will be found at the last, with lamps untrimmed and with no oil in them.

We will next address those of you who have been partakers of the Holy Communion. You professed to wish to be "Christ's faithful servant and follower." You professed your faith in Him, and your determination to be true to your religious obligations, to your life's end. You promised that "by God's help you would renounce the world, the flesh and the devil," and that you "would not follow nor be led by them." That help will ever be granted you, if you ask for it in humble prayer. You have met with trials and difficulties. Perhaps you imagined that you were to find your nature entirely changed—that you would never feel tempted to sin—that you would never be angry, even under provocation; that you would never be jealous of others, envious, unkind or unamiable. You may have expected some wonderful changes to be wrought in your own character and disposition by your obedience to God's commands. The blessed sacrament of the Lord's Supper, we do indeed believe is a sanctifying ordinance; but like the dew of heaven, its influence is gradual, often unseen and unfelt by the recipients, until manifested by the trials of life, or at the near prospect of death, when doubtful hope is changed into firm faith, and the Christian can say with

St. Paul, "for we *know* that if our earthly house of this tabernacle be dissolved, we have a house not made with hands, eternal in the heavens."

You have met with trials, perhaps, in the unkind remarks of others; they have asked for the fruits of your profession. It is true that you ought to exhibit Christian tempers, that you ought to be kind, courteous, meek and humble. Often may your friends have been pained to witness your defects, your apparent living so far below your Christian profession; but do not despair —you have placed yourself, with all your diseases of the soul, under the care of the great physician—we confide in His skill, we trust in His power and wisdom, and we know that if you will persevere, He will cure your spiritual maladies.

I shall conclude by addressing those who are about to make their public profession as followers of Christ, and for the first time, approach the Lord's Table in the Holy Communion.

On entering a new home, we regard with deep interest the first meal we take in that place. When the home circle assemble around the family board, they feel that this is a kind of consecration of their new abode. When you were about to leave home to go away for years, the last meal you took was a season of deep thought. When you return, and find yourselves once more seated at the family table, your hearts will overflow with gratitude for the goodness of God which has preserved you all, and brought you together again, crowning you with mercy and loving-kindness. And when a beloved member of the precious family circle is taken to join the family of the Redeemer in another world, how do we feel the void when the survivors gather together at table ; thus is the family board consecrated as the altar of domestic love and harmony, the suggester of tender and sacred associations.

The table of the Lord ! how solemn, how affecting the thought that our Saviour is here, with us, in Spirit—the bread and wine are the emblems of his body and blood given for us—he will bless to our use that holy feast—in it, we commune with the spirits of all Christian worshippers—with " the saints of all ages,"—here we meet in spirit with the beloved ones who, but a little while ago, knelt, bodily, with us at this table, but are now of another world ; we believe them present with us, rejoicing that we are following Christ in his commands—and that we shall soon be with them in Paradise.

It becomes those who are about to devote themselves to the service of God, to be humble, for they know themselves to be sinners in God's sight, and if reproached by their fellow-creatures as such, let them bear patiently such reproach, considering what persecutions their Saviour endured for their sakes.

It becomes them to be serious ;—shall a sinful creature of earth, permitted to approach the majesty of Heaven, lightly regard such a privilege ? Let thoughts of personal appearance, of the opinions of other human beings respecting you sink into nothingness, before the awful considerations which at such an hour should press upon the soul. You are beginning to take your first steps towards heaven ; with your eyes and hearts raised heavenward, seize upon that chain whose termination is in the spiritual world ; hold it fast—let it not be wrested from you till you find yourselves safe in the "bosom of your Father and your God."

—— 1856.

ADDRESS XVIII.

TO THE GRADUATES OF 1856.

You have now, my dear pupils, received the testimonials of honorable dismission from your scholastic duties. Some of you came to this place while you were yet children. The bud under our fostering care has blossomed ; and, in the bloom of womanhood, you are now to return to your respective homes. The years of your pupilage may have seemed slowly to pass away—but they are now all gone—and you, too, are to go with this departing, this departed school-year.

You who, for a longer time, have been pupils of Patapsco, will, more especially, be regarded as exponents of the system of education here pursued. Your success or failure in respect to the great business and objects of life, can never, either in your own minds or those of others, be entirely separated from the persons with whom, and the place where, your characters have, in some degree, been formed and moulded.

As the fruits which reward the cultivator are not all equally perfect, with the same degree of care and labor, so must moral and mental culture, ever be attended with various degrees of success. Health, energy of purpose, industry and perseverance, are necessary to form the thorough and accomplished scholar. Seldom are all these requisites found united ;—your deficiencies, for such the best will find in themselves, may it be your future care to supply, by improving all advantages which may be attainable. May you feel that so far from being proud of the attainments you have made, you should rather be humble because you have not done more. In this spirit of humility return to your homes—in this spirit enter upon the scenes of life, and you will render glad the hearts of friends, and secure the favor of strangers.

You are now to depart hence, to enter a new school—even the school of life. The school of life! where your teachers may be stern and severe, speaking harshly to you in trials and afflictions of various kinds, and in divers manners—but you must learn that "whom the Lord loveth, He chasteneth ;" and thus He prepares His children to leave this school of life with honor, and His approbation of, "Well done good and faithful servant, enter thou into the joy of thy Lord." If you have looked forward with solicitude to your school examination as a test of your preparation for an honorable discharge from scholastic duties, how should you ever bear in mind the termination of earthly scenes, and His scrutiny who having offered himself as your Saviour, is to be your final Judge. Think not then, that your trial is finished ;—this present, is only one stage in the drama of your life, but it is to make way for more serious and eventful scenes and duties, in which your attainments, principles and characters are to be tested.

Some graduates of former years, who, in the pride of youthful loveliness, and distinguished for talents and moral excellence, stood in the places you now fill, rest from their earthly labors, having left behind them a good hope of their Christian calling. Many others are now filling various stations in life with honor and usefulness; —when weighed in the balance, they are not found wanting. I say this in no boastful spirit, but in humble gratitude to God—for what they are, and for what they are not; both that they are pious and intelligent women seeking to know, that they may perform their duties—that they are not, the mere creatures of fashion, squandering health and reputation in scenes of thoughtless gaiety and dissipation. Often is the grateful incense of praise for their virtues wafted to me from the circles of life which they adorn, and where their genial influence is diffused. So may it be with you, who are now to leave the seclusion of academic life;—may you be prepared for admission into heavenly mansions should it be your lot to be called early from this world, or for a longer sojourn amidst the toils and trials of life—and though on earth we may never meet again, yet there will assuredly come a period, when, if we discharge faithfully the duties of our high calling, we shall rejoice together for all we have been, and all we have done, conformable to the dignity of our immortal nature, and of our Christian privileges.

The greater number of your class are professed followers of Christ. Several of you were baptized here. There was one* who stood with me as your sponsor; she was with us on the last anniversary of this day, but the Lord, whom she loved and served, saw fit, in a mysterious manner, to take her from us. May you cherish her memory, and emulate her bright example; and may each of you be to your parents, a blessing and an honor, as was my sainted daughter to her widowed mother. Let us bless God for all the saints He has given to earth, as an example!

The circumstances under which I take leave of your class are peculiar and affecting. While you go to begin the duties of life, I resign the office which for so many years has brought me into communion with young and loving hearts. Though rejoicing in the favorable circumstances under which I leave this interesting charge, and foreseeing for this institution, so dear to us all, a continuance of prosperity and usefulness, I cannot, without feelings which words may not express, bid adieu to my LAST CLASS OF GRADUATES.

* Miss Jane P. Lincoln.

PARTING HYMN.

ALMIGHTY FATHER! bow Thine ear,
  And listen to our farewell strain!
A sister band, behold us here,
  Thou knowest if we meet again!
For, far and wide, our pathways lie,
  And dangers wait our pilgrim band;
Uncertain all beneath the sky,
  Our trust is in Thy mighty hand.

For not to earth our hopes we bind,
  Sisters in Christian faith are we;
And oh, our Saviour! may we find
  In heaven, a home, and rest with Thee,
A "little while," the Saviour cried,
  And ye shall see your risen Lord,—
For us was Jesus crucified,
  For us, incarnate, was the "WORD!"

O Holy Spirit! 'tis Thy part
  To fit us for a heavenly rest;
Thy gracious influence on the heart,
  Alone can make us truly blest.
Our choral harmony of praise,
  To God the Father, God the Son,
And Holy Spirit, let us raise;
  The Omnipresent THREE-IN-ONE

Commencement, 1856.

CONCLUSION.

The course of this volume has been like the progress of life. We had our five times three-score and ten pages allotted us (for to the practical wisdom of publishers, authors are bound to submit.)—At first the period seemed long, and we indulged in making ample selections from the materials before us, but we found, as the middle part of the book was attained, we had made but slow progress. And so the pages went on, until there was, at the last, space for little more than the "Farewells." Is it not so with human life? Does not its termination, however protracted, come suddenly to all, and find much that was to be done, remaining incomplete?

We had intended to have given *Letters* written to pupils, while travelling in our own country and abroad. But having already passed the prescribed limits, we must omit them, with the intention, however, if life and health be permitted, to publish them at a future time, in a separate volume.

And now we part with our readers—we may have been but a dull companion, for we have discussed serious subjects, and perhaps have seemed austere in our sentiments; but what experience of life, the inspiration of conscience, and the word of God prompted us to say, we might not withhold.

At this very time, events are transpiring which speak to the women of America in louder and more solemn tones than our feeble whispers, of the dangers of yielding to the fascinations of pleasure. Parents and Teachers are thus admonished to be more sedulous in the moral training of the young, and to value above all other education, the proper development of the emotions and conscience, strengthened and sustained by a firm and well disciplined will. Thus only will women be virtuous, the safe and prudent conservators of domestic happiness, and public morals.

March 15, 1859.

ANOTHER CONCLUSION.

Nine years have passed since the author bade farewell to her readers—years of war and tumult in our country's history they have been, and never has there existed greater necessity for the wise training of the young than at this period, when the foundations of our civil government are shaken. Unless the rising generation of men and women shall redeem the country by freedom and patriotism, the "American Republic" may serve as a beacon light in history, to warn against the dangers of civil strife and partisan animosities. Though women may not bear a part in the government of the country, they can do much by their influence at home to save or destroy the Republic established by our political fathers.

MARCH, 1868.

THE END.

www.ingramcontent.com/pod-product-compliance
Lightning Source LLC
LaVergne TN
LVHW010150110826
845151LV00002B/477

* 9 7 8 1 4 2 5 5 3 6 8 3 1 *